Island in the Sound

Island in the Sound

By Hazel Heckman

Drawings by Helen Hiatt

SEATTLE   *University of Washington Press*   *LONDON*

For the Islanders

ACKNOWLEDGMENTS

For much of the early-day data in this book, I am deeply indebted to Betsey Johnson Cammon of Anderson Island. But thanks are also due the following persons, for assistance in the necessary research and for other help:

Mrs. P. L. Myers, Mrs. Ethel Gregory, Mrs. Etta Wallace, John Kucher, Ronald Kucher, Murray Morgan, Alfred Ekeberg, Mrs. Carrie Matthews, Mrs. Joan Johnson, Mrs. Jane Cammon, Mrs. Dora Zabroski, Mrs. Ellen Ehricke, Mrs. Lena Christensen, Mrs. Carl Greene, Miss Christine Anderson, Mrs. Gerda Johnson, Andrew Anderson, and Glenn Orr; Mrs. J. Ibbotson and Bruce LeRoy of the Washington State Historical Society, Mrs. Hazel Mills of the Washington State Library, Bill Goldman of the Washington State Bureau of Maps and Surveys, and the personnel of the Pierce County Assessor's Office and of Tacoma Title Company.

It would be difficult to list all of the published works in which I have found the answers to questions. But I would especially like to mention the Michael Luark diaries in the University of Washington Manuscript Library, which were brought to my attention by Mrs. Lucile McDonald's articles in the Seattle *Times*. Also, the May, 1939, issue of *Pacific*

Motor Boat Magazine; feature articles by Mrs. Gladys Sheaffer in the Tacoma *News Tribune Sunday Ledger;* the *Narrative of United States Exploring Expedition During the Years 1838-1841* by Charles Wilkes (Philadelphia: Lea, 1845), Volume IV; two books by Edmond S. Meany—*Origin of Washington Geographic Names* (Seattle: University of Washington Press, 1923), and *History of the State of Washington* (New York: Macmillan, 1924); two books by Ezra Meeker—*The Busy Life of Eighty-five Years* (published by the author, 1916), and *Pioneer Reminiscences of Puget Sound* (Seattle, Wash.: Lowman and Hanford, 1905); the souvenir edition of *Soundings*, published by the Personnel and Training Office of the United States Penitentiary on McNeil Island; and the Anderson Island *Gazette.*

I am indebted for botanical and biological aid to C. P. Lyons' *Trees, Shrubs and Flowers to Know in Washington* (Toronto and Vancouver: J. M. Dent and Sons [Canada], Ltd., 1956); Leslie J. Haskins, *Wild Flowers of the Pacific Coast* (Portland, Ore.: Binfords and Mort, 1934); Roger Tory Peterson, *A Field Guide to Western Birds* (Boston: Houghton Mifflin Co., 1941-61); Stanley G. Jewett, Walter P. Taylor, William T. Shaw, and John W. Aldrich, *Birds of Washington State* (Seattle: University of Washington Press, 1953); Muriel L. Guberlet, *Seaweeds at Ebb Tide* (Seattle: University of Washington Press, 1956); and E. A. Kitchin, *Distributional Check-list of the Birds of the State of Washington* (Seattle, Wash.: Pacific Northwest Bird and Mammal Society, 1934).

CONTENTS

x   *Contents*

APOLOGY

How shall I explain this book?

It is the story of a bit of land, little more than a pencil dot on the map of the state or of the nation, the casual biography of an island and of some of the people who inhabit it.

Much has been written, nostalgically, concerning the death of the small country community. Those who grew up in the warmth and familiarity of these once-isolated units see them engulfed by growing cities that reach out in every possible direction, to rob them of their geographical identity. They become outskirts, interlaced underground, in the name of sanitation, with an orderly pattern of waste and water lines. Dirt roads with green margins, and beaten paths, surrender to extensions of paved streets with curbs and gutters and to stone sidewalks, the sound of bird song to the roar and clatter of traffic. The fragrance of wild mock orange and of ocean spray give place to the stench of gasoline and carbon monoxide. The dignity of growing trees with canopies of foliage makes way for stark marching lines of creosoted poles that support a never-ending network of power cables and telephone wires.

In an island community, circumscribed by water, boundaries of demarcation, being fixed, are sharply delineated. Here such a submergence is all but impossible. If the island is small, the inhabitants are held together by the simple fact of their insularity and by the ecology of their common interests. In these small isolated worlds, lapped by tides that influence the days of their human inhabitants, as they expose the private lives of the limpet and the chiton, may lie the final exponents of those intimate neighborhoods so many of us remember. In these strongholds, a man's achievements, however slight, were noted, and he enjoyed a peculiar reciprocity whereby his fellows granted him absolution for his lapses.

Had I any real conception of the handicaps imposed by such a self-appointed commission, however, I suppose I might not have undertaken it. It is not that the story of the *Island* is so difficult to get down on paper. When writing is your vocation, it is a pleasure to talk about a place you have come to love. You can describe its fauna, its flora, its geographical aspects, the changing dress of its seasons. But if you are to tell the entire story, you must also include its people. And there is no place where the human inhabitants are a more integral part of the ecology than on an island.

The task would be simpler were the tale-teller to go away afterward, and never set foot in the community again. Were I not destined by inclination to live out my own span here, I would feel no hesitation in depicting its inhabitants as they are. After fifteen years, I am disposed to nothing save admiration, tinged often with more than a little envy, for their remarkable and courageous self-reliance, their independence, their classless simplicity of living. For the fact that I am obliged to expose them and their forebears to public view, I ask their indulgence. I know of no people as a whole whose everyday lives would stand up better under scrutiny.

If the historical portion of this story seems weighted somewhat on the side of the third family of settlers, the Bengt Johnsons, it is not to say that they were any more influential in the building of the community than were those who came before or after them. It is simply that I was privileged to have, in the person of Bengt's daughter, seventy-nine-year-old Betsey Johnson Cammon, a living source book.

Island in the Sound

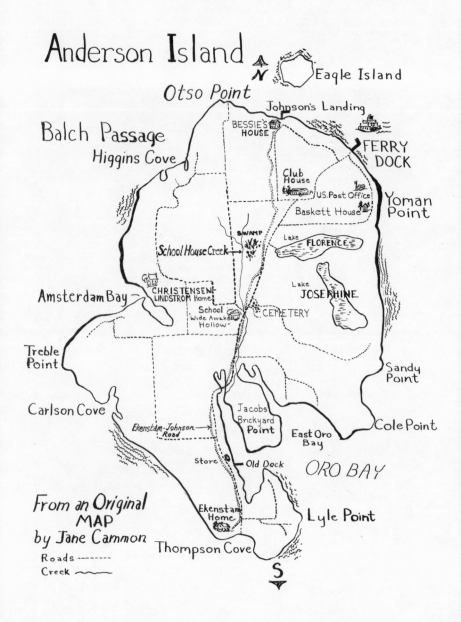

1

THIS LITTLE WORLD

Many years ago, back in Kansas, when I was in the fourth or fifth grade I suppose, we were obliged to commit to memory certain geographical definitions of terms almost totally outside our limited experience.

A *peninsula,* we learned in that dry country, was a tongue of land bordered on three sides by water. A *bay* was a body of water surrounded on three sides by land. A *sound* was an arm or recessed portion of the sea. An *island,* we all knew, and recited glibly, was a body of land smaller than a continent *completely* surrounded by water.

In that day, in our circumstances, people rarely traveled about with their children as they do now. To the age of eleven, I had never been outside the state of Kansas, and only once outside Montgomery County, in which I was born. I had been married for several years when I saw my first mountain, Pike's Peak in Colorado. I had my first glimpse of salt water other than Great Salt Lake and the Gulf of Mexico when I came to the Pacific Northwest, twenty years ago this coming summer.

As children, we could hardly conceive of a body of water larger than the small lake upon which we skated in winter and where we sometimes swam in the summertime. The only island I had seen, to then, was a tiny promontory of fossil-studded rocks embedded with the impressions of crinoid stems and lacy fan-shaped Bryozoa that thrust up out of the Verdigris River when that turbid stream dropped sufficiently in late summer to expose them.

But children are always intrigued by islands of whatever nature, just as grownups are. I can well remember the thrill of discovering, as we emerged from Hickory Hollow and came in sight of the river, that the little "island" had broken through. I recall vividly the eagerness with which I waded the waist-deep water in order to explore that first emergence. And I recollect subsequent visits as the flow continued to drop, to see what had lodged or sprouted there. The projection of a world sufficiently small to be explored exhaustively enchanted me. I returned again and again, until the water dwindled away to a trickle and the promontory was nothing more than a part of the exposed and dried-up river bed. Then I lost interest.

In the inner extremity of Puget Sound in the state of Washington (whether the proper term is "Up Sound" or "Down Sound" continues to be a moot point), islands lie chock-a-block, like raisins in a Christmas cake. Most of them are inhabited. A few, tied to the mainland by connecting bridges or linked by frequent ferry runs, are populous and fashionable. Lying like a quiet afterthought, Anderson Island, the innermost of these partially submerged hilltops, lays claim to neither of these dubious distinctions.

Until a small number of years ago, when the Island was

treated to a little flurry of unsolicited publicity in a local newspaper, few mainlanders even in the city fifteen miles distant could have told its location. They like to tell a story here about a sojourning Islander who was asked, once, "And just how and where *is* this little island of yours?"

"Well, I guess you might say it's in dire straits," he told his interrogator. He declares gleefully that she spread out a map of the Puget Sound country, where she had lived since childhood, and searched diligently for the straits in question.

Literally, this is an anomaly. To the Islanders, who make use of its gifts in a casual fashion and who take its natural beauty for granted as their heritage, the Island is a horn of plenty and a diminutive Eden. Insular living, most of them admit readily enough, may have its disadvantages, but they are quick to add that the advantages far outweigh them. I suppose it would be difficult to find an Islander who could be readily persuaded to live elsewhere.

Shaped vaguely like a head done by Picasso, or, as one reporter wrote, "like a Rorschach ink blot," Anderson is one of the smaller and less accessible islands Up Sound. In size, it comprises roughly nine sections, less than six thousand acres. It boasts approximately fourteen miles of shore line, most of it high bank and heavily wooded. By ferry, it lies about three and one-half miles from the mainland.

For a variety of reasons, Anderson is sparsely inhabited. The mainland is too far removed to make a bridge economically feasible. Only five scheduled ferry runs are made each day, none after six o'clock in the evening. The ferry, privately owned and under contract lease to the county, carries but nine cars, necessitating a tedious wait if there is an overload. With the exception of a little small farming and the gathering of wild greens for the florist trade, an independent vocation termed "brushpicking," the Island boasts no industry.

There was a brickyard once, before the turning of the century, but it did not last long. Island clay made poor bricks, the Islanders say philosophically. Competition with the Chinese, who used bricks as ballast for their incoming cargo ships and sold them on the mainland, could hardly be met, and the brickyard closed after a few years. About the only good that came of the brickyard, they tell you, was that a few Island daughters found husbands, and good ones, among the brick-makers.

The year-around inhabitants number less than a hundred people. The population figure is apt to range downward. Few new families come to stay, and the birth of a child is a rarity. Death takes its toll, but Islanders declare stoutly that people last longer here. "It's the pace of living," they say. "If you shift down instead of up, your gears don't wear out so soon." Long-time Islanders cling as stubbornly as the barnacles that line the Island shores. More than once I have heard some Islander say, "They're going to have to carry me feet-first to get me off this rock."

A few Islanders earn their living elsewhere. Clem Zukowski, a rugged transplant from McNeil Island, operates his own bait boat, netting and selling herring. His wife Crystal, a pretty great-grandmother whom the Island children affection-ately call "Cooky," accompanies the children across to neigh-boring McNeil each school day, to prepare the hot lunches for the children of both islands. A few Islanders work on com-mercial boats. Ivill Kelbaugh, a former West Virginian, works as deck hand on the ferry. Larry Gordon and Russell Cammon, both Islanders, serve as guards at McNeil Island Federal Peni-tentiary. Less than half a dozen commute by ferry to jobs on the mainland, even in the summer when the population swells to embrace that half-welcome invasion called "the sum-mer people."

A commuter must depart at a quarter to seven in the morn-ing and wait until six in the evening to return. The Island boasts no public night life, except for an occasional dance or local get-together. The only movies are periodic documen-taries or animated cartoons provided by the Sunday school or the Community Club.

All these factors, Islanders are convinced, keep their small world uncrowded. Occasionally one hears talk about a larger ferry that will carry more cars. *Islanders,* who plan their trips for uncongested crossings and follow an unwritten schedule of sailings, are rarely given to complaint. Lyle Carlson, the Oro Bay storekeeper, goes in with his big truck on Tuesday. The Johnson brothers, Rudolph and Oscar, milk and egg farmers, cross on Wednesday. Thursday falls to the Ehrickes, who operate a machine shop. This leaves Friday open for incoming week-enders and Monday for leftovers. An Islander who goes to town unnecessarily on a Friday is sometimes referred to as a "gooney," a name coined by Islander Peter James, an erstwhile deck hand on the ferry.

In the past few years, Island living has altered some, just as modern innovations have made living easier, if not less complex, almost everywhere. Early settlers, who lived along the shore for the most part, as do their descendants, communicated with one another by rowboat or by foot trails through the woods. Now, winding dirt roads, classified on survey maps as "light duty" and maintained by the county, make communication easier. Most Islanders own automobiles. Several have an "Island car" and a "town car." A simple intra-Island system of telephones, locally-owned and operated, ties the Islanders together on a single party line. Maintained by the subscribers, who pay ten dollars a year for the privilege and must vote on new members, it is known as "The Anderson Island Social Club."

As of very recent years, Anderson is connected to the mainland by an underwater Pacific Northwest Bell cable terminating in a single booth at Ehrickes' place. Incoming messages are dispatched about the Island by means of the Social Club phone, or by someone who is going that way. If an Islander wishes to call out, he makes his call, jots his name down in a book, pays his toll at Ehrickes', and adds a nickel for the privilege.

Earlier, before the booth was installed, the city phone, as it is called, hung on the back porch at Viv Gordon's place, down the road from the ferry. Beside the phone, on a shelf, sat a cigar box to receive whatever toll the operator specified. The caller counted his own change.

Recently electric power has come to the Island via an underwater cable across Nisqually Reach. Objections were voiced to this symbol of progress, just as objections were made, earlier, to the herd law, to the construction of roads, and to the inauguration of ferry service. Staunchly conservative Islanders opposed the power as distasteful government subsidy and foresaw the loan as a debt that could never be retired. Some feared a resultant influx of people. "If we wanted these things," they said, "if they meant a lot to us, we would not be living here but on the mainland where they are taken for granted."

Actually, the coming of power made little appreciable difference. Islanders read with both amazement and amusement the surge of publicity in mainland newspapers attendant on the event. "You'd think we'd been living in the dark ages," one remarked dryly. Most Islanders owned gasoline-burning power plants for lights and appliances, even television. Radios were battery powered. Refrigerators burned kerosene or bottle gas.

"It just goes to show," they say when a tree falls across an electric line, "life is simpler when you can cure your own ills with a wrench or a screwdriver and a trip to the outshed."

Even the ferry *Tahoma,* taking ninety-five years as a measure (the first permanent settler is said to have landed around 1870), is a recent innovation. And in the fundamentals, nearly a century of living has effected little change. Islanders grow their own fruit and vegetables. They take clams and oysters and firewood from the beaches, berries from the roadsides, and venison and fuel and building material from the woods. In autumn ducks and geese flock to the lakes, the coves, and the inlets. Habits and customs remain insular. Islanders arrange their own recreation, manage their own spiritual and social affairs, undertake in large measure their own building construction, and manage nicely within their tightly knit and narrow world without an officer of the law, a minister of the gospel, or a doctor of medicine.

"The only thing wrong with Island living," an Islander is wont to say ruefully, "is that it makes you want to live forever." More than one ailing Islander, even in my time here, has remained by choice to die alone in the house and on the Island where his best years were spent.

The pattern of relationship, too, is strikingly insular. Sons of Islanders married Island daughters, and brother followed brother across the continent and across the seas; it is largely their children and their children's children who make up the population now. I have long since given up trying to untangle the maze of relationships.

To further compound the riddle, certain sons abandoned their surnames, assumed their fathers' given names, and added "son" or "sen" to coin new names for themselves. Gus and Oscar Peterson, blood sons to Gustaf Carl Peterson, became Gus and Oscar Carlson. Bengt Johnson was the son of John Borgeson. An Aaraas became an Oros, and who could blame him? A Christensen became a Christy. "One thing's for sure," diminutive, blue-eyed Violet Ward, the Island librarian, chuckles. "This is one place you don't *dare* gossip."

The first settlers on the Island were Scandinavian—Danish, Swedish, Finnish, Norwegian—and Scandinavian names still predominate on the mailboxes and on the tax rolls and on the stones in the Island cemetery. These were not, primarily, plowmen, though John Ekenstam, the second settler, and Bengt Johnson, the third, proved up on Kansas homestead claims previous to their arrival here.

Mostly, they were men and women familiar with the sea— from living near to its shores—people at home in the forest and on the water. Those who had come from the north of Europe had known at home a climate and a flora similar to that in the Northwest. Accustomed as they were to a dearth of sunlight, to fog and skimpy summers and cold wet springs, they felt climatically at home. There was work to be done, and the work was fraught with perils. Scarcely a week passes in Northwest woods, even with modern safety measures, but that some workman loses his life while engaged in a forest enterprise.

But these perils were familiar, and Northwest pioneers did not, at least, suffer from cold and from heat, as did their counterparts on the plains. They were not plagued, as were the settlers of the Middle West, by wind and drouth, by dust and cyclone and locust. They had chosen, prudently it would seem, a temperate climate and a fastness stocked with natural resources, blessed with rainfall and lovely to look at into the bargain. On the land and beneath the water was food for the gathering, building material and fuel for the hewing, moisture to nourish whatever crops they planted. By contrast with the soddies of the Central Plains and the Southwest, their houses of fir and cedar were substantial ones. They found a forest ready and waiting for harvest, quiet waters for transport, a demand for the trees they hewed in their clearing.

But what of those who deliberately chose an *Island?* They put down roots in a narrow world cut off from civilization by miles of deep, cold water, by tides so strong and waters so turbulent and fog so dense at times as to render navigation of a small boat perilous if not impossible. Self-sufficiency is a necessity for survival on *any* frontier, and solitude is the common lot of pioneers everywhere. But what of those who chose an *Island?* Were they challenged by a world sufficiently small that they could encompass and explore and understand the whole of it? Perhaps that is what they sought. Perhaps, in a sense, they found it.

2

THE CARPETBAGGERS

Incurably Southwestern U.S.A. (we thought then), we arrived in the Northwest in midsummer 1946 following the end of World War II. The family consisted of my husband Earle and me, our fourteen-year-old son, Jim, and our ten-year-old Scottish terrier, Susie.

The war had had nothing to do with our uprooting, which had resulted from an internal mutation. But we had come, unawares, to a coastal city into which had poured during the conflict a vast influx of both service men and industrial workers from the Midwest and the South. The word "Okie," born of John Steinbeck's *Grapes of Wrath,* had had a rebirth. Our accents betrayed our origin.

It is no criticism of the people of the Northwest, and I do not mean it so, to say that we missed the warm, easy friendliness and unquestioning acceptance of strangers to which we had become accustomed. This is a condition prevailing nowhere that I have experienced except in sections of the Southwest and the South. After nineteen years here, my sole comment concerning native Northwesterners is that they are climatically smug. Following nineteen years of comfortable year-around living, I am bound to admit they may have reason to be.

We left Oklahoma in July. On the day of our departure the mercury in the shaded thermometer stood at 114 degrees Fahrenheit. The leaves on the cottonwood and catalpa trees hung like folded wings. The door latch was hot to the touch, the asphalt in the roadway soft and spongy. The grass along the roadsides was burned to a fawn brown. Even the ragweeds and the sunflowers looked spent.

We arrived in a cool evergreen country that seemed to our sunburned eyes a perpetual vacation land. Although my roots are fast here now, this continues to seem holiday country. Whenever I enter the openness of eastern Washington State, beyond the Cascade Range, I have the feeling that I am back where I more properly belong. I feel native and indigenous to a plains country. I always will, I suppose.

There seemed often, during those first years, something hostile and intrusive about these forests, as though if man were to lay down his axe and turn his back, the trees would push him and his puny efforts off into the Sound or the ocean and take over as uncleared wilderness again. Fences left untended were lost in a season to creeping undergrowth. Trails were obliterated by alder and salal, sword ferns and huckleberry and bracken, smothered in blackberry briars. Even grass or sorrel, uprooted and left to lie, I discovered, renewed itself. I found unwanted plants and bulbs, dug up and cast away in the autumn, blooming the following summer in the refuse pile.

We had our first experience of Anderson Island late in the year following our arrival. My husband's business associates owned a farm on the Island, and we were given permission to spend a weekend in the lodge-cabin there. The month was, I believe, September.

As we crossed the channel on the ferry *Tahoma,* I stood on deck facing the receding mainland and watched the wake in the gray-green roughened water. On the shore, the gloomy firs, marked here and there by the brighter, more showy foliage of the madroñas, grew down to the water line, almost obscuring the scattered houses. The boat bucked and jolted, throwing spray over the bow, as it nosed into the whitecaps in mid-channel. In the distance, seagulls circled and screamed. Long-necked grebes bobbed about like corks in the cold water, then turned tail and disappeared beneath the surface. Occasionally, a small silver fish, as bright as an arrow, darted into the air as though pursued and plummeted back again. Against the eastern sky, Mount Rainier arose like an optical illusion above a mauve horizon.

To a Puget Sounder, Rainier is simply "the mountain." Towering above the Cascade Range that resembles a string of foothills by comparison, Rainier is claimed, often fiercely, by both Tacoma and Seattle. From both cities, when visible, the mountain does dominate the landscape. Frequently during the winter months, and often in summer, visitors see only a veil of clouds and tend to doubt the mountain's existence. When the veil lifts, the cratered peak and shining glaciers provide a sight so magnificent and awe-inspiring that a stranger is inclined to see them as a mirage.

Rainier rarely looks tied to earth. As though mounted on a misty pedestal on silent rollers, the mountain appears to shift from one position to another, rarely wearing the same face more than ten minutes in succession. In winter, the entire mass may turn in a matter of seconds from a sparkling white to gray-green, and change as quickly to a spectral lavender-blue. Of an evening, touched by the reflection of the setting sun, shades range from delicate pink to the richest apricot. As the sun drops behind the Olympics into the Pacific Ocean, the color diminishes through all the tones of gray and purple to a ghostly pomegranate.

That day, Rainier was visible from snow-covered peak to mist-enshrouded foothills and stood up like a cardboard cut-out. A small cloud cap, like a halo, hovered above the crater, a sign Islanders regard as an infallible indication of an impending change in the weather. But that day, chilled more than charmed, I thought with nostalgia of a brighter and warmer climate. A light mist, termed facetiously "a dry rain," was falling. Remembering the seemingly unremitting rains of the previous November, December, January, February, March, and April. I thought that six or eight months of dour skies was a high price to pay for the relative comfort of a few weeks of heatless summer.

The deck hand, Peter James, who had asked our names and our destination as he took our tickets, stopped beside me. "It's going to be a fine day," he observed, "in the banana belt." I turned to look in the direction he pointed. Like a long green oasis arising from the blue-gray water, the Island lay bathed in sunlight. Through the slot of Balch Passage that separated it from neighboring McNeil, with its pale rise of penitentiary buildings, I could see a portion of the snow-dusted Olympic Range, etched saw-toothed and gleaming white against a clearing horizon. A little way back from the Island shore, sunlight touched the scattered houses against the green backdrop of a wooded slope behind them.

As we approached the slip, I watched the Island come into closer perspective. With its masses of madroña and dogwood berries, the white of the dogwood's second blooming and the scarlet of vine maple, the north shore is a pretty sight in September. Engines churning in reverse, the boat slid between the pilings. Peter James unhooked the guard chain, took up the rope with its knotted loop, and tossed it onto the apron. "Another successful voyage completed," he said with a grin, and leapt, as lightly as a mountain goat, onto the loading ramp. I have thought often since that day, how true his words were for us.

A visitor arriving by ferry, bound for Oro Bay at the south end of the Island, as we were, has his choice of two roads as he leaves the landing. We chose the left-turning one, that follows the curving shore around Yoman Point and up the hill and then turns right to climb into the woods to become Guthrie Road. A half dozen modest houses stood well back, all but

two of them obviously summer places. Beside the second, a
modern gray structure with a deep lawn shaded by cherry and
apple trees, a woman in a bib apron was at work in the garden.
Behind the house stood a small square store building and a
machine shop with a gasoline pump.

Up the hill, a little way beyond, we passed a gangling two-
story farmhouse, painted white and flanked by long red poultry
houses, obviously unused, and an old barn. A rough rock wall
of native stone set together and grown over with quack grass

ran around two sides of the yard. On the third side, the land
sloped away through a grass-grown orchard planted to fruit
and holly trees. Behind the house, a clipped meadow arose to
the wood's edge. A FOR SALE sign hung in a front window.

I remarked, I remember, that the house was rather ugly, but
that it had a nice view. Earle, who is exceptionally observing,
said, "That's the first real cottonwood I've seen in this country." I turned to look. The cottonwood stood behind the house,
its lower limbs touching the roof. (It is more than twice as high
as the tall house now.) We grew up in cottonwood country, in
southeast Kansas, where a single cottonwood, indigenous

there, will sometimes shade half an acre. In the autumn of the year the broad, heart-shaped leaves, that rustle enchantingly in the wind, turn to a bright, clear yellow, so transparent-seeming that you have a lost feeling when you look up into the foliage.

We drove past the old barn and turned to climb a steeper hill that curved away from the shore. Here, the dirt road was narrow and rutted, washed by recent rains. Along the sides, wild cucumber vines festooned the tangled masses of Himalaya berries, and bracken and Queen Anne's lace stood tall among the wide-lobed leaves of wild sweet coltsfoot. In the side ditches, sword ferns grew tall, and the pasture beyond the dilapidated fence was dotted with goldenrod and purple Michaelmas.

Near the top of the hill, the road plunged abruptly into deep woods. The feathered green of fir and hemlock and cedar, and the broadleaf green of madroña hung with ripening berries, made a canopy. Patches of pale chartreuse shone clean against the cinnamon satin boles of the madroña, and the green-leather leaves of the huckleberries were tipped with scarlet. A western wren paced us, flitting from bough to bough among the salal, and we saw the flash of a flicker and the flutter of band-tailed pigeons among the conifers. The road, barely wide enough for two cars to meet, appeared to close in ahead and behind us. In the quiet underneath the boughs of green, the car seemed an intrusion.

During the next three years, we returned again and again to the Island, and we always contrived to drive up the hill and past the old house. The For Sale sign still hung in the window. And, although the place seemed nothing for us, I knew a small secret feeling of relief each time I saw that the sign was still there. In the rock wall, a double bank of stones with an earth-filled space between, the quack grass grew tall and taller. In the orchard, the fruit trees, unpruned, put out long leafy suckers. The lawn grew thick with dandelions and sorrel.

But when spring came, the orchard was a pink and white cloud, and in the fall it was bright with apples and holly berries. Several times, we passed of a late evening or early morning and saw deer browsing underneath the Spitzenberg apple trees or nibbling at the leaves in the run-down rose bed. Occasionally, we caught a glimpse of a cock pheasant and his modest hen in the tall orchard grass. Often in summer, blue jays shouted from the locust tree or a chipmunk scolded from a gate post.

In the spring of 1950, four years after our arrival in the Northwest, our resistance wore thin and we accepted the deed for the place—the old house, some seven acres of woods and meadow, and the fronting beach and tidelands.

3

"HERE'S KINDNESS"

On the day we finally mustered courage to turn in and have a closer look at the Villa Beach place, which will always be known on the Island (I hope) as "the Baskett place," we met William Baskett.

Bill Baskett no longer owned the house, or even lived there, but he came with the place almost literally. It was he who had built the bulk of the house from its small beginning as a cabin and had cleared the land around it. Through the years, he had added and leaned on rooms as the need arose and as he could afford them. He added outbuildings, two modern twenty-five-hundred-bird poultry houses, a smaller five-hundred-bird house, a brooder house, a big combination hay and stock barn for his livestock, a milking parlor.

He had sold the house and the seven acres several years earlier, we were told, because it was too much for his wife Elsie, and the pair had moved to a little house at the top of the hill, overlooking the farm and the channel. Now that Elsie was gone, he was about selling the farm, too. But he had retained the right to live out his remaining years in the middle feed room of one of the poultry sheds. Whatever the plan might lack in comfort, it was one that suited him. He had spent his prime years on the Island. His children had grown up here. Elsie was buried in Island soil, as he wished to be.

In his late seventies, he remained a striking figure, tall and handsome, with piercing dark eyes in a lean high-boned face. He was a trifle bent at the shoulders, from hard work, but his step was quick and sure and he carried himself well. Until the

year of his death, he retained much of this youthful vigor of appearance.

We were told he held the key to the house for the owner, a mainland woman, and so we knocked on the feed-room door, and stated our errand. He was courteous but noncommittal. It was obvious that he did not care much, really, whether we liked the place. We were like all of the others, probably, who had looked at it during the four years it had been for sale. We didn't want a place to earn a livelihood. We were summer people, week-enders, in search of an escape from city living. At least that was the feeling he seemed to communicate.

All about us were evidences of the family's enterprise. Besides the barn, the cleared meadow, the orchard, the garden site, the sturdy buildings, there was the yard planting, the shrubs, the rock fence, the shade and holly trees. The rock fence alone, it was plain to see, represented a colossal amount of labor. The stones, many of which weighed hundreds of pounds, had been brought out of the fields by horse-drawn sled (we learned later). Mr. Baskett had set them in place with his own hands, spare-time work "to please the Missus."

"They both worked from can't see to can't see," one of the neighbors remembers. "The lights came on at three and four in the morning." It makes me ache a little to contemplate Elsie Baskett's grueling schedule here on the Island. She sold her own butter, eggs, poultry, and vegetables each week at the Pike Street Market in Seattle, traveling some forty miles by water each Thursday and back on Sunday. She purchased and sold produce raised by other Islanders, and picked berries in season to add to her display.

"It was my job to dress the chickens," Hallie Baskett Greene, recently retired to the Island, told me with a laugh and a shake of her head, as though she wondered at her own enterprise. "I was still in grade school here on the Island, so I couldn't have been more than fourteen. If school were in session, I stayed out on Wednesday. I could dress a hundred chickens in a day. For this I was paid a cent a head."

"Bill wasn't an easy man to work for," an Islander who had once hired out to him told us following Mr. Baskett's death. "He expected you to work until you couldn't go any longer, the way he did himself. But he was the best friend I ever had, I never doubted that. The thing was, I guess, *he'd* come up the hard way. He didn't know there was any other."

I came to value his friendship and was always glad to see him when he came. But I never quite got over the feeling he was looking over my shoulder to see how we were caring for the place. For as long as he remained on the Island, I left certain things to grow that I would otherwise have rooted out as not worth the time and trouble they consumed—the big ragged red peonies Elsie had planted, which he liked to take to decorate her grave on Memorial Day, the mass of American pillar rose sprawled across one end of the poultry house, the overgrown holly trees, the worn-out raspberry canes.

He said a thing to me once, toward the end of his life. It was as though with the words he accepted a fact, finally. Or perhaps he reminded *me*. We were talking about the place, of what it meant to both of us. I think he knew I loved it by then. "A man can't say he really owns anything in this world," he said with a little laugh. "The most he can count on is a lifetime lease on what he wants to keep." It occurred to me that with these words he relinquished the place to us, in trust for *our* lifetime.

I expect the time hung heavy on his hands. If I were at work in the yard when he passed on the way down to the store for his milk or bread, he stopped to talk about the place, or, more often, to lend a hand with whatever I was doing. To get at the quack grass in the rock wall, I had, literally, to pull the stones apart, and he helped me, moving the stones about with apparent ease with his long work-gnarled hands. When it came time to renew the soil for planting, he trundled wheelbarrow loads of manure down the hill from the old barn.

Sometimes he talked about the past, as elderly people do. He had been born in Missouri. His mother had died when he was two, and he had gone to live with his grandfather. At the age of twelve, he had left home and had worked his way to Seattle, where his father lived, with a second family, and then to Alaska during the gold rush there. Homesick, he had started the long trek back to see his grandmother. Obliged to stop off and work for a time in Chicago, he had taken the only job he could find, as a bartender.

There, in the restaurant where he took his meals, he met

Elsie, and they married and came West together. In Seattle, twin girls and then a third girl were born, while he worked, variously, at "laying ties," as a stock boy, and as the driver of a horse-drawn delivery wagon for Frederick and Nelson department store. When all three of the children contracted spinal meningitis, and one of the twins died, he obtained a job as caretaker of a farm on Bainbridge Island.

From there, following the birth of yet another daughter, Gladys, the family had brought their cow and their household goods by barge to Anderson Island, where they became the caretakers at the lakes place owned by C. B. Hopkins. By dint of scraping and saving, Bill and Elsie were able to buy the beginning of the Villa Beach farm.

"This was all woods, then," he said, "the house nothing but a little cabin in a clearing. There wasn't time to take the stumps out in the part we cleared that first winter, so we stump-ranched. You never saw such potatoes as we took out from around the stumps. Potatoes brought a good price that year. That's how we got our start."

It was easy to believe the story about the big potatoes. That first year our neighbor Ernie Ehricke gave *us* a potato that served eight nicely and that was white and mealy and unblemished to the center.

Through the years, the Basketts had cleared farther and farther, adding to the farm and stocking the place with livestock. They had added to the house, too, and it had been stoutly constructed. Now it was in a state of disrepair. But so long as the roof was sound and the place could be made snug in winter with the big circulating wood stove, I was willing to let well enough alone. When it comes to remodeling, I have no imagination. If the big, overgrown house was hardly gracious, it was at least spacious. The beach with its marvels was at the front door. The woods grew at the back. I was satisfied.

The man I married is of a different grain. He emerged from underneath the porch, festooned with cobwebs, to inform me that the supports were rotted out, the foundation sagging, the underpinnings gutted by termites. He went about tapping and measuring and dashing cold water on my enthusiasm. The high ceiling of drooping and scaling plywood panels would need to be lowered and tiled, the plumbing overhauled, a circulating fireplace installed, new windows set in. The floor dropped five inches from the front door to the center wall. The entire house needed to be jacked up and refoundationed. He cast a practiced and perfectionist's eye about the interior walls and stated flatly that he doubted there was a straight line anywhere.

There seems to be no record as to when the original cabin was built, and Mr. Baskett did not know. I do know that yellowed newspapers nailed to the wall underneath the layers and layers of wallpaper in the little downstairs bedroom (which Earle later made into a pleasant open workroom for me by cutting windows on the orchard and the water sides) headlined the assassination of President William McKinley, in the year 1901, and that a story on an inside page named the heads of state who had been invited by the Crown to attend funeral rites for Queen Victoria.

During that first summer we found little time for exploring the Island. Our method of reconstruction was accumulative. We accumulated paint, tile, lumber, plywood, wallpaper, nails, plumbing fixtures, firebricks, quarter round, varnish, adhesive, screws, nuts, bolts, hinges, insulation, and window panes, and heaped them on the floor in the big barn-like living room and set to work.

That is, Earle set to work. Having come, through his own efforts, to a bold conclusion that "anything someone else can do a lot of, I can surely do a little of," he set out to prove it. The fact that he had never hung wallpaper, laid tile, covered a drainboard, raised a house, designed and built a fireplace, or dropped a ceiling, daunted him not a whit. He did all these, and did them well, using only hand tools left over from his young apprenticeship as a pattern maker.

In town during the week, he hurried home from his job,

snatched up his dinner pail, and caught the last ferry to the Island, to work half the night by the light of a gasoline lantern. Each Friday, I was astonished by the transformation he had made. Faced with a particularly exacting and difficult task, he would admonish me, "Go outside and work in the yard. I'm apt to have to cuss a little." The yard, the garden, where, at least, I knew the names of things, was where I liked *best* to work. I was only too pleased to comply.

Hearing the sound of the hammer and the saw inside when he stopped, Mr. Baskett asked, "What's the Mister trying to do? Beat that old house to death in there?" I expect a lot of what we did seemed foolish. But he was generous in his admiration of the work, and stopped by often.

He carried away the cardboard cartons, to flatten into sheets and nail on the walls of his feed-room dwelling, which he kept as clean as most women would have done. He did his own washing, with a tub and board and an old-fashioned boiler. He spaded a tiny garden and planted potatoes and sweet peas and scarlet runner beans to run over the chicken wire that covered the nest rooms. And he planted a long row of "goose" beans to hull out for the winter.

I like the story of the goose beans that grew in almost every Island garden. Years ago, according to the tale, a Northwest hunter shot a Canadian goose and found a few strange-looking beans in its crop. The following spring, he planted the beans in his garden. From this beginning, he began to distribute beans to his neighbors, and their name and their fame spread, at least on the Island.

Goose beans are not especially suited for use as green beans, and so they are left to ripen and dry and then are shelled out for winter. This takes a good deal of time. But sitting in the sun to shuck oysters or to scrub clams or to shell beans or peas, even to pick chickens, as my mother used to say, has its compensations beyond the mere preparation of foodstuffs for the table.

Another story I came to like was that of "Mrs. Baskett's

flower." A great clump of this robust plant graces almost every
Island garden. One of these, as tall as a man, stood in front of
the house when we first saw the place. It died down in the fall,
but sprang up again in the spring and grew rapidly, a
boraginaceous-looking perennial, with coarse leaves, topped in
midsummer by a showy spread of delicate, lavender, bell-
shaped blossoms. I have yet to find a gardener who can call it
by name, and I have never found its like in any garden or wildflower book. "Oh, that?" the Island women said when I asked.
"Well, I don't know the name. The start came from the Baskett
place, so I call it 'Mrs. Baskett's flower.' " It occurs to me that
Elsie Baskett could ask no more appropriate memorial. "She
never threw away a bulb or seed," Island women say. "She dug
them in somewhere." Even now, yellow daffodils dot the roadside and spill over the bank to high-tide line each spring. In
summer, myrtle and moneyplant, saxifrage and St. John's wort
appear among the pink and white foxglove and the Queen
Anne's lace all up and down the roadsides above and below the
Baskett place.

On a bright day in April, that first year, Mr. Baskett showed
up with a spade on his shoulder. "Now, if you'll tell me where
you'd planned the vegetable garden, Missus," he told me, "I'll
spade it up for you." The truth was I hadn't thought of a vegetable garden. There hardly seemed time to bother with one.
"I reckon you won't want a very big one," he said, setting out
while I was trying to frame an answer, "just you and the Mister.
The best place would be over here. It's *good* dirt, for all it's
clay. With a little manure added, it will grow whatever you
want. And it won't dry out if you keep it stirred."

Each year thereafter, for as long as Mr. Baskett remained
on the Island, he and I sat down together in the early spring to
order seeds. He had his tried and true favorites, and I made no
effort to interfere with his choice. He did the planting, with
little help from me, and he kept the garden free of weeds.
He had his own homely remedies for diseases and insect pests,
and they worked remarkably well—black and red pepper, soda

and soapsuds and sulphur. He knew the moon phases most favorable for leaf or seed or tuber, and he planted in the pouring rains if the signs were right.

He had no use for commercial fertilizers. "High-priced sand," he called them. He was a firm believer in barnyard manure and dust mulch. "Keep the ground stirred," he said. "When it turns dry, stir the harder. That brings the moisture up." One of the tools he had kept from his farming was an oversize hoe with a blade as broad as his hand-span. Hearing a step on the gravel of a morning, I would look up from my typewriter to see him going down the driveway with the big hoe on his shoulder. If the day was warm, I carried him a beer and admired the garden. If it was cold, I asked him in to sit by the kitchen fire.

In later years, when we had television, he liked to come on Friday evenings to watch the fights. During our summers on the Island and of winter weekends, he frequently shared our evening meal. It was the only way we could repay him, and we liked having him. He had an ironic sense of humor, and he was invariably cheerful. He liked his liquor, too well sometimes; but he never came near when he had had too much. Often, when he came with his hoe or his spade, Earle would stop work and ask him in for a drink.

No connoisseur, he was fond of telling how all brands came from the selfsame barrel when he tended bar in Chicago and "nobody knew the difference." "There's none of it bad," he would say. "There's only good and better." He liked his whiskey at room temperature and without water to "weaken the jolt." But he never raised his glass without the ritual of his own particular toast, "Here's kindness!"

Setting out toward the mainland on the *Tahoma* on winter Sunday nights, we marked the lonely pinpoint of light from his kerosene lamp, a dim glow behind the curtain of fog or rain. But he had a choice. He and Elsie had worked hard and saved well during their working years. He could afford to live elsewhere. Or he was welcome at his daughters' homes, he knew that. But he was an Islander, and this was the way he wanted it.

One Saturday morning, Earle found him stretched on the floor beside his bed, where he had fallen. His hip was broken. But all he asked for was a drink of water. Nor did he complain during the wait for the ferry to bring the ambulance. The doctors did a good job of piecing the bone together, and he was able to return to the Island for a time. But he was obliged to give up after a while and move to a convalescent home on the mainland. I visited him there many times. He longed for the Island with the intensity of a homesick schoolboy and was eager for news of it, but he remained cheerful and uncomplaining. "When I get back to the Island," he would say, knowing as well as I that his return would be "feet first," as the saying went. But we both pretended.

For a long time after he returned, to be buried from the community clubhouse, his door remained locked. The blackberries and the honeysuckle sent out long runners to smother the mailbox, and thistles and fireweed grew tall in his potato patch. We counted eleven swallows' nests that following summer on the rafters of the wire-front section that served as his storeroom.

We have a few belongings he gave us—a ten-gallon stone jug that he and I filled with cider one autumn Sunday, a grubbing hoe too heavy for an average-size man, a big pitchfork, a washboiler. But it is in the small remembered incidents that he remains alive. I rarely plant a seed but that I wonder whether I have the blessing of the zodiac. And whenever I hear a toast proposed I recall his fervent and sincere, "Here's kindness!"

4

ELLEN

Among the richest rewards of Island discovery, for all of us, was coming to know Ellen Ehricke, who kept the store down the road.

The store, where Ellen presided (there is no other word for it), dispensing "flow of soul and feast of reason," along with flour and yeast, hops and malt, bananas and snuff and bandannas, was a wonderful place to go. The little, square, inadequately-lighted building was served by a kerosene refrigerator in which she kept Island-produced milk, and butter, and a bit of meat, sometimes of Island kill. In a vented cooler cupboard reposed the slab bacon and the salt pork the Islanders liked, and the big longhorn cheese daisies she weighed out in pie-shaped slabs on her counter scale.

The native lumber shelves nailed along the walls and the center counters held, besides the canned goods, every manner of merchandise—shirts and socks, greeting cards and fish-hooks, rope and kerosene lamp wicks, shoe laces and paraffin candles and lanterns. One of the rewarding things about visits to the store, especially during the week, was that business was never rushing. A good brisk business day in winter, when no week-enders or summer people were abroad, probably saw half a dozen customers. That first summer I fell into the habit of dropping in, almost daily, to sit on a beer carton beside Ellen's packing-box desk, to visit.

Like the poet's Dr. John Goodfellow, "offering solace and answering prayers," Ellen bent a sympathetic ear to the several Islanders who came to her with their problems. She kept house

for her husband Ernie and her son Bob in the gray shake dwelling her menfolk were about remodeling when we first came, dividing her time between her household chores and the store, which, no matter what the hour, was always opened when a customer came. During her "spare" time, she worked among the strawberries or in the big vegetable garden.

If a customer arrived and found the store closed, he knocked on the kitchen door and was invited inside for a cup of "Mamma Ehricke" coffee, made by the old-fashioned method of boiling the coffee in the water and allowing the grounds to settle out. Many times I watched Ellen make the coffee, which was delicious; but, as with her Yorkshire pudding, I was never able to achieve a like result.

Ernie died during our second year on the Island. Following Bob's marriage to an Island girl, Sylvia Johnson, Ellen moved into an upstairs apartment over the shop in order to give the house to the young couple. When she retired from the store, after a while, she moved her business quarters into the shop and kept books and waited on customers when Bob was busy or away on a job. There, between a homemade oil drum heater and an old battered desk with a captain's chair, she still "presided," as it were.

Ellen (who once told me casually that Sigrid Undset was "some kind of distant cousin") was a believer in ultimate good. Often during our talks she reiterated her conviction that greed, and greed alone, stood in man's way. One day, she believed, he would come to see this. Unlike the poet, she believed that the good men did lived after them. The weight of this accumulated good, passed on from generation to generation, would eventually prevail, she declared firmly, and men would live together as brothers.

Ellen not only prescribed to this philosophy, I came to see; she lived it. It was her habit to look for the good in all of those with whom she came in contact, and to point it out to the rest of us. I liked this. "When Ellen came to the Island," Mr. Baskett told us once, "she was a beautiful girl." Beyond middle age when we first met, she was still lovely to look at (and is now). When she is amused or pleased, her delphinium-blue eyes blaze up as though a light had been turned on behind the irises.

"Mrs. Ehricke's a *queen*," Jim said admiringly one day, shortly after we had made her acquaintance. Watching her move about the shop in her old sweater and canvas sneakers and homemade apron, pumping kerosene from a drum or searching through a cluster of greasy bins for a nut or a bolt a customer wanted, I was pleased by his perception. She *did* have a regal air. It came, I thought, from inner resources that gave her self-containment. Years later, one who knew her well summed her up by saying, with a trace of envy perhaps, "Ellen's a challenge to *any* woman." And so she was, and continues to be.

But she proved adept at business, too, and could be firm when the need arose. Islanders laugh about the morning at Sunday school when she demonstrated the "singleness of purpose" she frequently cited as a necessity for any enterprise. Asked to pass along the page number of a hymn, she glanced at the blackboard where the number was written. Preoccupied, probably, with Monday thoughts, she read out promptly, "A dollar ninety-seven."

Through Ellen, as through Mr. Baskett, we came to know, during our first years, a good deal about the Island and its inhabitants, and to meet a number of them. I remember with especial pleasure some of those early encounters. At Ellen's store one day I met Mrs. Esther Gulseth, a widow who lived alone in a three-story "picture-book" house on the north end of the Island, a big midwestern house that bristled with gables and overhangs.

"You live in the big Baskett house, eh?" Mrs. Gulseth asked as we shook hands.

"Well, I live in the Baskett house," I acknowledged. "But *your* house would make two of *ours,* you know."

"However did you happen to *build* such a big house, Esther?" Ellen put in. "With not much family to fill it?"

The widow counted her change carefully, her lips moving. "*I* didn't build it," she said. "*Gulseth* built it."

"Well, then," Ellen persisted, "why did *Gulseth* build such a big house?"

The old lady took up her basket to start the long trek home, but turned at the door. "When I get to heaven," she threw back grimly, "that's the *first* thing I'm going to ask him."

One afternoon I entered Ellen's store to see a stooped octogenarian negotiating over the counter for a can of house paint. "It's to paint the window sills of my new place down by the

beach," he explained to Ellen. "When I get that job done, I'll
be all through."

"Fine," Ellen said. "I guess you'll be moving in soon, then?"

He shook his head in the negative. "Not yet," he said, "not
for a while, anyway. I built that house for my old age, you
know."

I see him go by in his rowboat sometimes, a bent figure leaning to the oars. A fishing pole protrudes, or the boat is piled
high with bark gathered for fuel along the shore. An Islander
tells a story about having seen the old man out in his boat one
day, resting his oars. Seeing him later at the store, the Islander
remarked the fact. "Saw you out fishing this morning, Al. Did
you catch anything?"

"I wasn't fishin'," the old man corrected him. "I was just
a'loafin'."

"Uncle Al," as the Islanders call him, is only one of several
solitary senior Islanders who live alone and enjoy their lives.
Like Mr. Baskett, they could live more comfortably on the
mainland, but this is the way they want it. You do not even
think of them as aged. Invariably, I am surprised to learn how
old they really are. Younger Islanders keep an eye on them,
without seeming to. But no one prevails upon them to stay
out of boats or to go to town where they could receive care.
For the man who catches his own fish and gathers the fuel to
cook it, life remains a challenge.

Because she was well acquainted with the needs of her customers and kept a careful list, Ellen's goods rarely languished
on the shelves. She carried packages of dried hops, for Islanders
who were not satisfied with the degree of hop flavor to be had
from the ready-prepared malt mix. She stocked saccharine for
the diabetic, salt substitutes for those who needed them, and
the special brands of cathartic preferred by the chronically
constipated among her customers. She bought blue bandannas
for the man who had an aversion to red ones. Shirts and socks
and fishing lures were purchased to suit her customers, whose
sizes and tastes she knew as well as she knew her own.

"Summer people," as we were, and still are, learned to use the brand of toothpaste or of powdered pectin, the grade of cheese or the kind of soap the Islanders preferred, or they did without.

Nor was Ellen's store unique in this peculiar and, to us, admirable discrimination. A young mainlander told me once that he had walked into an Island store and asked for a bottle of milk.

"Sorry," the storekeeper (not Ellen) told him, "I'm out of milk."

Walking about the store, the young man declared, he opened a refrigerator door and saw a number of bottles of milk on a shelf. "But there's milk *here*," he protested.

The Island merchant, a man of few words, wasted only six on his mainland patron. "That milk," he said laconically, "is for the *customers*."

But when we were genuinely in need, we were treated to so prompt and generous a response that we forgot we were summer people. Time after time, I asked for an item at the store only to have Ellen say, "Well, I'm out of that until Thursday. But I've got some at the house I can let you have." And, whether it was soda or soap or vanilla, she would leave the store and paddle across the turn-around to her own kitchen to get it for me.

Frequently I went home laden with more gifts in my basket than purchases—a box of red ripe strawberries, a jar of jam, a cucumber, a big meaty tomato, a pan of cinnamon rolls, or a golden sweetmeat squash from Ellen's garden. Often I enjoyed a snack at the store while we visited, a cold coke, or a candy bar, or a paper plate of cheese and crackers.

Although we traded mainly at Ellen's store, being north-enders, we were treated equally well when we drove across Island to the south-side store. Because the proprietors conducted other enterprises, such as selling live bait from the boxes at the end of the old dock, running an occasional taxi or freight load, they had at times to be sought out or to be brought down from their house on the hillside by the sounding of the horn. Receiving no response, once, I was about to drive away, when the proprietor appeared from the beach below.

"Sorry to bring you up," I apologized. "I'm about out of gasoline."

"That's all right," he said, giving me his characteristic grin, "I was just down there tossing rocks into the water."

Having had a bad morning, I was tempted to ask whether I could join him.

Quiet by disposition, he too was as obliging as you could ask. When Earle stopped one day in search of a mousetrap, the young merchant looked in vain about the shelves. "I seem to be out of traps," he regretted. "But if you'll wait a minute, I've got one up at the house I'm not using just now, and you're welcome to it."

Earle recalls with admiration an occasion when he had prevailed upon an Islander to haul several boxes of building material from the mainland, sharing the load with supplies for another part-timer. Asked what we owed for the trip, the hauler considered for a moment and then replied: "Well, I really ought to charge John eleven and you five, because his load was the bigger by half. But he's complained so much lately, I'd better charge *you* the eleven and *him* the five, to keep peace between us." Charmed by such frank and logical reasoning, Earle paid the eleven, which certainly was not excessive, without a murmur.

One lesson we learned early was to adapt ourselves to Island pace. When Earle, who likes to get things done the moment he conceives of them, was about building the circulating fireplace, he needed some welding done. "'Sure, I'll come up and do it," Bob Ehricke, a Washington State graduate of the school of engineering, assured him.

When a day or two passed and Bob had not come, Earle devised a diplomatic approach. "You go down," he instructed me, "and ask him *not* to come before five. Say I won't be home until the afternoon ferry to show him what I want done. That will remind him, in case he's forgotten, without seeming to nudge him."

Bob, who has blue eyes exactly like Ellen's, gave me a boyish grin across his lathe. "You tell Pappy for me," he said, readjusting his goggles, "that he's getting Goddamned subtle."

I seem to recall that he came a week from the following Wednesday. Of one thing I am sure—had the weather turned cold suddenly, he would have come at once, and would have worked all night if necessary.

Frequently we heard some elderly Islander refer to Bob as "indispensable," and we came to believe, along with a good many others, that it was true that he could, as the saying went, "keep *anything* running." "If he or Ernie can't find a part for whatever you have that's broken down," Mr. Baskett told us, "they'll *make* it out of something and it will work better than a factory job."

The 1929 Reo the Ehrickes drove, and still drive, as an Island car, was a smoothly functioning example of their ingenuity. We saw cars and tractors in deplorable condition and of incredible vintage dragged into the shop and driven away under their own power. Like the small-town medical practitioner, Bob was a specialist in every phase of his business because he had had to learn to be. He looked upon a broken-down piece of machinery, not as a chore, but as a challenge.

But he could be independent, too. "He told me he'd fix up the *old* car," an elderly Islander related. "He said he didn't want anything to do with the new one." Bob repaired the former, as he had promised, and she still drives it about the Island with confidence, although it has almost reached the antique carriage class.

One day Bob emerged from underneath a hood to ask a commuting Islander, the owner of a third-hand Plymouth, "How long do you plan to drive this car?"

"The way I reckon," she said, "it will be about seven years before I can *afford* a new one."

"O.K.," he said, not at all perturbed.

"He would hardly speak to me when I drove up in the new car," she told me a few years later. "He acted as though I had cast an aspersion on his ability by buying it."

"If anything goes wrong while I'm gone, get Bob," Earle told me unnecessarily, whenever he set out on an extended trip from the Island in the summer. On rare occasions when Bob planned to be gone for more than a day, he saw that cars in need of service were attended to, empty propane tanks replaced, and stove-oil drums replenished. We were at first amused by and then joined the flurry of activity attendant upon the news (any Islander will tell you that news moves at the speed of sound here) that Bob was about to "leave the rock" for a few days. Generally, his departure was delayed a few sailings by Islanders who needed looking after.

Like Oscar and Rudolph Johnson, who had long since accepted the responsibility of keeping the Islanders supplied with clean milk and fresh eggs at a price all could afford, Bob (a World War II veteran) quietly accepted his self-appointed commission for keeping the fires burning and the wheels turning when he returned to the Island from his tour of duty in the South Seas. The Island was where he wanted to live. He liked the people, most of whom had known him from babyhood, and he liked the pace of living.

One evening, before the miracle of electricity came to the Island, I was a guest at the Ehrickes when a somewhat anxious second call came in on the intra-Island telephone about a balky Kohler plant. Bob said a few soothing words to the caller, to the effect that he would come when he could, and calmly returned to his supper. "People who get hysterical about a light plant," he observed, "have no business living on an Island." He might have added that Island stores sold paraffin candles at six cents each and that it was a good idea to keep a supply of them for emergencies, in case you had been so foolish as to discard your kerosene lamps and lanterns.

5

THE DAY THEY BURIED TED

The first funeral I attended on the Island (services for Ernie Ehricke were held at a chapel on the mainland) was that of a man named Theodore Roosevelt ———.

I do not know what brought Ted to the Island in the first place, his own solitude, perhaps, the need to belong, or the fact that he could live comfortably on little income. I was surprised to read, after his death, that he had been a blacksmith on the mainland, and even more surprised to find his name mentioned in a sports column as having been a memorable baseball player, who had played every position by turns in a matched game once.

I was amazed, too, to learn that he was in his sixties at the time of his death. He seemed little more than a youth. I scarcely knew him, really. I had given him lifts several times when I encountered him on an Island road, going my way. I had driven past his house often.

The house—small and modest, and very old—did not belong to Ted, he only lived there. Perhaps he paid rent, or perhaps when he needed a house, this was the only house on the Island that was vacant, and so he moved in. That is the way it is often done.

As houses go, it wasn't much of a house. But it was adequate for Ted's needs, which were simple, and it had a certain charm, because of its background (backdrop, really) of wooded hillside. The building stood on a rise, a little back from the road. A tumbling clear creek, referred to on the Island as "Schoolhouse Creek," where Island children fish for trout, ran a stone's throw from the back door. That was Ted's "running water."

Take any season, and it was a pretty spot. In summer, the wild grass was kept neatly mowed around the dooryard. Often a white cat sat on the porch. The cat came with the house, I guess, or perhaps the house belonged to the cat. For I had seen her or one of her forebears there, even before Ted's time, after the death of the earlier occupants, two aged brothers called "the Freese boys."

During the Freeses' time the garden was in use and a thing of beauty and productivity. We passed often and saw the cat, or one like her, seated near one of the old men, who stood as unmoving as a scarecrow until we had passed from sight. The cat sat watching a mouse run. After the Freeses had gone, she hunted among the oxeye daisies and the Queen Anne's lace that grew in the abandoned garden plot across the road from the house.

After Ted moved in, we saw overalls and socks and shirts on the line. Ted always looked clean. He had no car and so he was obliged to walk to the store or to his work at odd-jobbing about the Island. He rarely had much to say when I picked him up. But he was always pleasant and courteous. He seemed content enough.

Ted died as he had lived, alone. He had mentioned not feeling well, a few days previously, to a widow he was helping with her wood. A neighbor found Ted slumped over his table, dead of a heart attack.

We heard that his worldly goods, besides his personal effects, consisted of a handful of coins in his pocket. An Islander for whom he had done odd jobs obtained a burial allowance from the Social Security Administration. Because he had served as a marine during the war, the American Legion offered assistance.

Services for Ted were held at the community clubhouse, with the Island women in charge. The funeral car, with Ted's flag-draped coffin, arrived on the eleven-thirty ferry, along with musicians supplied by the Legion, a mainland minister, who had probably never heard of Ted, and two or three relatives, of whose existence few Islanders had been aware prior to his passing.

The month was January, the day chill and gloomy. A fire blazed in the massive hand-hewn stone fireplace. The mantel had been decorated with Island greens, fir and huckleberry and salal. Potted plants brought in by the women stood about. At the back, behind the rows of folding chairs, a buffet table centered with flowers had been prepared for the visitors. There was hot coffee and hot substantial food.

The scene was memorable, the flag-draped coffin, with its backdrop of drawn stage curtains and indoor plants, the greens-enshrouded mantel, the leaping fire, the quiet diners. Before the meal was finished, more Islanders began to arrive. There was, as always for a funeral, a considerable turnout. The newcomers accepted coffee, spoke naturally of Ted, went on to other subjects—the weather, the local news, the coming election. They were quiet but not intimidated by the occasion. The women went about gathering up the remnants of the meal, packing baskets, serving dessert. The chairs filled gradually.

As the minister went to the front to begin the service, a few in the back rows still held coffee cups. The big club pot simmered on the stove. The rich smell of coffee mingled with the fragrance of burning alder, the spicy aroma of the mantel greens.

"I never knew Theodore Roosevelt ————," the minister began thoughtfully, "nor saw him in life. But what you have done and said here tells me all I need to know about him. I heard one say, 'No matter what it was you asked Ted to do, he did it well and cheerfully.' Another said, 'Ted never asked for credit. He paid for what he bought. If he didn't have the cash, which was often the case, he did without.' Still another said, 'He seemed always in good spirits. I never once heard him complain about his lot.'

"In my hour or so here, I have heard nothing said of Ted save of his good qualities. That which you have done here, this meal, these decorations, are in themselves a tribute. You are his friends, his neighbors, the people he knew and who knew him best. I have heard you remark his friendliness, his helpfulness, his cleanliness, his integrity. What better can you say of a man than these things? There is nothing that I, who did not know him, can add in the way of eulogy. . . ."

We followed Ted in our cars, along the curving road that winds through the woods and up the steep hill to the burial ground. Island women had been there ahead of us and had set baskets of greens beside the gate. We watched the final crumbling of earth over the coffin, watched the funeral car depart with decorous haste to catch the three o'clock ferry. In a brush-enclosed recess, a neighbor waited with his tractor to fill the grave. Here was decency and dignity, and death seemed a natural thing. The wind blew cold, but the Islanders, warmed by this thing they had done together in tribute to honesty and simple cheerfulness, wandered among the graves, remembering and reminiscing.

I have been to a number of Island funerals in the years since Ted's death, and it is always much the same. People take time out from their own enterprises to bury their dead. The cemetery is made decent for the new arrival. If it is the blossoming season, flowers stand about, as though the earlier dead held open house to welcome the newcomer. Even to visit the cemetery alone is to have a feeling of community. Wander among the graves of those you knew, and of those about whose lives you have been told, and they seem to stand before you. The names carved on the earlier stones, worn and weathered, are the names of those who founded this small world and who made it a good place to live.

Following Ted's death, his house stood vacant for a good while, until another who was needful came along to occupy it. During that time we saw the white cat on the porch, or hunting in the orchard, crouched patiently beside a mouse run. I expect he found living thinner without his saucer of Island milk and the scraps from Ted's table. The grass grew tall in the dooryard, and we noted as we passed the absence of washing on the line and, at night, the loss of the faint gleam of light that had shone from the kerosene lamp on Ted's table.

"I wish someone would move into Ted's house," I remarked to an Islander that following summer. "I miss the light of his lamp from the window."

"So do I," she agreed, and paraphrased, "Never ask for whom the bell tolls. It tolls for us all! Especially here."

6

TO CONTROL SNAKES, IMPORT MONGOOSES

Any isolated community, I suppose, would serve as a prime example of coexistence. But it has been said that nowhere so much as on an island is the relationship between all of its organisms, both animal and vegetable, so close and so apparent. I remember with chagrin an abortive effort on my own part, a few summers after our arrival, to meddle with that admirable interdependence here.

I suppose the most maligned wobbler of Mother Nature's balance wheel in the Pacific Northwest would be the misguided Scot (if Scot he was) who is said to have brought from his native heath a handful of broom seeds, to plant in his Oregon dooryard or on the Nisqually prairie where he was (allegedly) employed by the Hudson's Bay Company. Perhaps the Englishman who is said to have imported the first pair of starlings would rate at about the same level.

My own interference occurred, innocently enough, when I attempted to introduce two dozen Kansas hoptoads to the dubious delights of Island living. Unlike the mistaken Britons, I was not prompted by nostalgia. Nor was it I, precisely, who imported them. Actually, the toads were the fault of Ezra Taft Benson, the then Secretary of Agriculture, and my niece Barbara, a biology student at the state college in Manhattan, Kansas.

The affair began with my having received in the mail a government bulletin entitled *Slug Control*. I have always been a sucker for government bulletins, especially for those of the agricultural variety. My bookcases are stuffed with them. If someone with authority takes pains to write a thing, and the busy printing office in Washington takes the trouble to put it into type, and my congressional representative compiles a list which I may have gratis, I feel duty bound to order the maximum allowable.

Motivated by desperation, I read this one with avidity. Previous to the time that we took up "small farming" on the Island, as the bulletin facetiously described our dawn-to-dark labors those first years, I had yet to encounter a garden slug. On many a "dew-pearled" morning, as a child, I had watched the slug's cousin, the shell bearing *Gastropoda,* a rather charming mollusk that wears a decent covering, creep across "the thorn," and I had collected many a matchbox full of his delicate abandoned shells. I still recall my feeling of revulsion at the first sight of his slimy relatives, *Deroceras* and *Limax,* on the Island here.

My notion of the worst of all possible worlds, I can say without reservation, would be a planet on which the common garden slug predominated. Whereas I avoid stepping on a beetle and will go to great pains to capture a house spider and carry him outside, I can, and frequently do, scissor slugs in half with a malevolence that shocks my family.

From the time the dews and damps set in of early evenings until the grass dried off of mornings, from long before lilac time in the spring until frost, our bit of earth here was literally carpeted with these repulsive, slow-moving creatures, in three colors—black, brown, and unpleasantly mottled.

Like the hoptoads, which seemed for a brief and happy time an answer to the slugs' depredations, they are nocturnal feeders. They can be found during the day, nestled cheek by jowl, in moist places—under boards or rocks, in crevices in the earth, underneath piles of trash, hidden in the root crowns of plants, especially of the blade variety, or plastered cozily against the underside of large protective leaves such as chard or rhubarb, or (the baby ones) glued to the ventral side of the one lettuce leaf you neglect to examine before tossing it into the salad.

That summer, slugs were more prevalent than usual. I set rows of cabbages and marigolds and went out the following morning to find quarter-inch stems or no trace of my labors at all. I planted expensive seeds, and the sprouts disappeared as they broke crust. Slug bait, a commercial product made from apples, took its toll by the hundreds. But it was as though fresh and hungry slugs arose, phoenix-like, from the slime of their dead companions.

Even before *Silent Spring,* I was something of an organic gardener. Having grown up in the sulphur and coffee grounds, ladybug and red pepper era, when the only pesticide we knew was Paris green, which we used on potato beetles but nonetheless mistrusted, I was always on the lookout for natural remedies. *Deroceras,* according to the bulletin, had few enemies, because, understandably enough, few creatures could stomach him. The sole exception named was the common hoptoad, which was endowed with some mysterious enzyme for rendering the slimy secretion that marks the slug's passage not only digestible but palatable.

I mentioned the interesting fact about the toad's digestive system, I remembered afterward, the following autumn during my annual visit back on the farm in Montgomery County, Kansas, where, just as during my childhood, a grandfather toad, fattened on sowbugs and the like, lived among his lesser relatives in the cellar drain.

On a Sunday evening preceding my April birthday the next spring, I ferried back to town frustrated after two days of "small farming" spent, largely, in a vain attempt to save a few rows of seedlings from the ingestive inroads of the common garden slug. I entered the house to the sound of the ringing telephone and sprinted up the steps to answer.

"This is the post office," a reproachful male voice informed me. "We've been trying to reach you all day. We've got a special delivery air mail package of live frogs for you."

"Sorry," I panted. "Wrong number."

"Is your name Heckman?" the voice asked sharply.

I admitted that it was.

"Then I've got a package of live frogs for you," he insisted. "I'll be right out to deliver them." I heard the lonely sound of the dial tone.

When I opened the front door several minutes later, the uniformed gentleman who confronted me looked mildly relieved, having half expected, I suppose, that the recipient of live frogs might appear astride a broomstick, or at least with a black cat in the offing. He handed over a small cardboard box, conspicuously labeled LIVE FROGS RUSH PERISHABLE, and covered with airmail stickers. "I think they're dead," he said, all reproach again. "I've not heard a peep out of them since morning."

Because it had been literally thrust at me, I accepted the package. "I'm sure there must be some mistake," I said. "What would I want with live frogs?"

My question went unanswered. Having done his duty, the postman disappeared in the night. I heard the diminishing "pop, pop" of his cycle.

I carried the box, at arm's length, to the light. Unmistakably, it was addressed to me. The return address was that of a biological supply house in Topeka, Kansas. Mystified, but curious, I set the box on the table and took a knife from the drawer. Having cut the tape, I lifted the flaps.

On top of a dampish mass of newspaper lay a card, with the message: HAPPY BIRTHDAY FROM BARBARA. As I pondered this, an ugly head emerged, followed by a pair of long legs. Not a frog, but a toad! It seemed an answer to almost prayer when I had absorbed the connection. I shoved the animal back and clapped the lid shut.

The box on my lap, I sat down to think. For a toad's skin to dry out meant death, I had read somewhere. The newspapers in which my friends (probably a pair) were swathed were only slightly damp. They would be thoroughly dry by morning. The poor things had already been confined for twenty-four hours in the small box, which smelled, definitely, toady.

I set the now-silent container on the table and dialed an acquaintance who, I knew, had worked in a biology lab at the University of Washington during her student days. "Why don't you put them into the bathtub with a little water?" she suggested, when she could stop laughing.

Fortunately, Earle was not at home. I was all alone in the house. Who would mind . . . or know, for that matter? In the bathtub, they would have life-sustaining water, and freedom of a sort, until I could get them across to the Island.

In the bathroom, I ran an inch of water into the drain end of the tub. In the other, I constructed a little island of damp crumpled paper. I set the box carefully in the tub and again, more cautiously this time, lifted the flaps.

Like the animals from the ark, or, more aptly, like the clowns in the small-car circus routine, toads emerged. I readjusted my estimate to two pairs, to four, to a half dozen. And still they came. One by one, they broke cover, flexed long-cramped muscles, and leapt at the porcelain walls of their new prison. They fell back with soft wet plops, and leapt again. I gave up trying to estimate their number. It was like attempting to count a plate full of Mexican jumping beans. The tub was alive with toads, all jumping and splashing at once in a grand jamboree.

When they had stopped coming, I took the newspaper out of the box. A last toad lay, belly-up, at the bottom. But, like the delayed-action jester, he came to life at a touch. Thoroughly soaked now, or exhausted, the others gradually ceased their leaping and flattened themselves on the floor of the tub so that

I was able to count them. I counted twenty-five, a baker's two dozen!

During the night I awoke again and again to the sound of soft guttural croaks from the bathroom, and was obliged to orient myself. In the morning, the weakling, or I supposed it to be he, lay belly-up again. The others appeared content in their new white world and quiet, until I began to gather them up to return them to the close confines of their shipping box, which I had filled with fresh paper.

It took a while to corral them all. Just as I thought I had a firm grip on a slippery captive, he would slide through my fingers and be off as though on springs or by jet propulsion. I caught one by the hind legs as he went over the side. Another made the shower head in two leaps, where he perched like a warty gargoyle and allowed me to brush him into the box. I took up the "dead" one to carry him to the trash bin.

Recruiting strength and momentum, he uncoiled his legs, negotiated the kitchen in a series of leaps, and disappeared through the door into the living room. Minutes later I hauled him, palpitating, from beneath the sofa and restored him to his companions, burrowed, by now, silently into the depths of their unfragrant container.

Nor did they utter a single croak during the long drive to the ferry slip. "I've got a box of hoptoads here," I told obliging Peter James. "I wonder if you'd take them up the hill during your morning layover and turn them loose around the garden."

"Now, I've heard *everything*," he said. "Do you want me to catch some flies for their lunch?"

"They'll do fine on their own," I told him smugly. "They're going to live on garden slugs."

All the same, I felt a sense of almost maternal responsibility for their welfare. That afternoon, I called a commuting Island friend, a teacher, to ask whether she would mind stopping by the Island house on her way home, "to fill the bird baths." "I've sent over twenty-five hoptoads," I said. "They just might take off for the pasture pond unless there's water handy."

"How's that now?" she asked. "For a second there, I thought you said *hoptoads*."

When the phone rang the following morning, the awakening began. "Don't ask *me* to water your toads again," she opened indignantly. "I've still got a queasy stomach. I met a snake at your gate last night with a toad head-first down his gullet, and still kicking!"

"Didn't you even rescue the toad?" I wailed.

"I turned green and fled," she said. "I was completely shattered."

Chamber of Commerce brochures from west of the Cascades invariably point to the fact that this area contains but one snake, a harmless nonpoisonous *Thamnophis* of the grass or garden variety. I had seen a few in the garden and had welcomed the sight, knowing that they accounted for a good many harmful insects. I should have remembered, alas, that all *Kansas* snakes, including *Thamnophis*, were also inordinately fond of amphibians. I remembered that a bull snake had taken over the cellar drain one summer, depleting the toad popula-

tion there. It was only when he was accidentally dispatched that they made a comeback.

I hurried to the Island the following weekend, resolved to account for every snake I met. Actually, I never accounted for but one. And then I was riddled by the feelings of guilt that invariably follow my taking any life, save that of a slug (I cannot explain this). He was stretched full-length on the rock wall, taking the sun, and I struck in a fit of umbrage.

Previously, as I say, I had seen a *few* snakes around the place. The following spring, word must have gone the rounds of the snake world that a CARE package had arrived. One week, I counted five snakes, the next, seven. I saw more snakes that summer than I had previously seen on the Island, and more than I have seen any summer since. They lay about in the sun, suspiciously fat, and thrust out their tongues when I approached too close. One took up residence underneath the foot scraper at the back door and emerged on warm afternoons to lie on the sidewalk.

Occasionally, I saw a Kansas toad. One passed his days in a little aperture underneath an ivy-covered piece of driftwood at the back, from which he emerged of evenings to flick beetles off the sidewalk with his incredibly swift tongue. Slugs emerged, too, from underneath the selfsame bit of drift, and headed for the cold frame, leaving trails of slime behind them. So far as I could see, Toad failed to notice them. I could only conclude, charitably, that he remained blissfully ignorant concerning his own peculiar enzymes. He was, after all, a native Kansan.

To tell the truth, we *did* note a certain abatement of slugs that summer. And, although I dislike to contemplate the theory, the Kansas toads may have been indirectly responsible. One night, Toad failed to appear. Nor was he in his "Hall" when I looked there, hopefully, each following day for a week.

Something like a week later I came suddenly upon what seemed an abnormally large *Thamnophis* zigzagging his way across the ivy. Positive that here was Toad's assassin, and incensed, I raised my hoe to strike.

A shadow fell across the sidewalk. "I wouldn't do that if I were you," my neighbor Murph, a seasoned Northwest gardener, admonished mildly. "That's one of your best friends, you know. Accounts for more garden slugs than all the bait you can pour out of a box."

I lowered the hoe. "You don't *mean* that?" I gasped.

"Darnedest thing you ever saw. They eat slugs the way you'd eat peanuts. I read somewhere they secrete some kind of acid that breaks up the slime."

I watched the serpent disappear with a flick of his tail in the heather. "Maybe," I muttered, "you read it in a government bulletin."

"Might be," he agreed. "But I doubt it. I don't often read 'em. . . . Only other critter I've ever seen would touch a slug was a big Indian Runner duck I had once."

I tried *that* panacea, too, a few summers ago. And, by George, he was right. One warm afternoon I stopped at Lake Florence, a lovely jewel of a lake on the highest portion of the Island, for a dip in the swimming hole. I was surprised to see a big white duck with a broken wing being pursued in and out of the water by excited children.

Whom did he belong to, I asked. He must have escaped from somewhere. A newcomer, driving in, volunteered the information that she had seen just such a duck at the R's house.

It seemed unlikely that a bird with a broken wing could have come so far, I thought. But, if the children would help me catch him, I would take him there.

By the time we had reached the R's, we were close friends, the duck and I. For all of his considerable bulk, he insisted upon riding on my lap, where he kept up a constant chatter as he nibbled at my earlobes. Certainly he was someone's pet, and a lovable one. I drove into the R's driveway feeling like a Scout who had done my good deed for the day.

I was unprepared for Mr. R's not-so-very-pleased look. "He *was* our duck," he admitted. "I took him to the lake this morning to get rid of him. But thanks all the same. Just leave him and I'll take him back there."

"No such thing," I told him, considerably embarrassed. "I'm going that way. I'll just drop him off."

"If you're sure it'll be no bother."

"Did you raise him?" I asked, lifting my voice so as to be heard above the duck's loud protests.

"Mrs. G. gave him to me," he said. "Someone gave him to her children as a duckling. She got so she couldn't stand his slug-eating habits, so she brought him over here and gave him to us. But he makes such a mess. . . ."

On the drive back, as though he sensed that he was about to be abandoned again, the duck grew even more loving. Dropping his voice to a husky little-more-than-whisper, he poured his woes into my ears, the while he billed them. "If you do this," he warned, "I'll not last the night, with all the 'coons around. Tomorrow you'll find my bones and feathers in a heap on the bank."

I slowed for the lake turn all right, but could not bring myself to make it. "But I *can't* take a *duck* home," I argued. "What would Earle say? We're only week-enders now. We can't be hauling a big hunk of poultry back and forth. And what would I do with you in town?"

"Just let me out of the car in the driveway, behind the hedge," he said, finally, "and let *me* handle it."

I was upstairs changing into dry clothing when I heard Earle's shout. "There's a *duck* here. Where in thunder do you suppose he came from?"

"A *duck?*" I echoed. I leaned from the window to look. Earle was squatted on the sidewalk. The duck stood tall in front of him, talking in his sibilant pianissimo, the while he nibbled lovingly at his master's earlobes.

We kept him for two months, until cold weather. During the week away, I prevailed upon Ellen's granddaughter Cindy to feed him and put him away each night in one of the poultry houses and to let him out in the morning.

It would be difficult to say, in that time, how many slugs he accounted for. Perhaps he did not eat slugs at all when we were away, only the corn with which we provided him. I have a notion that he may have eaten slugs only to show off, or to secure his position. I grew extremely fond of him, as did Earle. When we drove into the driveway on Friday evening, he came to meet us, relating the news of his week's activities.

During the day, he sat on the patio, a soft white mound of feathers, with his head tucked out of sight completely. This required, naturally, a good deal of scrubbing. But he was worth every ounce of energy expended, and I think he knew it. Step outside the door, and he was on his feet in an instant, his head going up and down on his long neck, his soft voice imploring you to bend down so that he could express his affection.

Following a prolonged session of that, he moved off toward the orchard, his head still bobbing, the while he coaxed you with many a backward look to accompany him. We took profitable and pleasant walks together, he and I, I lifting boards and turning over leaves to expose the long fat cigar-shaped slugs which he consumed with apparent relish. One day, by actual count, he ate twenty-one.

His crop was so distended and heavy that it dragged in the grass as he made his way to the plastic baby tub that served as his water basin. There he stood, blowing bubbles in an effort to clear his bill of the gluey slime that had all but cemented the two parts together. At such times, like his former owner Mrs. G., I turned away from the sight. But, following alternate periods of dunking and blowing, and honing on the grass blades, he emerged with his bill as bright and beautiful as ever.

When we went East for an extended business trip in the autumn, I was obliged to find a home for him. "Just for the winter," Earle promised. "We'll bring him back in the spring when we move to the Island for the summer."

But the new owner, a tidy housekeeper, was appalled by the mess he made and passed him on to another party, where, I fear, he may have served as a Thanksgiving *pièce*. I refrained from asking. In any case, he was gone from the Island, and from the earth, probably.

But, in fond memory, I still see him assemble himself as if by magic from a heap of sleeping feathers, to greet me with his gentle persuasive monologue as we set off on a slug hunt. In the moments when I can bear to contemplate his probable end, I cannot help wondering if he tasted a trifle peculiar, and whether the resultant gravy may have had a slightly "epoxic" consistency.

7

IN THE BEGINNING

Geologically, the Island is scarcely dry behind the ears yet. In all probability, its birth as a land mass dates back around fourteen thousand years, to the post-Pleistocene, when the long finger-like lobes of the Cordilleran Glacier began to retreat, as the climate tempered.

Grading from boulders down through rocks, pebbles, and sand to a clay so impermeable that it sets up like concrete, it is the land mass that tells the story. Whatever may have happened in a more recent epoch, the bulk of land gives evidence of Quaternary debris, unconsolidated drift rubble, ground down by the movement of the ice and left in a thick mantle over the Tertiary deposit below.

During the ensuing ages, the Island has been added to, just as it has been subtracted from. Since the first pale shoots broke through to light and air, seasons of growth and of decay have built on the land mass. In less than half a century, shore lines have receded as much as eighty feet in places with the ebb and flow of tides that take their toll each year. On other shores the banks have filled out and extended, as slides have changed the contour.

Early maps list Island soil as "poor soil" or "second-rate."

And so it is for the most part, rocky and thin and acid. But it supports a lush growth of acid-loving plants, huckleberry and salal, mahonia, fir, hemlock, alder, cedar, and madroña, that tall, broadleaf evergreen the natives call "madrone" and visiting Canadians refer to, correctly, as "arbutus." And in certain areas, added to by the accumulation of leaf and needle drop, soaked by winter rains and protected from wash, and cultivated lovingly, the soil is deep and rich and productive.

So far as is known, the total years of *man's* influence on the Island as permanent inhabitant come to less than a century, which, geologically, is nothing. Long before settlement began, trees were cut here for cordwood and "square timbers" and piling, bound for distant ports. Sparse records of the Hudson's Bay Company at Fort Nisqually across the channel known as Nisqually Reach mention "the little island" as a source of logs as early as 1850. Even before the Island was named, the British cut its trees to build the stockade around the Bay trading post, and rafted clay across the Reach to use in the fort's chimneys.

Sailing vessels from San Francisco came up the coast during the gold rush of '49, dropped anchor in the Reach, and sailed back with logs from "the little island," to be used in the construction of wharves and pilings. The first export cargo to go out of the Sound, on the bark *Rosalind,* is said to have been poles cut on the Island for the Bay company, bound for Hawaii.

The Island was named three times. It was first called Anderson, in 1841, by Commander Charles Wilkes of the United States Expedition, sent out to explore this northwest country. "Twelve miles more brought us to the anchorage off Nisqually," Wilkes wrote in his *Narrative,* "where both vessels dropt their anchors about 8 o'clock. Here we found an English steamer [*Beaver*] undergoing repairs. Soon after we anchored I had the pleasure of a visit from Mr. [Alexander] Anderson* who is in charge of the Fort and Captain McNeil. They gave me a warm welcome and offered every assistance in their power to aid me in my operations." Grateful for his welcome, Wilkes sought to repay his hosts' kindness by giving their names to the two nearby wooded islands.

The Wilkes expedition of 1838-42 charted 261 names. Present-day maps of the Upper Sound are peppered with the appellations of those on board the Wilkes steamers. At least three Island place names, those of Oro Bay and of Yoman and Otso Points, are credited to Wilkes. Mineralogists, naturalists, philologists, botanists, artists, even a surgeon connected with the expedition left their names on waterways, channels, inlets, passages, islands. We must assume, however, that Wilkes was a modest man, or a forgetful one. There is no record that he ever named a single thing for himself.

But if the name Anderson appeared, then, on ships' charts, some following explorers, especially Captain Inskip of the British frigate *Fisgard,* which was on this station from 1844 to 1847, chose to ignore the mapping of the American expedition. Inskip renamed the Island "Fisgard," gave the name of Duntze Island to McNeil (in honor of Captain John A. Duntze), and

---

* Alexander Caulfield Anderson was born in Calcutta on March 10, 1814. He became a chief trader of the Hudson's Bay Company and was located at Fort Nisqually during the years 1840-41. After other service in the company, he retired in 1858 and took up residence near Victoria, British Columbia. He died in May, 1884.

sought to change Oro Bay to Rodd Bay, in honor of his first lieutenant, John Rashleigh Rodd. Whether or not Wilkes had named Thompson Cove at the south end of the Island, it was charted in honor of the Reverend Robert Thompson, the chaplain on board the *Fisgard*. Cole Point honored the master on the *Fisgard*, Edmund P. Cole. Even Nisqually Reach was called for a time Inskip Bank. The third name, "Wallace Island," commemorated the death of Leander C. Wallace, also of the Hudson's Bay Company, who was killed in an Indian skirmish at Fort Nisqually in 1849. The gold excitement having brought about a rush of pioneers to California, Chief Patkanim of the Snoqualmies decided to realize his dream of driving out the white men while they were reduced in number. As a ruse, he quarreled with the Nisqually tribe and took his warriors south. Once at the fort, he entered and demanded that the white men leave.

When a gun was accidentally fired, the warriors on the outside, mistaking this for a signal, began to attack the fort gate. The gate was closed with Patkanim *inside*, his forces without. The swivel gun in the bastion was brought into use, and the battle was quickly ended. Leander Wallace was killed at the gate by the first volley. A Bay employee named Lewis died of his wounds later.

Chief Quallawort, a brother to Patkanim, and a Chief Kassass were tried, convicted, and hanged in May. In July, Fort Steilacoom was established, and the Indians were finally convinced that the white man could not be so easily evicted.

Obviously, the name of Wallace Island prevailed for a time locally, however the Island may have appeared on navigational charts. The baptismal certificate of Betsey Johnson Cammon, dated October, 1886, bears the name of Wallace Island, and the name appears on other official records up to the time of the admission of Washington Territory to statehood, in 1889. Then, for whatever reason, the name of Anderson was resumed.

The name is more in keeping, really. It is interesting to note that whereas British and Indian names prevail in Upper Sound, the titles given to the coves and the inlets, the roads and the landings on the Island are largely Scandinavian. Anderson, Otso and Carlson, Johnson, Vega and Brandt and Ekenstam express, surely, the early settlers' nostalgia for the shores and cities of their childhood, which few of them were to see again. It is doubtful whether they ever hoped to go back. They were not adventurers or traders, as were the British here. They had sailed the seas to put down roots. The years sped by and there was little time, or means, for travel.

On an April day in 1854 an Indianan, thirty-five-year-old Michael Freeman Luark, set out in the rain aboard a scow for "Wallace's Island," to cut cordwood. Luark was accompanied by a man named Ballard and "a team," he neglects to say whether horses or oxen. In all probability they were the latter, for he writes later, during his several weeks' stay on the Island, of working "three yoke of cattle," and then, having "lost one yoke," of working two.

The Luark diaries consist of twenty-five volumes recently acquired by the University of Washington, finely written sheets of lined notebook paper, yellowed with age but well preserved. The fact that Luark bothered to keep the diaries, under adverse conditions of living, seems a rather remarkable circumstance. His shelter on the Island consisted of cedar boughs, with Indian mats hung about the inside to keep out the rain. Most men, as one Islander remarked, would have "sacked out" after a hard day's work instead of writing about the day's doings.

Luark had come into the Northwest Territory the year previous with his brother Patterson and had staked a claim much further south, at Beaver Creek Prairie. He writes of buying a crosscut saw for ten dollars and fifty-seven pounds of salt at five cents a pound, and of having taken a job for a brief time at a lumber mill on the Deschutes River near Olympia. That was in October of the year 1853.

Early in the spring of '54 he came north, looking for work for wages. In the city of Steilacoom, which he refers to as "a stirring town . . . full of logs and stumps," he obtained a job as "woodcutter and roadbuilder" on Wallace's Island. Probably he meant skidroads for the chuting of logs.

Luark appears to have landed on the east side of the Island. But after two days of work, he moved his camp to the west side, in the vicinity of a bay (obviously Amsterdam, near Drayton Passage), to join a group of pile cutters there. During the move he noted the abundant springs on the west slope above the bay, the "deer signs," and the "otter." He also noted the growth of "blackjack pine," in addition to the fir, cedar, and hemlock, and spoke of "laurel" growing "two feet in diameter." It is supposed he must have referred to madroña, called laurel by the early settlers.

Although he cut as much as three cords of wood some days, Luark found time to observe and to explore the Island, as well as to set down his observations. He spoke of the fine rich valley that girdled the Island between the two bays, which he refers to as "our bay" and "Cod Bay," now Oro, on the southeast side. It is nearly all boggy land between Amsterdam and Oro bays. But for a slight rise where jackpines grow close together in a separating wood, the Island would be divided into two islands here. The narrow strip between the bays is a flyway for the big blue herons that work both bays at low tide, and from the time the rains begin in autumn until early spring, wild mallards swim about in the shallow lakes that form like catch basins in the green meadows. Luark noted that men named Orr and Thompson took a claim in this valley. The rest of the Island appeared to Luark to be rocky and sandy. He dismissed all of the soil in the territory "north of the Skookumchuck" as "poor, thin soil, full of rocks and gravel."

On the twelfth of April, six days after Luark's arrival on the Island, the "barque *Areana*" sailed into the Reach and dropped anchor, to be loaded with piles. On one day, Luark cut "six piles." Exploring in the *Areana*'s longboat, he and his fellow loggers discovered on the southeast corner of the Island "a good claim" upon which stood an abandoned house, vacated by "two men" who had held the claim and who had cleared it to the appearance of "a sheep pasture."

One Sunday, Luark climbed a "300-foot bluff," remarking that "Mt. Rainier was visible today in all her grandeur." On the top of the bluff, one of the higher portions of the Island, he came across "a large body of fresh water about 1½ miles in length, with an average width of 80 rods." He saw fish sporting on the surface and large ducks swimming about. Following a little stream from this lake through the woods, he discovered a second lake, with an outlet falling, by way of a gully, two hundred feet to salt water. These would be Lake Josephine and Lake Florence, which lie like an eye and a teardrop in the skull-like shape of the Island.

Excited by his discovery, Luark stepped off rough measurements and was at pains to jot it all down in his diary. Seeing no signs of man, and feeling (no doubt) that he was the Sir Francis Drake of this small circumscribed world, he christened the lakes "The Twin Sisters," and observed that "the island would be beautiful for a rich man's retired residence."

Following the outlet down the gully, Luark discovered that the southern point of Gove's Island (now Ketron) lay due east of where he stood and that the entire country to the east lay in view. Adventuring further, a few days later, he obtained a canoe from "an Indian grave on a small island nearby." This could only be Eagle Island, where, it is rumored, Indians placed their illustrious dead in canoes high in the fir and hemlock trees. This canoe, along with Luark's axe, were cherished possessions, obviously. For he speaks of having to hide the canoe and of having to "cane" a man named Dudley for stealing his axe. Once the canoe drifted away, and Luark was obliged to swim the cold water in order to retrieve it.

Luark seems to have had no compunction about helping

himself to the dead chieftain's canoe, but he writes with strong disapproval of an occasion when a girl of fifteen and her mother, "Ft. Simpson Indians," visited the Island from Fort Nisqually. The mother hired the girl out to Ballard for four dollars, Luark wrote, adding that this was a universal practice, carried out with as little shame as would be felt in hiring a horse. One of the Indians, on the following day, "became saucy and received a welt on the head from Ballard." Remarking further about such traffic, Luark cites the case of the owner of "a store, eating saloon and tenpin alley," and observes that this deplorable business is not only practiced by the common man but among those who "move with the upper ten."

Once Luark writes of paddling home from Steilacoom in a storm that threatened to swamp the canoe. In May, he recounts having found a fern stock (presumably bracken) that measured six feet, one inch, in height and of having observed that the dogwood and black huckleberry were in bloom.

On another occasion, having paddled to Steilacoom, he attended "Indian Catholic services" in a blacksmith shop and came away impressed. The Indian priest, he wrote, chanted or sang in Chinook jargon from two parchment scrolls, which he unrolled as he proceeded with the service, and followed with a sermon that chided the white man for selling liquor to the Indians.

Another day, Luark attended a horse race in Steilacoom, climbing a tree in order to attain a better view. He observed a group of Indians underneath the tree making bets. The game, it appeared, was in the nature of strip poker. Each Indian stripped solemnly, adding his garments and his belongings to the pot. The Indian who had placed his bet on the winning horse collected the lot and went his way, while the losers departed with dignity. Luark could not help contrasting this quiet transaction with the noisy quarrelsomeness of his fellow Caucasians at the track.

On June 1, the bark *Sutton*, which Luark had been helping

to load, sailed for San Francisco with "sawed lumber and square timbers," and Luark shortly left the Island to help to build the first Pierce County court house, at a wage of $3.50 per day. In July he returned to his claim on Beaver Creek Prairie, having observed that the only good soil he had seen in the northern part of the territory appeared to be in small parcels. Previous to his return he had found two adventures of note to write about: putting a large raccoon up a small cedar, and killing a bald eagle that measured seven feet, three inches from wing tip to wing tip. But this latter was on the mainland and not on Wallace's Island.

Eventually, the wood camps closed down. The scars healed over. The Orr mentioned as having staked a claim with a man named Thompson was obviously Nathaniel Orr, whose son Glenn, at eighty-four, still lives in Steilacoom in the house in which he was born. Orr built a cabin on his land. But he never moved his family to the Island. His wagon-making business was, after all, in Steilacoom; and he felt that the Indians were too obstreperous about that time to make living in a lonely outpost completely comfortable.

After the wood camps closed, the Island waited, a long hooked hump of land with a forest on its back, for the first settlers. Mainland Indians probably continued to visit Island shores in their cedar canoes during those years, as they did later, after the settlers came, to dig clams or to gather berries, or even on hunting expeditions. Beach excavations at Oro Bay have disclosed "kitchen middens" of clam shells, as though from some shore feast or potlatch, and an occasional arrowhead or bird point is found among the gravel. The Ekenstam girls, daughters of the second family, told of having found what seemed to be an Indian burial ground on the hill above Thompson Cove. But there was no dearth of hunting grounds on the mainland, then, and the deer population, long-time Islanders say, is far greater now than it was before clearing for homesteads began. And it is doubtful whether berries were so plentiful before the settlers' axes and saws admitted warmth and sunlight. Huckleberries and salmon berries, currants and gooseberries and blackcaps, salal and Oregon grape, all of which the Indians used, must then have fringed the Island shores. But blackberries, both the trailing *Rubus macropetalus* and the escapee, *Lacinatus*, which overrun the Island now, are followers and not progenitors of civilization.

8

YESTERDAY, TODAY, AND TOMORROW

My first real explorations of the Island were of its flora. I
had come into the Northwest from the plains country, bringing with me, as we carry useless burdens from place to place, a
box containing several hundred mounted and labeled botanical specimens, collected in a five-state area of the Southwest for
my own information and pleasure. Here in this green and
growing country flanked by salt water, I was confronted by a
bewildering array of fauna and flora, both marine and land,
to which I could give no name.

Nor did I learn much during those first years of living in the
city. To visit a museum, an aquarium, or an arboretum is not

the same as to take field guide in hand and wander through woods and over meadows. Nor does one learn as much or retain as well when he is exposed to a conglomeration of specimens removed from their natural environment.

Here on the Island, armed with books and charts and slides, I began to explore in earnest. Some of the flora differed little, I found, from the flora of the cooler, moister portions of Colorado and the Ozarks, even from that of parts of Kansas, except there was more of it, and it grew to greater heights and bloomed more prolifically. Often, it went by different local names. For example, fireweed, which grows in abundance in burned-over areas in Colorado, is known there as "blooming Sally."

"Not only did we have *trees* in Kansas," I was able to tell the doubting Northwest Thomases (who appeared to have driven hurriedly across *western* Kansas, if, indeed, they had ever seen Kansas at all, on a hot day in August), "we even had oak and maple and ash, elm and cottonwood and hackberry." Madroña we did not have, nor Pacific dogwood nor fir nor alder nor hazel. But where, on the other hand, was *their* Osage orange, their shagbark hickory, their sycamore, their Kentucky coffee? But these things were said in pique, to those who poked fun in order to see me bristle. In truth, I was filled with awe and with a gnawing desire to know.

Presently, we began to spend more days of the year on the Island than on the mainland. Then I could observe the seasonal changes. Gradually, I became less aware of the rain, the gloom, the morning fogs; I began to like them, rather. "There's this about it," Earle said, as we sat by the fire one November evening and counted the fact that we had served three hundred meals to guests (all of them welcome) the preceding summer, "this kind of weather, there's not something forever breathing down your neck to be done."

The Island continued to seem a wonderful discovery, the peak of a submerged mountain, on the shores of which I had somehow landed. As with the island in the Verdigris, I wanted

to know all about it that was to be known. I could learn something of its fauna and flora from regional books and from
observation, and I was coming to know its current inhabitants.

But in order to come at any kind of understanding of a place,
one must know something of its earlier years. How had the
community begun, and how had it progressed through time?
Change in such a place is slow, but constant. The seasons and
the years come and go. The story of a community is made up of
the everyday lives of its people, of their defeats and their suc-
cesses, of their plans and ambitions, of the tragedies that touch
their lives and of their achievements. A country is settled, a
community is developed by the restless, the visionary, the val-
iant, the stubborn, the rebellious. The opportunity to know
who these people were and what they had done came unexpectedly.

At Christmas time, I received in the Island mail a card from
Betsey Cammon, a woman in her seventies, whom the Islanders, even the children, call "Bessie." For the past several years,
she wrote, she had been about the compilation of a record of
the Island's past and of those who had built it. This was something, she said, which she wished to leave as a memorial to
them and as a heritage to their descendants. Would I care
to help?

I did not know Bessie Cammon well, but I had come to
admire her a good deal. She is a tall, spare, clear-eyed woman,
who shows her Scandinavian ancestry, in her case Swedish. I
knew that she was a widow and that she lived alone at the north
end of the Island, near Otso Point, in the big family house in
which her three sons had grown to manhood and where she
had lost her only daughter.

With the exception of a few years during the early part of
her marriage spent at Still Harbor on nearby McNeil and at
Kapowsin, she had lived all of her life on Anderson. She had
taught the Island school and had been married in the first
wedding held on the Island. A few years previously, as a teacher

in the nondenominational Sunday school, the only strictly spiritual organization the Island affords, she had sponsored the young people in the publication of a mimeographed newspaper, *The Island Gazette*. She had contributed, each week, a page pertaining to the early years. I knew that she could be relied upon to be painstakingly accurate. I replied that I would indeed like to help. This seemed precisely what I was looking for.

Bessie's is a charming house. Standing hard by the north shore, it is surrounded by luxurious growth, a spreading hazel tree, a pine festooned with ivy, big bing cherry trees, an evergreen hedge. Flower beds are filled with old-fashioned perennials, phlox and primrose and Michaelmas, sage and snowdrops and geraniums. Bird houses made by her children and grandchildren hang about. Each summer a wisteria with a parent stem as thick as a man's arm drips blossoms in the front yard. A second wisteria, where her big cat Jerry sleeps, his tail hanging down like a latchstring, drapes the back pergola.

Everywhere, inside and out, are objects picked up on the beach, driftwood and shells and dried starfish. Old pictures decorate the walls, along with art work done by her grandchildren. The wide mantel holds mementos of a family that went down to the sea in boats. "Cluttered," Bessie calls the house. But it is a charming and clean accumulation. Hers is a house filled with memories, of birth and death, but of loving and living and laughter, too. You feel it when you enter, by the back door, always. The front door faces the water.

It is a place of good smells, for Bessie is always canning or making something—chili sauce, or apple jelly, cinnamon rolls or pumpkin pie or sauerkraut. Once, because we had talked of it, she served me a bowl of Scandinavian fruit soup. Or we had tea and skorpa.

The windows of the kitchen, which is heated by a wood burner, look out across Balch Passage to McNeil and across to the wooded arm of the Olympic Peninsula called Longbranch.

On a clear day, the snow-powdered peaks of the Olympic Range stand out in a ragged saw-toothed line, like mountains on a picture post card.

Often one of the little freight boats the Islanders call "grain boats" or "beer boats," the *Skookum Chief* or the *Skagit*, the *Indian* or the *Lovejoy*, passed by as we sat talking. Or we stopped to watch a sailboat taking the breeze, or a long gray Coast Guard boat. Perhaps an Island fisherman rested his oars as he drifted along the edge of a tide rip. Occasionally, if the tide were running fast, as it does both in and out through the Passage, a tug with a raft of logs in tow swung in to stand by and wait until slack.

Sometimes a really big freighter or a transport passed, under its own power or pushed or pulled by tugs, like an elephant on leash. Often a log patrol boat nosed along the shore in search of logs escaped from booms, or Islander Clem Zukowski's bait boat went by at a good clip, out for herring. Occasionally, the little skiff from next door, where Bessie's son Russell lives, pulled out from shore bearing her grandchildren, John and Michael and Betsey.

The big boats sent in wake waves that pounded along the beach in a soft liquid rhythm. Waves from the smaller boats struck the shore gently, in a rolling motion, rocking the skiffs tied out to their moorings and rolling and turning the clean-washed gravel. On a still morning the hammer of the tugs' engines could be heard from a long way off, and on days of fog the hoarse voices of the boats struck back echoes from the Island bluffs and trees, as they had in the old days when it was by means of echoes that the skipper kept his bearings.

During the months that followed, I spent a great deal of time at the little table in Bessie's kitchen, listening, poring over yellowed maps and census books, clippings and photographs and school records, in an effort to piece the story together. We digressed often, for there was much to be speculated about. We were dealing with human beings and there was human emotion and motivation. There was tragedy touched with comedy in which pathos played an integral part. There were absorbing and sometimes hilarious stories that, for the sake of charity, could not be told.

Invariably we got around to the same questions: What brought people here? How had this small world remained relatively unchanged in a rapidly changing society? How was it that in an age of hurry-up, life on the Island still moved in low gear, still retained the ease and the dignity of deliberation?

Was it the isolation, the fixed geographical boundaries? Did it have to do with the smallness, the closeness to nature with her lavish bounty, the fact that the Island assured generous living space?

We talked a good deal about the probable future of the Island. Much of the land is held by long-time owners, or by the sons and daughters and grandchildren of early settlers and homesteaders, who, as their forebears, dread to see the Island change. It is the Islanders who really set the pace of change, we concluded. The accumulation of material goods, the march of progress is held of less importance than is living space. There is little concern for more than enough.

9

FIRST COMERS

The precise identity of the first settler on Anderson Island is uncertain. But this much is known: He was a son of Hans and Dorathea Smith Christensen. He hailed from Denmark. His name was John, or Andrew, or Christian. He probably first saw this wooded world in 1870.

The lineage of the Christensens is an interesting one. The grandmother, the daughter of a German baron, eloped with a footman and was disinherited. Her son, Hans (who came eventually to the Northwest, but not to the Island), married Dorathea, the daughter of a Danish minister. Following an invasion of Denmark by Germany, Dorathea vowed that none of her children should ever fight for Germany, and so she shipped them out to sea as soon as they were old enough.

Andrew, who went to sea at the age of fourteen, was shipwrecked in Puget Sound and subsequently landed on Anderson Island. Although the records do not indicate whether his brothers John or Christian had already landed here, it is generally accepted that Christian, the eldest, was the first true settler. John and Andrew, a brother named Peter, and a sister, Christine (later Christine Kuthman), are also known to have lived here for a time.

Of the family, only Christian lived out his life here. He is buried, along with his wife Helda, his son Daniel, and three of his daughters, in Island soil. Now only Dan's widow, Lena, a retired Island postmistress, remains. She lives next door to Bessie at Otso Point, "in the house Dan built," and her house, too, is filled with memories.

Andrew and John (who took the name "Christy") borrowed a "stake" and built a raft of logs, hoping to float them to a mill at Port Blakeley. When the raft broke up, the logs were lost in a storm in the channel. Shortly thereafter these two left for the mainland. Andrew's daughter, Etta Wallace, has in her possession a logging agreement drawn up between the two brothers, whose knowledge of English, or lack of it, comes through delightfully in the businesslike wording of the contract.

Walals Is. Pears Co. Wash Territory

We agreet upon this 1 dae of Oct 1872 that ve Andrew N Christensen and John F. Christy vel log of the N.E. qua of N.E. Sec. 5 . . .

1. By agrement, John F. Christy vel pae 25 cent per thousan for all the tember on sait N.E. quarter . . . four poles are conted one thoussen feet of lumber.

   Ve forteymore agreet upon that ven fennesing logen sait tember ve vel comens to make road and holl the tember off vich is call the nole enclouet the tember laing N. and W. of the haf mile post. Ve vel comens and tack all the tember vich vel fall on level and go to the North end of my svale and end about the rens of the corner post of the Railrode fortey. Ven done ve vel comens at the S. end of the E. of the strem and log of all the tember vich the chopers leffet to chop til ve get to the line of the Railrode fortey. Vich end our agrement.

2. Agrement about Seder

   Ve, A. N. Christensen and J. F. Christy agret upon that after fin-ichin holling the fur tember, ve vel hol the Seder. If not ve vel move to my Hous. Wile holling the Seder, I, A. N. Christensen vel gae to J. F. Christy $2.00 per dae and bord and $1 per dae for oxen feid.

3. Agrement about fires.

   Ve agreet upon that thar shall be no fiers bilt on the logen gronds, excepcon on dae wich is cold. Ve haf the prevelech to bilt a fire the 15 dae of Aug if ve vess to do so.

4. Agrement about manoars [this probably refers to "manures"]. J. F. Christy haf agreet that A.N.C. shal haf da manoar for to years from the 1 dae of April 1873 and the balans vel belong to J. F. Christy.

5. Ve, A.N.C. and J.F.C. agreet upon des 12 dae of Oct 1872 that if enny question should rise between us, it shal be settlet by tacken a half dolar and tos oup 3 tim and hae that get, to have right and it vel be sattisfatury to the other.

En witnes har-of thad this agrement and rols vich comencet on page 4 and ends on page 8 are doly tru and agreet upon by J. F. Christy and A. N. Christensen.

Such charming entries continue through two hand-written books, a rich lode. One of these books notes the occurrence of an earthquake in December of 1872, the year of Christian's marriage, and lists the Island witnesses to the event as "Christian and Helda Christensen, Andrew and Jette Christensen (Andrew's wife), Peter Christensen, and John Christy."

The third brother Peter remained for a time. But then he too left the Island. So far as is known, it was in the year 1870 that the young Dane, Christian, signed on as a member of the crew of a Danish ship bound for the northwest corner of the United States of America, still territorial in status. When the ship dropped anchor at Port Gamble in the Strait of Juan de Fuca, Christian "jumped ship," and worked his way Up Sound to land eventually on Anderson Island, where he staked out a claim for himself.

How long this took is not a matter of record. For a would-be settler to use this means of coming to the new country was not unusual. Time after time, in stories of the settlement of the Northwest, the sentence, "he jumped ship and took up homestead land," appears. Some were pre-emption claims, whereby the settler took an option to purchase. The Donation Act, signed in 1850 and known as the Oregon Land Law, had come to an end by limitation in 1854.

Christian first settled on Amsterdam Bay on Drayton Passage and began to clear land. The name of the bay appears on earlier maps as "New Amsterdam." Early boatmen referred to it simply as "Dutch Harbor." The location would seem to have been a wise choice. The inlet was of considerable depth at high tide, affording protection for small boats. Fresh water, a commodity needed in quantity by wood-burning steamers, sprang from the hillside above. Side- and stern-wheelers, on the increase in the Sound, furnished a ready market for the cordwood he cut in his clearing.

Christian obviously made no large initial investment, as did his brothers with their log raft. He built a woodyard on the Bay and offered his cordwood for sale there, dragging it down the hill by means of oxen—a cheap, if slow, source of power. The Island lay on a direct route between the booming pioneer town of Olympia, which was to become the state capital, and the thriving young towns of Tacoma and Seattle. The steamers burned up to sixteen cords of wood a day. Christian built a dam to impound fresh water from the springs and a landing for the boats he serviced. By 1872, he felt so well established that he wrote back to Denmark and asked his cousin, Helda Maria Cathrina Cardell, to join him as his wife.

Helda was eighteen, twelve years Christian's junior. She had not seen him for two years. It is doubtful whether there had been much communication between them. In those days, a letter from the northwest coast of the United States to Denmark traveled for a long time. For a girl of eighteen to set sail for a tiny wooded island to make her home in a log cabin must have required considerable courage.

A faded photograph, taken in Denmark, shows her as a slender, delicate-looking girl in a high-necked dress. Informal camera shots at Island neighborhood gatherings during her late years show her as a stocky woman with a strong serene face. "She *was* a strong woman," Bessie remembers. "She had initiative and energy. She was a real force in the building of the community."

Helda arrived at Fort Steilacoom in February, 1872, accompanied by Christian's brother Peter. She had brought along a wedding dress, painstakingly made, but the little church afforded no privacy in which to change. She and Christian were married in a mass ceremony, along with sixteen other couples who planned to establish homes in the territory. Following the nuptials, the young couple set out by rowboat for Amsterdam Bay, between nine and ten miles away by water.

Helda and Christian spent fifteen years on the Island together, and they were crowded ones. Helda's first child, Kate, was born in June of 1873, with an unknown Indian woman from the mainland in attendance. The woman had seen Helda once, early during her pregnancy, and foretold the precise day of the child's birth. And, although Helda did not see her again until that day, both baby and midwife arrived on the day specified.

Kate Christensen grew up on the Island and married the Aaraas who became an Oras. Those who remember her as a young woman say that she sawed and chopped wood, tended stock, helped to build a wharf. When a new family, the Dahls, for whom Lake Josephine was first named, came to live on the lakes, sixteen-year-old Kate hitched up the Christensen oxen and hauled the newcomers' furnishings over the rough wooded trail from Johnson's Landing. Previous to Kate's ninth year, the Island offered no school. But records show that she was still in school at age nineteen. Kate died recently in a rest home at Poulsbo, Washington, at the age of ninety.

Young Helda's second daughter, Julia, arrived when Kate was two, and a son Daniel was born four years later. Christian was obliged to officiate alone at at least one of the births. "Help yourself to wood and water," he is said to have called in a harassed voice to the captain of a steamer that had pulled up beside his dock. "The cow's having a calf and my wife's having a baby!"

Mainland Indians stopped often at the little cabin, where Helda spent much time alone with her children. As curious and as cheeky as children, they paddled into the bay, climbed the rise, entered the cabin without a by-your-leave, and pointed to whatever it was that struck their fancy.

"They especially liked her homemade bread," Dora Christensen Zabroski, Helda's daughter, told me. "She couldn't understand their language, which was a kind of jargon, and they couldn't understand hers, which was Danish. She was always a little nervous about them and gave them whatever it was they asked for. Once, it was the ornamental buttons off her basque dress, and she cut the buttons off and handed them over." Little Kate, who was afraid of strange white men, had no fear of the Indians and always ran to meet them when they came. Sometimes they brought quarters of venison, which they sold for fifty cents. A big fresh salmon brought a nickel.

When Helda was thirty-three, Christian, who had been ailing for some time, died of pneumonia and asthma, leaving her with six children and a seventh, Dora, on the way. With the help of a manager, Helda carried on alone for two years. Then she married another Islander, August Lindstrom, who established a woodyard of his own at Otso Point. Helda bore him a son, Conrad.

"We were a happy family," Dora remembers. "For all that we called our stepfather 'the old man,' we liked him. He was kind to us. And we adored our little half-brother, 'Cunnie.' Whereas we now lived at Otso Point, we kept the old place at New Amsterdam and went back to the old house often, rowing the distance in our skiff."

On a January day in 1897 tragedy once again entered Helda's life, this time in double measure. Dora, who was going on ten that year, remembers that "the old man had gone over to Amsterdam to do some work, taking Cunnie with him. Julia and I followed later. I climbed the hill to the house and found the old man dead on the floor. I thought he was asleep and went to tell Julia. We went back to the house and found that Cunnie was dead, too. Both of them had been shot. The old man had left a note saying he didn't want a son of his to grow up in this 'rascally world.' "

"Mamma was expecting another baby in June. People said that when she heard the news, she put a hand on her breast, and that's why the baby, Myrtle, was born with a mark like a bullet just there. People believed such things, then."

The house where the tragedy took place still stands, a gaunt unpainted structure perched on the side of the steep slope overlooking the mouth of Amsterdam Bay. The interior has

been remodeled tastefully by the current owners. But it is known on the Island as "the haunted house." Kept awake on windy nights by creaks and groans, an earlier owner added a sturdy room at the side, into which the family could escape when the sounds were especially persistent.

During the year following the two deaths, Helda was to lose two more children, baby Myrtle and seventeen-year-old Helda Maria Christensen. The record of these events, briefly noted, reposes in Helda's Danish Bible, on two yellowed and brittle pages that tell the story of a voyage through time. The earlier dates are recorded in Danish, the latter in English, as she learned the language. Born, the daughter of a sailmaker, in Assens, Denmark, in 1853, Helda Cardell Christensen Lindstrom died in 1933 on Anderson Island, half a world away.

She gave birth to ten children, nine of them living and one of them still-born, all without a doctor in attendance. Childbirth in those days was looked upon as a simple elemental process, involving a certain risk but nothing to consult a doctor about. Doctors were for such things as broken bones, and smallpox, if you could persuade them to come, and for tuberculosis. Even the "consumptives," it would seem, rarely left the premises here. At several Island farmsteads, a "little house" was constructed. In this, a tubercular member lived out his life in hopeless isolation, cared for by a devoted member of the family, who fetched and tended. Some of these "little houses" still stand, memorials to the victim of a dread and incurable disease, and tributes to the memory of a tireless devotion.

The second family of settlers, comprised of John and Ann Ekenstam and seven of their eleven children, arrived from Sweden by way of Kansas on a February day in 1879. They came to the Island by steamer and landed at the southernmost tip, in the gentle inlet known as Thompson Cove. Steamboat traffic to the Island was at the whim of the tides in those days. "The tide was well in," Louise Ekenstam Ostling, one of the daughters, wrote afterward, "and we were able to land on the dock built out into the water (obviously by one of the Christensen brothers), but the cow was pushed overboard and had to swim."

"Father had bought 212 acres. He came from Kansas where a small farm was no good, and he was bound to have a big place. He at once found it necessary to try to raise our own wheat so that we could make our own bread. He got a couple of mules and they plowed up so that he could sow wheat that very spring when we came there first.

"A part of the land had been cleared, and a house and a

barn had been built in the clearing. There was an old orchard that was quite nice, or had been. But it had been torn down by wild cattle."

Various theories exist concerning the wild cattle, which a good many early-day Islanders remember. They may have been left over from the closed-down logging camps. Or the beginnings of the herd may have crossed the Reach from the Bay Company's open range on the Nisqually prairie. "We were terrified of them," Dora Christensen Zabroski told me. "We always tucked away or covered up every bit of red we were wearing before we set out on the long wooded trail from our place on Amsterdam Bay to the schoolhouse in the center of the Island."

Until the third family came in 1881, no school existed on the Island. And this, too, was a problem that faced the Ekenstams. "But we children were three girls and four boys," Louise wrote, "and being so many, we felt quite contented and happy to be by ourselves. There were lots of Indians around (on the mainland), but they seemed pretty good-natured. The only time we were afraid was when the Victoria Indians would come up our way in big boats and lots of them at once. My oldest brother told us to be very friendly and kind to them and let them have all the fruit they wanted. With the home Indians, we never needed to worry. They would be across on the Nisqually Reservation and we could get fish and things from them.

"The beauty of the island was that we had all the food we could possibly eat or use and an abundance of deer. As soon as it got dark, the deer would be all around and, of course, we could get all the fish we liked because the Indians would come around and sell us nice big salmon for five cents apiece. By fixing up the orchard, we soon had every kind of fruit we wanted, and we never had any trouble with pests. . . ."

An Ekenstam granddaughter, Edna Ostling Myers (Louise's daughter) of Longbranch, tells a story, handed down, of one late August when a group of "Northern" Indians came in canoes and systematically stripped the orchard of its ripened fruit, carrying the fruit down to the shore in big cedar baskets. But for all the loss of the fruit, the tale has a happy climax. During the unscheduled harvest, an Indian came to the house, pushed open the door, and entered. Terrified, Ann was about to whisk her children out through another door and so to the fields where the men were at work, when the eldest, Carrie, took matters into her own hands and confronted the visitor.

There ensued a lively exchange in signs and gestures. Mindful of her brother's admonition, the girl even managed to wear a smile of sorts. To the women's relief, their guest finally departed. And so too, presently, did the laden canoes.

Ann and the girls walked down through the orchard. The marauders had been thorough. Not one good apple, not a presentable plum, not a sound pear remained of the fruit they had counted on. When they had reached the beach, they stopped in amazement. There on the sand stood one of the long Haida canoes they had so frequently admired as the boats sped by on the water. Red on the inside, shining black on the outside, it boasted on the prow a handsome carved figurehead. The facts were obvious. Without knowing it, Carrie had made a deal by her nods and gestures. The canoe had been left in exchange for the harvest.

"Grandfather still had it when I was a little girl," Edna remembers. "Sometimes he took us for a ride in it. It was a gift well treasured. When it disappeared from the beach one day during a storm, we mourned its loss. But it had changed our opinion of the Northern Indians, who had made a bargain and had kept it."

The Ekenstam house, built by John and his sons, remains standing on the hill overlooking the cove. An old rookery of a building, from which all of the windows have been broken, it is a haven for birds and rodents. But, with its alcoved bedrooms, from the wall of which hang bits of still-bright wallpaper, and with its magnificent view looking out to the cove across the old orchard, it still wears an air of elegance.

"It *was* an elegant house," Edna remembers. "Or so it seemed to me. Built of planed lumber floated in from a mainland mill, it was furnished with heavy walnut furniture upholstered in crushed velvet."

Outside the kitchen door, a tall gnarled oak tree stands. Planted by John Ekenstam as a symbol of the family name, which means "oak stem" in Swedish, it drops leaves and acorns each year on the ancient moss-grown roof. Interestingly

enough, the only portion of the Island upon which oak trees flourish is at the south end, between the cove and Lyle Point and along the southwest shores of Oro Bay.

Faded snapshots taken on the island show Ann Ekenstam as a frail-looking woman of slight build. Islanders say she had left a servant-operated home in Sweden. But she spun and wove and managed to feed and clothe her large family. The eleventh and last child of the Ekenstams, a girl, was named Elva, meaning "eleven." The young Ekenstams, growing up on the Island, were a gay and lively lot. The big barn built by

John and his sons served during the eighties and the nineties as a social center for both McNeil and Anderson.

All of the Ekenstams of the original family are dead now. The four sons died without issue, so the name is rarely heard here. On early survey maps, the names of Edward and of Will Ekenstam, two of the sons, appear on parcels of land on the northeast portion of the Island, where they bought and built, to live as bachelors, and the name of "Charley" Ostling, who married Louise and who lived for a number of years on his own land on East Oro Bay, is spoken often. The name of Ekenstam appears on present-day maps only on the Ekenstam-Johnson road that bisects the Island from south to north, from Thompson Cove to Johnson's Landing.

This seems too bad, really. For they were a sturdy family with pride of lineage. They had considerable influence on the Island in the establishment of a school and in the building of the community, which consisted of a good many families before the last of the Ekenstams was taken away to be buried on the mainland.

The third family, Bengt and Anna Johnson and their baby son, Gunnard, landed on the Island in the spring of 1881, two years after the Ekenstams came. As had John Ekenstam, Bengt had already homesteaded land and proved-up in Kansas. Strangely, of the first four families that formed the nucleus from which the community grew—the Christensens, the Ekenstams, the Johnsons, and that of Nels Magnus Petterson, who was to follow shortly and settle on the shore of East Oro Bay—only the Christensens had come other than by way of Kansas. It pleases me to think, as I prowl the Island roads, that this fact may account for the original planting of the several "real Kansas cottonwood trees."

10

BESSIE CAMMON'S ISLAND

"Although Papa Johnson was fifty at the time of my birth, in 1886, and seventy at the time of my marriage," Bessie told me, "he never *seemed* old to me. Nor did Mamma and the other Island women seem as *young* as do women in their thirties today. Maybe it was because of the long skirts they wore, or because of the fact that women did not wear make-up then. There was less emphasis on a woman remaining young-looking. Too, they all had large families, so I suppose there wasn't much time to devote to keeping young."

Bengt was born in Vega-Halland, Sweden, and came to America as a young man. He stopped in Chicago first and then migrated out to Lindsborg, Kansas. He had proved-up on his claim before he met Anna Nelson, who had come from Eno-Kane, Sweden, to stay with her sister Olivia. Bengt was forty-two and Anna was twenty-two at the time of their marriage.

Bessie doesn't know why her folks came West, really. "I only know they came to stay. In those days you didn't make a trip to look a situation over. You couldn't afford to. You made the decision and then pulled stakes and moved for keeps, trusting that things would work out." Several Scandinavians from around Lindsborg had already come West, and Bengt and

Anna may have been influenced by that fact. Bessie thinks some others may have come at the same time. The trip was by train to San Francisco, and up the coast on the steamer *Idaho*. They settled first at the foot of Mount Rainier, near the town of Enumclaw. But the bears were too numerous and too intrusive, and they broke camp and continued looking. At this juncture, in the town of Steilacoom, Bengt encountered a Swede by the name of Larsen, who asked him whether he had considered settling on an island.

Bessie doubts whether Bengt had thought of such a thing. But as he stood looking out across the water, he could see Anderson Island (then called "Wallace") to the left of McNeil, where the territorial jail was located. Wallace was comprised of some nine sections of wooded land, he learned, and only two families—the Christensens and the Ekenstams—had settled there. More important, the Island harbored no bears.

Christian Christensen's woodyard at New Amsterdam was already well established. But cordwood was much in demand for the steamers that were already, in 1880, plying the waterways Up Sound. Bengt's desire was to farm, as he had in Kansas, and to raise livestock. But he reasoned, as had Christian, that while he was clearing to farm, here was a cash crop ready to harvest, as well as fuel for his own use and choice material for building.

The north end of the Island seemed a good site, and land was available there at two dollars an acre. The Christensens had settled on the west shore, the Ekenstams on the south. Behind little Eagle Island, off the north shore, the water would be comparatively slack for easy landing. Some of the land Bengt bought then, or later, was railroad grant land.

In old title books, transaction after transaction names the railroad as "grantor." The land was granted to the railroad companies in sections by the United States government, "to induce and finance" the building of the roads deemed so necessary to the settlement of the country. The grants consisted of alternate sections, six—sometimes fifteen, twenty, and even sixty—miles on either side of the proposed routes. The total of such land granted is estimated to have been in the neighborhood of 131,000,000 acres.

On a May day of 1881, baby Gunnard's first birthday, Bengt and Anna landed on the Island, bringing their household goods from Seattle on the stern-wheeler *Messenger*. These boats did not draw much water and could approach fairly close to shore at high tide, and they carried long gangplanks. No clearing had been done on the land Bengt had purchased, and so the Johnsons lived for a time in a small abandoned cabin on the point of land that bisects Oro Bay, known now as Jacobs' Point. When the cabin was built, and by whom, is and will probably always remain a mystery. All trace of it is gone now, and Bessie remembers only that Anna (who was expecting a second child) spoke often of having cooked on "a smoky fireplace." Bengt, meanwhile, had set to work to clear and build a cabin on his land at the north end, three miles away by rowboat.

I like to think how the Island must have been when Bengt and Anna came. There was less of deciduous growth and of broadleaf evergreen, early Islanders say, before the removal of the big trees admitted light and gave the alder, the maple, the dogwood, the madroña a chance to establish. But, take any year, and the Island is at its best in May.

Although madroña has a habit, disconcerting to the tidy gardener, of shedding its leaves at intervals to make way for new foliage, it is, to me, the loveliest of all the trees on the Island. In May, the madroñas are covered with clusters of creamy urn-shaped flowers among the glossy green-leather leaves. Trees of irregular growth, they bend and twist, but always with grace, to accommodate their environment, which may be a steep overhang or the edge of a dark conifer wood, to which, in any season, they lend a splash of spectacular color.

Following the creamy flowers of May, pendants of berries ripen to a bright orange among the shining silver-lined leaves. In late summer, the defoliating bark peels back in ragged curls to reveal a tender chartreuse, which has turned to a soft pinkish-cinnamon by November. It is a splendid tree in *any* season.

In May the frail blossoms of the bitter wild cherry trees are like lace edging along the banks above the beaches, and the Pacific dogwood displays its showy green-white bracts against the varied greens of new conifer growth. In May and June, the foamy pyramids of red-berried elder mingle with the pale tassels of vine maple, lingering red currant, coral-flowered salmon berry, and the rich cream tips of aromatic sticky laurel, called "summer lilac" or "mountain balm."

Although there is flowering from February, when the heavy leafless heads of sweet coltsfoot (butterbur) appear along the roadsides and the yellow spathes and spadices of skunk cabbage open in swampy places, until frost lays a hand on the golden-rod and Michaelmas and Queen Anne's lace, it is really in May, here, that summer comes. She may change her mind in June, withdraw, with glum skies and chilly nights, and hold up gardening plans and projects. But you can count on May, usually, to be a month of blue skies and blue water, of fragrance and of color.

The cabin into which Bengt and Anna moved that fall was typical of early-day houses here, which were added to as families grew to need more space. It consisted of two rooms and was made of logs, chinked with burlap held in place with plaster. Because of their resistance to decay, cedar logs were used as a foundation, with fir above. Small trees were felled and peeled to use as uprights and as rafters. The roof was of hand-split shakes. Stumps eight to ten feet high served as scaffold supports. When the cabin fell apart, after eighty years, many of the logs were still almost as sound as when they had been put together.

Feed sacks were tacked over the inside walls and covered with newspapers, printed in Swedish and in English, which could be replaced when the walls needed freshening. The floor was of bare planed boards, which were scrubbed on hands and knees, with a brush and homemade soap made from saved fats. Bessie still makes her own sometimes, convinced, even now, that soap made from Anna Johnson's recipe is a better product than can be bought in the stores, besides saving fat that would otherwise go to waste.

When the house was finished and the roof in place, Bengt set to work to build a landing for the steamers. Because of the tides, it was necessary to extend the wharf a long way out, below low water. The pier was built on pilings, cut and dragged down to shore and driven deep in sand and gravel. To supply fresh water for the steamers, he dug a storage reservoir into the side of the hill. This "cistern," as it was called, was fed from springs above by means of homemade wooden troughs which were called "spouts." Additional spouts carried the stored water down to the landing, where it was supplied gratis as a part of the service. This was termed "watering up." (Later, after the steamers had installed condensers, they reused their own steam.) The reservoir served a dual purpose. Covered over, it was a "springhouse" where milk and butter and other perishables were kept.

Anna's second child, also a boy, arrived in October and was named John. She was to bear five more children on the Island, all without a doctor or nurse in attendance. Anna had grown up on an island in Sweden, where her father had bleached and dyed materials as a vocation, spreading them out on the ground in the sun to dry. But that had been a tiny island, close to the mainland, from which the Nelsons had poled back and forth. On Anderson Island, Anna and Helda, dependent upon each other in time of need, lived more than two miles apart, through dense woods or by frequently rough water.

One morning Anna went down to the milk lot, leaving three-year-old Gunnard and baby John alone at the cabin. Returning to the house with her full milk pail, she looked up to see the baby teetering on the window sill. As she ran, he fell and lay screaming with pain, his leg doubled underneath him.

Anna, who was expecting a third child, was alone with the children. Bengt had taken the rowboat, and she had no means of transportation. The tide was coming in. Obliged to walk along the beach for help, Anna knew that it would be necessary, in places, to wade the cold salt water, and therefore dangerous to try to carry the injured child and lead the other.

Her first act was to nurse baby John to sleep. She cut wooden splints and set the bone as best she could and wound the leg about with dish towels. Having tied three-year-old Gunnard to his bed, she set out. The tide was even higher, by this time, than she had anticipated. Frequently, she was obliged to wade waist-deep water, to climb over shifting logs or through overhanging branches, hampered by her long skirts and by the fact that she must carry the injured child carefully so as to avoid a compound fracture. And, whether or not as a result of the strenuous trip, Anna was to lose the unborn child she carried.

A fourth child, Emil, born the following year, lived only one month and became so far as is known the first interment on Anderson Island. A daughter, Augusta, was born in 1884. Bessie was born in 1886. There were to be two more sons, Ben and Otto, both of whom have retired to live on the Island.

Only a little more than a decade had passed since the birth of Helda's Kate, and already the Island was teeming with children. By the time Kate was twelve years of age, Helda was the mother of six—Kate, Julia, Dan, Helda, Christine, and Grace. At the south end of the Island were the seven young Ekenstams. A road of sorts had been built to bisect the Island roughly from south to north; the handful of Islanders set to work to establish a school. The community was on its way.

"There are times," Bessie said one day, "when it occurs to me that I have not progressed very far in seventy-nine years." She was born October 5, 1886, in the little log cabin above Johnson's Landing. Presently she lives less than a mile away, in the big family house her husband Oscar Cammon built on the land she inherited from her parents. Although a few of her married years were spent elsewhere, Bessie admits to being an incurable Islander. At seventy-nine, she can hardly conceive of living on a mainland anywhere. Indeed, she cannot conceive of living anywhere except at Otso Point on Anderson Island, from which she can look across at the mountains and watch the boats pass through the channel.

The boats are vastly different from the side- and stern-wheelers she knew as a child, boats that stopped at New Amsterdam, lined with summer cabins these late years, and at Johnson's Landing. Nor do they sound the same. But the hammer of the passing tugs and the hoarse whistles that bounce an echo off the Island hills and trees on foggy mornings take her back to her childhood.

"One of my earliest recollections," she said, "is of being ridden up and down on Papa's ankle as he sang to me in Swedish. I remember the song, so I must have heard it when I was older, too. Probably he sang it to the younger children, then. It went like this:

Rida, rida, Ranka. Hasten heter Blanka.
Hvar skall han rida? Till en liten piga.
Hvar skall hon bo? I en liten ho.
Hvad skall hon heta? Anna Margaretta.

In translation it reads:

Ride, ride, Ranka. The horse's name is Blanka.
Where shall he ride? To see a little girl.
Where does she live? In a little village.
What is her name? Anna Margaretta.

"From the earliest, I remember Papa as a small man with a black beard. Of course, it turned white later. Although he was a strict parent, he was good to us children. But he didn't have much time for us. He was always busy. Being busy was a habit he couldn't break, I guess. Even after the woodyard was closed, when the steamers had stopped coming, and after the children were grown and gone, he still chopped and carried wood as a hobby.

"Mamma had a great deal to do, too, with six children to tend and the teamsters to cook for. But she took time for such as music, too. She sang a great deal at her work. Mostly, she sang hymns in Swedish or English. It came to seem to me that when she was the most troubled about something she sang more. One song I remember she sang a great deal was 'Sweet Hour of Prayer.'"

Anna had brought a musical instrument with her from Sweden. She called it a "solmonica." Bessie has the instrument, along with a book of psalms set to music. The psalms led us to wonder if the name might have been "psalmonica," and we set off on a research project to find out. We found a description of such an instrument, consisting of an oblong wooden sounding box with a single string. Musical dictionaries defined it as a "monochord . . . an ancient invention for the mathematical determination of musical intervals." The nearest we could come to a possible explanation of the name, then, was that it really was a "solmonica" and that it came from the word "solus," meaning "alone," a solo instrument with one string.

Isolated together as they were, it would seem only natural for these early Scandinavian families to keep to their own customs and their own language. But Anna Johnson was determined that English, the language of the new country, was the only tongue to be spoken in the home. The children eventually learned Swedish. But they learned it at the Swedish Lutheran church in Tacoma, where services were conducted in *both* languages.   .

Anna talked little of her home in Sweden and of her journey to America. She had come "steerage," she said, and the journey had taken a long time. Passengers of that class were obliged to bring along their own food for the journey and to sleep on a floor of the boat, wherever they could find the space.

Anna had brought her food in a deep wicker basket. It had consisted of Swedish "flatbrod" and dried meats. She had brought a carafe filled with three quarts of coffee. On the Island, the carafe was used for making boiled coffee by adding hand-ground coffee beans to water. The basket was used as a repository for magazines, mending, all sorts of things, just as Bessie uses it.

"I suppose there *were* a great many ways in which we copied the customs of the old country," Bessie told me. "But as young people, we were impatient with some of the old ways, too, just as young people are today. I can remember feeling secretly glad that Mamma wore a hat instead of tying her head in a kerchief, the way some of the other Island women did. *Now*, even the *young* girls wear kerchiefs."

Most of the Scandinavian customs followed on the Island had to do with foods. Lutfisk (still eaten here at Christmas time) was more or less a holiday dish. But Islanders ate a good deal of fruit soup. The Swedish name for the dish was *frukta soppa*. Made with different ingredients, depending upon which fruits were available, the soup was a clear amber in color, and slightly thickened, usually with old-fashioned pearl tapioca. With a basic stock of raisins and prunes, plus dried apples, lemons, and other fruits at hand, the dish contained neither fat nor sugar. Served hot, as a first course, it was followed by meat and vegetables. "There may have been other ways of making it," Bessie said. "But that is the way we were taught. We also ate a great deal of clabber. The milk was soured quickly for this, not left to sour until it turned bitter."

With the closest grocery store miles away across the channel, women were obliged to plan a long way ahead, especially during the winter months. The store boats that came later were a real convenience. Staples were bought in quantities and kept outside in a storehouse built for the purpose. The woodchoppers who wished to do so drew on these as a part of their wages.

Women baked their own bread. If the starter was lost, they prepared their own yeast. To make the yeast, they boiled dried hops, raised in Island gardens, and added sugar and grated potatoes to the water. "We often ate dough balls," Bessie remembers, "tiny balls of bread dough, baked hard and brought to the table heaped in a big bowl. They tasted something like the bread sticks you buy today. We children used them for a game we called 'odd or even.' Beef and chicken were plentiful and most Island families had plenty of milk and butter. I can remember milking five cows night and morning. In addition to the lutfisk, which was soaked out, boiled, and served with a cream gravy, boiled rice and milk was a dish traditionally served at Christmas time."

Skorpa was kept on hand to serve with coffee to visitors. A bread resembling rusks, skorpa was made from a rich sweet yeast dough containing eggs. Baked in a loaf, it was cut into thick pieces and baked again, slowly, until it was brown all the way through. To keep the skorpa from absorbing dampness and becoming soggy, the housewife put it into a cloth bag and hung it above the stove. Skorpa was often dunked in tea or coffee and eaten dripping. Lump sugar for visitors was a must. The sugar was not dissolved in the beverage, but eaten between sips.

Stockings were hand knit of hand-spun yarn. Island sheep supplied the wool. Garments were made from hand-woven stuff. A few Island wheels, handed down, exist as heirlooms. One of *my* prized possessions is a hand-woven blue and yellow rug, made by Bessie on her old basement loom, which I purchased a few years ago at an Island bazaar.

In addition to all of these tasks, Anna Johnson somehow found time to garden. During her first year at the Landing, she planted a bed of crocus to form the digits 1 8 8 1, to commemorate the date. For years afterward, these were clearly discernible at blossoming time. On a rainy February Sunday this year, I walked in past the ruins of the old house and saw masses of white and green snowdrops raising their heads above the dead bracken, an annual resurrection.

"After the cemetery was laid out in the center of the Island," Bessie said, "we used to take flowers there. My brother Emil, who died before I was born, was the first death on the Island so far as we knew. He was buried before the cemetery was laid out the way it is now, in the woods on the high part of the Island. A stone was put up for him later, inside the fenced part, but his remains were never moved. I used to know where the grave was and to take flowers there. But it's lost now."

One grave Anna tended was that of a young Islander, Guy Gardner, who had gone over the Cascade Mountains into eastern Washington at seventeen to help drive stock across for early settlers. Guy fell ill and died on the trip, probably of pneumonia, called "quick consumption" then. He was brought back to the Island for burial. His parents moved away soon afterward, and they asked Anna to care for his grave, which she did as long as she was able. Bessie still decorates the grave, with its simple epitaph, "Our Loved One," each Memorial Day, because of the promise Anna made.

After Bengt and Anna had been on the Island for a year or so and felt settled, they sent for Bengt's father, John Borgeson, to join them. Grandfather Borgeson made it from Kansas as far as San Francisco all right, in company with Charlie Carlson, a potential Island teacher who was making the trip West. But when the steamer was ready to leave San Francisco for Puget Sound, he was nowhere to be found, and the Carlsons were obliged to leave without him. He was found by San Francisco police, wandering and lost in a city park, and sent up by a later boat, to live and die on the Island.

Although they kept busy supplying wood for the steamers those years, the Island settlers had not lost sight of their original aim—to have cleared farms stocked with sheep and cattle, and fruit trees sufficient for their families. To keep the cattle out, they fenced the orchards with rails—made by hand-splitting the logs—dove-tailed end to end. The fences, consisting of six or seven rails, ran a little zigzag, giving rise to the name of "snakefences." Fences around the houses and outbuildings were made from hand-hewn cedar pickets.

Making my way through tangled woods, I come across remnants of these sometimes, like the sections of a staff upon which music is inscribed. Moss-grown, the split lengths hold aloft a burden of sword fern or of little salal bushes, or of a red huckleberry whose roots have found nourishment in the moss that is in turn nourished by the decaying wood in which its roots have wedged a foothold.

Red huckleberry (*Vaccinium parvifolium*), fairly common but not prevalent as is the black huckleberry, has an affinity for old wood. Seeds dropped by birds or animals take root in the hollows of decaying stumps, and the delicately graceful shrubs arise like impressionistic Christmas trees, hung, in late summer, with clear bright balls of fruit.

"I don't think it occurred to anyone then," Bessie says, "but I have thought, often, about the cords and cords of fine wood that went into the hungry maws of the steamers. Now it seems a frightful waste of good building material. But in order for the country to open up, the steamers had to operate, and with clearing for fields and orchards, they all had to go." Less valuable trees might have served the boats as well. But alder and madroña, like blackberries, are opportunists that spring up when fir and cedar and hemlock are gone.

In order to keep up with the demand for cordwood, the woodyards hired whatever men could be persuaded to come to the Island to work. Some of these were transients. But many chose this way to work out a stake to buy and build on their own places. Chopping was hard work, and the pay was less than that for the teamsters who did the hauling. Some of the woodcutters brought wives. Others batched around in shacks or cabins. Several lived on McNeil, rowed across each morning to work, and returned of an evening to their own chores. Like the Island settlers, most were Scandinavian. Bessie remembers a Charlie Johnson, Erik Myberg, Chris Steen, and a man named A. S. M. Anderson, and called all of it.

The woodcutters worked in pairs, with a crosscut. The men stood on a springboard about five feet above the ground. With a big tree, this left a considerable stump, six, eight, sometimes ten feet across, to be grubbed out by hand. Often, two men worked an entire day to remove a single stump, hacking it down with an axe and taking out the roots with a mattock. The tree was limbed and then sawed into four-foot lengths, which were split with sledges and wedges.

The teamsters hauled the wood down to the yard where it was ricked up ready to be loaded onto the steamers. A cord of these four-foot logs, measuring eight feet in length and four in height, at one time brought two dollars, which was considered a high price.

Occasional storms took their toll of trees, especially of the shallow-rooted, and these too went into the furnaces of the steamers. Earlier settlers had used oxen for the hauling, but as horses became more plentiful most farmers preferred them because of their greater speed and ease of manipulation.

The woodchoppers worked ten hours a day, six days a week, and were paid sixty cents a cord. This came to around nine dollars a week for a fast worker, considered a fair week's wage.

At the end of each working day, woodpiles were measured and each man was credited in a record book with the amount of wood he had cut and ricked up. When an hourly wage basis became the custom, about 1893, and Tacoma area choppers were drawing twelve and one-half cents, the Island paid fifteen cents.

The Island was considered a good place to work. If you were not too particular about your "diggings," you could get room and board for two and a half dollars a week, and Island get-togethers were lively. Dances and parties and picnics, held on either McNeil or Anderson, lasted the night through because of the long row home after dark. A wooden vat, located somewhere on the east side, supplied Island-made whiskey.

Staples brought in on freight boats and kept in the storehouse where the teamsters slept consisted of sugar, bags of flour packed in barrels, Arbuckle's coffee beans, slabs of salt pork and bacon, plug cut chewing tobacco, and wooden pails of salt herring. It was said, and believed, that no Scandinavian could live without salt herring in his diet.

In the year 1893, flour was listed at $3.75 a barrel. Sugar sold for six cents a pound. Butter cost thirty cents, cheese eleven, and bacon fifteen. Copenhagen snuff, called "snoose," came in gallon stone jars, jug-shaped and of a rich cream color, with a good glaze. Several of these handsome jars can be seen on the Island today. The wide use of snuff resulted partly from the fact that smoking in the woods would have been dangerous. Regulations to do with closing the woods in dry weather were nonexistent then. But, neither were there engines that might have set a fire.

One woodchopper several Islanders remember was a hunchbacked man named Mattias Iverson. Because working in the woods was difficult for Matt, he was given a job as general choreman about the farm. Matt cleaned the cow and horse barns, helped with the feeding and the milking, and cut and sawed wood for the stoves.

Some cook stoves boasted a reservoir at the back for heating water, but all of the water for house use at the Johnsons' was heated in kettles or in the wash boiler. Frequently, these boilers were handmade from the big tins in which the light-house tender *Manzanita* delivered mineral oil for fueling the Eagle Island stake light.

The heating stove, oval in shape and with a nickel bar where you could toast your feet on chilly nights, had isinglass windows across the front. The flames showing through these and the cheerful reflection on the walls, Bessie remembers, made you *feel* warm, whether you were or not. On the top of the stove set a fancy spire. When the spire was pivoted to one side a flat surface was exposed. Here you could set the cast iron teakettle if you wanted a cup of tea. The kettle was heavy even when empty. When it was filled, Bessie remembers, it was all she could do to lift it into place.

For wash day there were two other iron kettles, even larger and heavier, and a copper wash boiler. These, along with the ridged washboards and three graduated wooden tubs, made up the laundry equipment. Matt Iverson often helped Anna with the washing, doing much of the hand rubbing on the board. Bessie remembers that he often embarrassed her by asking, "Bessie, *when* are you going to stop wetting your panties?" But the children, as well as the woodcutters, all liked Matt, because of his rich sense of humor, and he became indispensable around the farm. "It occurred to me later," Bessie said, "that he may have laughed and joked in order to help himself through his bad days. In addition to his hunchback, he suffered a hip deformity that was often painful to him."

One woodcutter the Islanders called "Friday" came to chop for the Lindstrom yard at Otso Point. Friday lived in a small shack he had built out of fir poles and cedar shakes, a house so small his little stove would hardly fit in at the head of his bunk, leaving space only for a box, used as a table, and a small stool where he sat to eat.

On the first night in his new home, Friday discovered that his bunk was too short for his considerable length. After a few uncomfortable nights of sleeping drawn up, he cut a hole in the wall at the foot. Awakened one morning by a scratchy feeling on his bare feet, he declared, he found that a pair of grouse had taken up a perch on his ankles. He solved the problem by nailing an empty coal oil tin over the opening, and slept with his feet in that.

Once the Johnson yard employed a Chinese woodcutter, a strange little man who lived to himself in a small dirt-floored cabin he had made from fir poles, roofed with cedar shakes, and furnished with a straw-covered bunk. "Because we so rarely saw people of another race," Bessie recalls, "the house, which we came to call 'the China cabin,' held an aura of mystery for us. After he had gone from the Island, we went again and again to search the place. I don't really know what we expected to find. We never found anything at all.

"There *was* a mystery connected with his departure. He simply disappeared without a trace. It was during the Chinese trouble in Tacoma that culminated in the expulsion of most of the Chinese from that city. No one knew whether he was involved in the trouble or whether he was simply caught up in the expulsion. He had gone to town by steamer, as he sometimes did, to visit other members of his race. He never returned to the Island. The house, if it could be called that, remained 'the China cabin' until it fell apart.

"Although Tacoma was less than twenty miles away, the Chinese trouble, as everything else that went on on the mainland, seemed far removed from our lives. It sometimes occurs to me that the way we feel detached here on the Island from whatever is going on on the outside is not altogether to our credit. Our parents read the newspapers brought in by the steamer crews just as we read and listen to the radio and watch television now. We like to know what's going on outside. But we are somehow lulled into half believing that only that which happens here on the Island happens to us.

"The Island was a fine place to grow up, really. It was our entire world in a manner of speaking, and we felt we knew it from end to end and from side to side, all of the woods and clearings, and the channel, and the trails that skirted the McNeil penitentiary. We were not so many young people, here and on McNeil, but we visited a good deal. By foot or rowboat, it was a long trip. And so we often spent the night, to make the trip pay. We had to wait, several hours sometimes, for the tide to turn in our favor before we could start home."

"How did you know about the tides?" I asked. We chart all of our water activities by the tide table we keep hanging on the kitchen wall.

"Well, the tide was always either *in* or *out*, or coming or going," she said. "We simply ran down to the shore and *looked*."

"Didn't your mother worry about you, when you were away overnight, with no way to notify her you had arrived safely?"

"No, I don't think she ever worried. The Island trails were safe enough, and we knew how to handle a boat. I guess she didn't have *time* to worry. We had been taught not to take risks. If the water whipped up, we simply stayed off until it calmed again.

"But I think it was more than that, too. She just didn't have any use for fear or timidity of any kind. Once, when we were swimming in the cove near the Landing with some town girls, my sister Augusta got too far out and began to flounder and gulp water. One of the girls had the presence of mind to push a limb out, and Augusta got hold of that. We were all so scared that we wouldn't have gone back to the cove to swim. But Mamma said, 'You're going back there tomorrow. You've learned your lesson and I don't want you to grow up to be afraid.' "

All Island children learned to row soon after they learned to walk. When a child was tall enough and strong enough to lift the oars and set them into the oarlocks, he set out, even if he had to stand in order to manipulate them. One year, the Christensen children—Julia and Dora and young Dan—rowed from their home at Otso Point to McNeil Island to finish out a six-month school term because only three months were offered on Anderson.

"Often, we were obliged to row against a strong tide in Balch Passage," Dora told me. "Across on the mainland, a man by the name of Snyder was said to sneak in at night and tow away Islanders' logs. We had heard this so often that Snyder had become a kind of villain. When the tide was running hard, we used to say that time and tide and Snyder were against us. We didn't know enough to be afraid. We just believed in our ability to handle a boat, and I guess our parents had confidence in us, too."

"I was afraid of everything *but* water," Bessie says. "Water seemed something open and to be trusted. On the other hand, the woods were dark throughout most of the year, and filled with creaking sounds. Often the fog lay thick between the trees. Birds rattled or hooted or started up unexpectedly, with a great flutter of wings. My brothers would say, 'That was just grouse, silly.' But it didn't help me any. The pileated wood-peckers made a terrible racket. They were as big as young roosters and made a loud squawking noise when they flew. Little 'coon faces looked down like spooks out of high nests in the trees. Deer leapt suddenly.

"The woods were full of wild cattle, too, or so I thought. The deer were shy and leapt lightly, so that you were only startled. Mostly, they saw you before you saw them. But you came on the cattle and they whirled and stared as though they were about to charge, and then went blundering and crashing away through the underbrush. I saw a wild bull behind every tree."

As the Island settled, the wild cattle gradually disappeared. They were killed off for meat, or joined the domestic herds. Prior to the extension of the herd law to include the Island, cattle had free run. The lead cow of each herd, chosen for her gentleness, wore a bell. After browsing all day on the tender wild peas that grew in the clearings, she set out for home at milking time, and the rest of the herd followed. Occasionally some stray hung back. The owner's "Co, Boss. Co, Boss," could be heard as he walked through the woods in his search. Each settler's bell had a different tone, and the children learned to distinguish one from the other.

Open range was an accepted thing until the first automobiles came, after ferry service was established. Then Island visitors began to complain of the animals on the roads. A petition was circulated asking that the mainland herd law be extended to the Island. Islanders were outraged. Why, they asked, should a handful of mainlanders in search of "free pasture" for themselves deprive the inhabitants of forage for their animals? And who, after all, was to see that the *deer* kept off the roads? If a visitor drove with his lights on high beam and at decent speed, he wasn't going to strike an animal in any case.

A meeting was called and the issue was hotly debated. But the summer people had their way. Obliged to accept the fact, for the first time, that the Island was a part of the county and the state and not an autonomy in its own right, Islanders grumbled, but they built fences.

On a Saturday last summer, I went by for Bessie and we drove down to the northernmost terminus of the Ekenstam-Johnson road and walked in through the gateway along a weed-grown trail to have a look at the remnants of Bengt's and Anna's cabin and of Johnson's Landing.

Not much is left. Time and tide have taken their toll here as elsewhere. For Bessie, the visit was a reliving, a picking among the ruins of her birthplace, a memory of the "Gee" and "Haw" of the teamsters, the sound of the axe and the sing of the crosscut, the splash of a steamer's wheel and the bellow of her whistle as she approached the Landing . . . the feel of the beaten path beneath a little girl's bare feet as she ran down the hill to watch the tying and the loading.

The day was warm for this area, the kind of windless day when all of the odors of the leaves and of the grasses mingle together and are intensified by the heat from the sun. We left the car at the main road and waded through waist-high bracken and tangles of trailing wild blackberries to the remains of the log house. The squared logs had been stacked up along the trail and numbered, with a thought to reconstruction of the cabin down by the big house. The timbers are roughly hewn. Many of the long wooden pegs that held the logs together remain in place, as do the big square nails that supported them.

In the old orchard, planted more than three quarters of a century ago, before Bessie was born, pear trees had already set the year's fruit. Most years Bessie still gets her autumn canning here. Half smothered by the wild grass and bracken and by the ever-present Himalaya berries, heavy now with their bearing, we found trailing hop vines, descendants of the vines Anna Johnson planted for making yeast, and a vigorous bed of mint. The climbing pink rose she trained beside the storehouse almost covers the building. That day you could hardly see the leaves for the blossoms.

The "new" section of the original cabin, moved up from the landing, remains attached to the floor of the old part, from which the roof and the walls have fallen. "I remember the day Grandpa Borgeson's body was laid out in this room here," Bessie said. "I was six at the time. He hadn't been well. That morning when Mamma went out to hang the clothes on the line, she said to me, 'Look after Grandpa.' When he began to gasp, I ran out and told her, 'Grandpa wants a drink of water.' She rushed into the house, but he was already dead.

"No one thought of calling an undertaker. I doubt whether one would have come, so far out, to an island. The neighbors came in and prepared the body and put him into a homemade cedar coffin, which was hauled to the cemetery in a wood wagon."

She paused briefly to examine three upside-down steps from an old staircase, the treads roughly sawed and worn half in two by years of climbing feet, and a fallen plank with a row of big thread spools for hanging clothing. "I go back in mind, often," she mused, "along the wood paths we walked and ran as children. Mostly, it seems to me we ran."

The ruins of the house stand high above the ruins of the Landing. The trail down to the wharf is grown over by a tangle of trees, fir and madroña and alder, and by huckleberry and bracken. All that is left of the Landing are a few half-rotted logs embedded in the earth. A portion of worn doubletree, some rusted harness buckles lie underneath the fallen roof of the barn.

We stood above the water and looked across at Eagle Island, like a round cake, at high tide, frosted with trees. Close by the bulkhead on the mainland side a barnacle-encrusted rock protruded a little way off shore. "That rock was always there," Bessie said. "It was always covered at high tide, but we knew to watch for it when we rowed out to tend the stake light."

As we made our way back up the grown-over depression that was once a road, she remarked that the trail seemed to grow more steep each year and that she did not come back very often.

"How does all this make you feel?" I asked. It is one thing to remember from a rocking chair, where the images are pleasantly blurred by time, and quite another to go poking in fact among the shards.

She weighed the question for a moment, as we watched a gray gull draw a slow circle around the dead spire of an ancient fir on the little island. "It makes me feel a little bit as though time has run out from under me," she said finally. But she said the words cheerfully. "I guess the Island means something different to each of us," she had said to me once. "I reckon you might say each of us has his own Island." This was her Island, this memory of the wood paths and of the steamers, just as the rolling hills of southeast Kansas will always belong to me. Whatever happens here, no one can deprive her of this heritage.

11

WIDE AWAKE HOLLOW

By the time the third family arrived on the Island, in 1881, the community already boasted several children, but no school. Kate Christensen, who was nine, had had no schooling. The second Christensen daughter had turned six. The Ekenstams had four children of school age. The fourth family, the Pettersons, with one school age daughter, Anna, arrived soon after the Johnsons. These seven formed the nucleus for the first Island school, a three-month term held in a small abandoned house overlooking Oro Bay. This may well have been the house "discovered" by Michael Luark, as related in his 1854 diary. Who built it, and when, may always remain a mystery.

The session was taught by a young man from the mainland, Calvin Wilt. There seems to be no record either of the salary paid Wilt for his services, or of his education, or of the books he used. The curriculum was up to the teacher, as was the decision concerning the level to which each child could attain. School months were June, July, and August, the only months considered fit for children to be trekking over the wooded trails and through the bogs. No provision was made for heating the building, nor was there money to pay a teacher more than three months out of the year.

But an "intent" was filed at the territorial county courthouse by the serious-minded Islanders. The district was given the number "24," which meant that twenty-three school districts had already been established within county boundaries. Islanders received no financial help with their project. Children ranged in age from five through twenty, and each child proceeded at his own level of learning.

Most of the overworked teachers who taught the school during those first years boasted little schooling, but I suspect they were pretty good. Initiative was a quality they had to have, and they were dedicated. Otherwise, surely, they would have been doing something more lucrative and less exacting. It is interesting to note that the most modern schools have returned to an ungraded system. I am prejudiced, no doubt, from having started my own schooling in a one-room ungraded rural; but I think the method, even then, had a good deal to be said for it.

An island is sometimes in a peculiar position concerning school land allotted, and Anderson was no exception. In her case, the portion of such land that did not lie under water lay at the extreme southeast point of the land mass, cut off from the majority of the settlers by a band of boggy ground, too wet during the spring, fall, and winter months for the children to negotiate.

The problem was solved, finally, by Christian Christensen's brother Peter. Although there is no record that any of his children ever attended school on Anderson, he donated ten acres from his own claim, in the approximate center of the Island, to serve as a school site. Here the first schoolhouse was built, in November of 1883, when District 24 was a year old.

The building was twenty-six by sixteen, fashioned from rough one-by-twelves, with narrow battens over the seams. It was not sealed for three years, and was never painted. N. M. Petterson, the fourth settler, did the construction. The lumber, brought from a mill at Lake Bay on the mainland, was floated over and hauled in by oxen. The cost of the lumber was $30.27. The charge for labor came to $83.60, making the total investment in the one-room school $113.87.

The next several years must have seen an increase in value, at least in the minds of the Islanders. For in an 1892 report, the schoolhouse was estimated to be worth $350.00. During the early 1880's, and, indeed, for the following decade or two, there occurred a considerable influx of families, both transient and permanent. With the woodyards in full operation, many woodcutters came. Several took claims or purchased land and settled. Small transient logging operations sprang up from one end of the Island to the other.

Most of the Island children attended school more or less regularly, once it was established, though there were no restrictions or truancy laws. As soon as there was an adequate building that could be heated, and funds to pay a teacher, the term was extended to six months. Books, supplied by the parents, were handed down until they were worn to tatters. There was no set amount of work to be covered in any one year. When students had finished one book, they simply started another. When the last day of the school term came, they wrote "left off here" at the end of the last lesson learned. Here they began when school reopened six months later.

Paper, being expensive and difficult to come by, was used only for very special work. Slates were a must. The slates, approximately nine by fourteen, were much better to work on, the children were convinced, if washed with saliva, which formed a glossy coating. This was called "the spit rub." The more tidy teachers objected to the "rub." But, being both alert and speedy, and equipped with long sleeves for drying as well, the students managed, when pedagogical backs were turned, to achieve an adequate polish.

Seats were all double, and two pupils sat at a single desk. The box-style heater occupied the center of the room. At the rear stood a rough bench, holding a water pail and a dipper.

The pail was filled each morning from Schoolhouse Creek, which arose in the swamp, crossed school land, and terminated in Oro Bay.

During recess and the noon hour, the older boys, assisted by the teacher (if he chanced to be a man) worked with axes and saws, mattocks and "grub hoes" to clear the grounds of trees and stumps, thus burning up a good deal of energy that might otherwise, parents believed, go into mischief.

The school grounds had no limits as such, only the surrounding woods, where the children might range at will, so long as they kept within sound of the teacher's bell. Arriving in the morning, they put their bottles of milk into the cold waters of Schoolhouse Creek. At noon, they ate lunch seated on some shady moss-covered log and then foraged for wild flowers or for berries.

Trillium grew thick in the woods along the creek (as it does now), and bright orange tiger lilies came into bloom late in the school year. Sweet-scented honeysuckle twined about the trees and tumbled over the rotting stumps. Mock orange per-

fumed the air about the building, and, by mid-July, foamy showers of ocean spray draped the edges of the clearing. Bessie recalls that once a boy brought in a skunk cabbage blossom. The teacher, unfamiliar with nature, exclaimed over its exotic beauty and put it into a vase. "She went around wrinkling her nose and looking for a civet, while we hid behind our slates to giggle."

Wide Awake Hollow, as the school was named, changed teachers often. The Island was a remote place for a young teacher. There was no recreation, and the pay was not much. The teacher was obliged to room and board at some settler's house and to walk the long wooded trails, build the fires, chop his own wood (if a man), and serve as his own custodian, as well as to plan the curriculum, decide who belonged where, and how much could be mastered.

The teacher's salary for a three-month term came to around $110, all told, an average of $36.60 per month. This was considered a fair wage. The number of daily recitations that must be heard was usually about eighteen.

Even so, some of the teachers assumed extracurricular duties. Early Islanders remember a Miss Mary Cox, who went to town by steamboat on Friday evening, but who returned early Sunday morning, to teach a church school class of the same pupils in the same building.

"I started school at the age of five because I didn't want to stay at home alone while the others were away (I thought) having fun," Bessie says. "I can close my eyes now, and see landmarks along the two-mile wooded walk, certain rocks that protruded in the middle of the road because they were too large to move, certain trees and stumps. Trails from homesteads on the west and the east shores came into the main road, in itself little more than a trail, with grass and sometimes stumps and stones between the wagon tracks. In summer, dust lay deep in the tracks and came up between our bare toes. After the rains came, we wore boots and were obliged to wade through the wet places.

"Whoever came along the trail first laid fresh fern fronds on the road, so that the others would know they had gone before, and not stand and wait. I'm sure I didn't learn much that first year. In the afternoon, the teacher, a Mrs. Lizzie Shutt, bedded me down in her coat on one of the benches, and I took a long nap.

"My most vivid memory of those first years is of running to keep up with the others, because I was terrified to be left alone. The road led through dense forest, where I had to look straight up to see the sky. I would lag behind until the others were out of sight, and then run as fast as I could, with my heart in my mouth, until I could see them again.

"It was not until I was six that my education really began. Mrs. Mary M. Eade was the teacher that year, and the first thing I learned was to sing the A,B,C's. Mrs. Eade, who was a very religious woman and quite dedicated to our morals, gave us each a New Testament to use as a text. I know that religious teaching is frowned upon in the schools now, but I doubt if we were harmed by it. We had Bible reading each morning, which seems not a bad way to start a day, and sang hymns from the Gospel Hymn Book.

"One hymn I remember we sang a good deal was 'Pull for the Shore.' That one had real meaning for us Island children. At whatever level in school, we were obliged to memorize a good deal. I know that is not done much any more, either, and I expect some of the verse we memorized was not that which is now considered very good, or literary. I know that Henry Wadsworth Longfellow is not now considered a good poet. But we considered him so, and I am sure our teachers did. And surely the textbook people did or they would not have included so much of his work.

"I am bound to admit that the morals Longfellow pointed out were pretty obvious ones. But, still, there was something about the recitation of such poems as 'Life is real, life is earnest' that kept the lessons with us. To be sure, we often rattled off verses without any attention to punctuation or to meaning. But then, through the years, as experience widened and deepened with living, those words took on meaning. At least they did for me. And some of the poems we learned, such as 'Thanatopsis,' are still, now, and will always be considered good.

"We learned 'The Village Blacksmith' and 'The Mountain and the Squirrel,' 'The Arrow and the Song,' and 'The Camel's Nose,' and they may not have been literature at all. But they created an image for us and stirred our imagination. I think they taught us something besides just words, too. They were company, for me, as I walked along fearfully through the darkening woods. I suppose it's sentimental, but I think, too, that some of the lines learned then have helped some of us along other, figuratively darkening, trails, encountered in our later lives."

Bessie also risks being termed "old-fashioned" and says that she thinks "mental arithmetic," which was taught from a separate book, filled cover to cover with thought instead of drill problems, was good training, however tough it seemed at the time.

For the first six years of its struggling beginning, only three months were offered each year at Wide Awake Hollow. But in 1889, the statehood year, the first six-month term was realized. Even so, there was a month of vacation between the two halves. Pupils attended through April, May and June, stayed at home during July, so that the boys could help with the haying, and went back for August, September and October. The five rainy months made up the long vacation period. The school term always ended with a program and a dinner.

"During all those years of growing up and attending school," Bessie told me, "it was my constant ambition to be a teacher. But whenever I mentioned this in Papa's hearing, he said firmly, 'No, Bessie. I want you to learn to work.' It was an Island teacher, Miss Emma Tripler, who made the suggestion that turned the dream into a reality."

The year was 1905 and Bessie had turned eighteen. Wide Awake Hollow was still ungraded, and she had gone through all of the books and subjects offered. She thinks this would have amounted approximately to an eighth-grade education.

She had stayed out of school for a year when she was twelve, to visit cousins in Idaho, making the journey by train and taking all of her belongings in a trunk.

At the age of sixteen she had gone to Montana to work for a transplanted Tacoma family. But, by the spring of 1905, she had returned to the Island and was restless and in need of something to occupy her time. Carl Petterson, the superintendent of the Sunday school, asked her to direct the Easter program, and she accepted.

During the two-mile walk home with Miss Tripler, following the program, which had gone off well, Emma said, "Bessie, you ought to teach school."

Of course, it was what the girl wanted to do more than anything she could think of. But she was sure the teacher was joking.

"No, I mean it," Emma said. "There's to be a six-weeks normal course in Tacoma this summer. Why don't you attend that and then try the teachers' examination?"

And so it was that Bessie found herself, in September, in possession of a teacher's certificate, and, on a morning in October, in front of her first pupils, thirty-three children ranging in age from six through eighteen, on Mount Solo in Cowlitz County, a Finnish community.

Her chief difficulty lay in the fact that only three of her pupils spoke English. She could have managed Finnish-Swedish, she thinks, but the language spoken was Finnish-Russian.

Without the three English-speaking children, whom she used as interpreters, she would have been at a total loss. On the playground, the Finns made no attempt at English. As though her appearance were some kind of signal, Bessie remembers, they would stop whatever game they were playing, band together, and speak rapidly in their own language.

"I don't know how much the students learned during my three-month term at Mount Solo. But I was happier than I had ever been, I think. Teaching was every bit as rewarding as I had thought it would be. I dreaded to see the term come to an end." It is easy to believe that Bessie was a dedicated teacher. Her eyes light up when she talks of her time in the class room. A woman of probing mind, she has never lost her interest in learning, and she has the kind of affectionate authority that makes a good teacher.

Not long ago, I attended a party at the clubhouse, where tables had been set up for cards. When some of the younger children became restless and a trifle boisterous, Bessie left the table quietly and made her way to the end of the room where the youngsters were running and scuffling. Presently all were seated in a circle, absorbed in some game of their own. Bessie, who sat among them, seemed to be thoroughly enjoying herself.

During the times we worked together in her kitchen, her grandchildren drifted in and out of the house as though it were their own, as, indeed, it looks to be. Their possessions are everywhere. When four or five young Islanders prevailed upon her, a few years ago, to follow the meandering course of Schoolhouse Creek through the tangled woods and across the overgrown swamp to its mouth, Bessie donned slacks and stout boots and set out. "I'm getting a little ancient for that kind of strenuous exercise," she laughed. "But we made it, and it was a fine trip."

A week after the end of Mount Solo's school term, Bessie was back on the Island with a commission to teach the spring term at Wide Awake Hollow. Here, too, her pupils numbered thirty-three and included all eight grades. But these were no strangers. Most of them, including two of her brothers, Ben and Otto, she had known since babyhood. But the salary was a whopping forty dollars a month, and she could stay at home and save a board bill.

One day a thing happened that she still trembles to remember. A fight broke out on the school ground between two of the big boys. Powerless to pull them apart, shaking inwardly, she said as sternly as she could, "If you boys don't come into the schoolhouse, you will have to go home."

To her astonishment, they left off fighting. One of the boys came in. The other went home. When he failed to return the next day, or the next, she inquired, only to learn that the father thought the boy had been expelled. After she sent a note to the parents, the boy returned, and nothing at all was ever said about the matter. Last summer, sixty years later, the boy returned to the Island for a visit, and he and Bessie laughed over the incident. "But it seemed," she says, "an earth-shaking thing, then."

Bessie might have gone on teaching the Island school. But in the summer of 1906, she was maried to Oscar Cammon and went to live at Still Harbor on McNeil, from which Oscar and Martin Cammon (the name had originally been Kammen, but it had been changed along the line somewhere), made a livelihood by fishing for shrimp and by towing with their boat, the *Anna B.*

The *Anna B,* a steam tug, is well remembered on the Island. "Made more money during her work years than she could carry," old-timers say. Built at Longbranch for the Cammon brothers, she was named for Miss Anna Butsch. "Anna was an earlier girl friend of Oscar's," Bessie says. "They used to tease me about that."

The pair was married on the lawn at Johnson's Landing, underneath a flower-decked paper bell. Following a picnic breakfast, they set sail for Tacoma on board the *Anna B,* took the train from there to Moclips on the ocean, and spent a three-day honeymoon, the only time they were to have really alone.

"Martin took it for granted he was to live with us," Bessie laughs, "and neither of us had the courage to tell him different. Once, I did go so far as to suggest he might be happier in the house that stood a little way down the beach from ours. He wasn't offended, as I was afraid he might be. He just said, 'No Bessie, I don't want to break up the family.' And that was that."

Bessie's first child, a girl, named Anna (who was to die at

the age of fourteen), arrived the following year. Bessie contracted "gastric fever," she recalls, and spent three weeks in a
Tacoma hospital, at a total cost of sixty-three dollars. That was
in 1907.

Bessie and Oscar lived several years on McNeil, where two
of their three sons were born, but they never really left
Anderson. During this time, they were summer people, week-
enders. They set about building the big house where Bessie
lives alone now. When it was finished, they persuaded Bengt
and Anna to move into it. But the elder Johnsons never felt
at home there, and moved back after a while to Johnson's
Landing.

The closing of Wide Awake Hollow in 1958 brought forth
the customary howl of protest. Although one-room rural
schools were closing all across the nation, Islanders reasoned
that the school was the nucleus of the community. But, from
a record enrollment of forty-eight in 1907, the Hollow had
dwindled to seven, the number for whom the school had been
started.

Because all of McNeil Island was government-owned, the
children remained under the jurisdiction of the Anderson
board. They continued to gather at the Hollow for church
school, and school board meetings were held there. After a
while, new playground equipment was installed and the school
yard became a public play area. To the children, the daily
boat trip was a novelty. On McNeil, there were hot lunches,
better equipment, and more competition. And, because the
ferry schedule to the mainland must be maintained, two-thirty
was dismissal time!

Lately there has been talk of consolidation with a larger
district on the mainland, a movement that would result in
the elimination of old 24. Islanders are reacting in the only
way they know—by writing strong letters of protest. To send
children of six and seven across to the mainland on a 6:45 A.M.
ferry for a ten-hour day away from home, they declare, is simply unthinkable. They look upon the suggested move as an-

other threat to their rights as responsible citizens. District 24, they feel, is just about their last claim to identity as a community.

Island children are looked upon as a community commodity. If any child falls ill or is injured, every Islander is anxious. If one is awarded a special honor, the entire Island shares with the parents the feeling of achievement. The reason, I suppose, lies partly in the fact that the children are so few. Many homes, currently at least, are childless.

But it occurs to me, also, that the children here have a special quality. The Island is their world, and they know that. The knowledge of being universally cherished gives them poise and self-confidence. Whatever and however they are elsewhere, they are at ease here, where they call all adults by given names, just as they address each other.

I am constantly impressed by their knowledge. I have encountered few adults anywhere who are more aware of or better informed about their surroundings. The woods, the beaches, the water make up their playground. Forced by insularity to find their recreation and by scarcity of numbers into participation in the adult world, they form friendships at every age level. Isolated from interests taken for granted by the urban child, they explore for fun, and learn without being aware of the accumulation of knowledge.

Their charm comes of an abundance of good health, I think. But they have inquiring minds, too. They are inveterate collectors—of shells, agates, driftwood, birds' nests, marine specimens, curios of nature. Social activities are planned to include them; as in the early days, they go along.

With fourteen miles of beach to explore, they never seem at a loss for something to do. There is no safer nor more enchanting playground for even the youngest than a sloping saltwater beach. Twice daily, the tide comes in with its gifts, and ebbs away again to expose them to the young collector. A child has only to lift a stone on the beach, and away goes a tiny crab, as comical as anything in an animated cartoon. Hermit crabs in their borrowed houses provide endless fascination. Agate hunting is a never-ending pastime, and they are all experts at it.

"Children growing up in the country take their images of integrity from the land," Hortense Calisher wrote in *A Wreath for Miss Totten*. "The land with its changes is always about them, a pervasive truth, and their midget foregrounds are criss-crossed with minute dramas which are the animalcules of a larger vision."

And so it is with children who count the woods and the Sound, and the shore that lies between, as a daily playfield. Their heads are crammed with knowledge gained from simple observation. Nearly all these children go away when their school-days are finished. But title maps of the Island are dotted with the names of natives, both young and older, who hope to return when their work on the outside is done.

12

JOHNSON'S LANDING

Frequently, in Bessie's kitchen, the talk turned to boats. Boats make up the life line of any Island. For Anderson, they had a special meaning: they were directly responsible for her beginning as a community.

For nearly two score years, side- and stern-wheelers, called "paddle wagons," stopped by Island woodyards daily to take on cordwood. Johnson's Landing alone dispatched more than eighty thousand cords. It would be impossible to estimate, all told, how many cords the Island yards accounted for. Christian Christensen had been about cutting and selling wood to the steamers ten years prior to the Johnsons' coming. Before the turn of the century, a third yard, that of August Lindstrom, who was to become Helda's second husband, sprang up at Otso Point, only a mile or so from Johnson's Landing.

"These woodyards were beans and bacon, in one way or another, for most of the settlers," Islanders say. "The chances are the Island would have been a long time settling without them, and that it would have been quite a different place." Save for the brief sojourn of the brickyard at Jacobs' Point in Oro Bay in the nineties, woodcutting and hauling has constituted the only industry for which wages were ever paid here since settlement began. Even those who farmed cut wood as a side line to augment the meager income to be derived from their farm produce, which posed a transportation problem before it could be turned into cash. During the brickyard era there were those who laid down their axes and their saws to become brickmakers. But when the brickyard closed, they took them up again.

Like all long-time Islanders, Bessie loves to talk of boats. Boats have been the lifetime concern of most of her family. Her four brothers, Gunnard and John, Ben and Otto, were boat men; and her husband Oscar Cammon, along with his brother Martin, made his livelihood by shrimping and by towing with his own boat. Bessie's late son Roger had his own fishing boat, the *Peso*. Another son, Robert, built a fifty-foot ketch, the *Bobcat*, on the Island, with the help of other members of the family, and sailed the boat down the coast, through the Panama Canal, and up the Mississippi River to his home in St. Louis, a matter of eight thousand miles.

Even after the end of the steamboat era, for more than a quarter of a century mail and passengers were carried by a variety of commercial craft that touched in more or less regularly at Island shores. Now only the ferry *Tahoma*, referred to as "the bottleneck," survives.

Volumes have been written about boats in the Puget Sound country. For more than a half century, from the time settlement began until the railroads came, the only access to and from the lonely little settlements huddled in clearings along the shores of the Sound, both on the islands and on the mainland, was by water. Previous to the coming of the white man, the comparatively calm waters of the Sound were negotiated by the long cedar canoes of the Indians. Channels and passages served as the only highways. Sailboats preceded the stern- and side-wheelers.

As early as 1836, the Hudson's Bay Company's steamer *Beaver* lay at anchor off Nisqually Reach, hard by the Island. People here like to talk about the *Beaver*, the first steamboat to serve the settlers. Built in England, on the Thames, she was 101 feet long, with a twenty-foot beam and a depth of eleven feet. She could not carry much fuel and so made the trip from the Thames by sail, taking 163 days (more than five months) for the journey.

When she came into Puget Sound, then called "the Inland Sea," her boiler and engine were put to use, and she became a wood burner. It is said, here, that the *Beaver* burned as much as forty cords of wood per day. Cordwood to fuel her furnaces may well have been cut on Anderson, Islanders believe, though there is no substantiation of this.

By 1853, the first of the American steamboats had come to serve the pioneer settlers around Puget Sound. These "river boats," as they were called, came from the Columbia and from as far south as San Francisco, and made a steady influx into this sea of bays and reaches and islands. In the quiet inner waters of the Sound, the side- and stern-wheelers worked efficiently. For work among the islands, where the boats were obliged to stop often for fuel and water and to pick up and deliver cargo, the stern-wheelers proved best. Because of the location of the paddle wheel at the stern, these latter could come closer in to shore and enter water of a lesser depth.

"But the side-wheelers, with their decorative wheels that looked like lace doilies turning at a distance, were more graceful and picturesque," Bessie recalls. It would be difficult to hazard a guess as to how many boats stopped in at Island woodyards during the steamboat era. But they were a great many, and they became very familiar to the Islanders.

The *Capitol City,* the *City of Aberdeen,* the *State of Washington,* the *Nisqually,* the *Greyhound,* called affectionately, "The Pup," all stopped regularly at Johnson's Landing. "We took the boats more or less for granted, I suppose," Bessie told me. "But I can remember, too, that we never tired of watching them come in and leave.

"We could hear them coming when they were still a long way off, out of sight in fog or around the bend. We learned to distinguish them by sound, a steady over and over. There was always the sound, too, of surplus steam popping from the safety valve beside the stack when the boat was tied at the Landing. It must be remembered that these steamers could not shut off their source of power the way a modern vessel can by simply shutting off the engines. The wood kept burning in the furnaces and the steam kept generating and had to be exhausted somehow, or the boilers would have blown up at the wharf.

"In times of fog, the captain blew the whistle and listened for the echo against the trees or against the land to tell him how close he was to shore. Some of the whistles made a gurgling noise, as though there were water inside the whistle pipe. We learned to distinguish each boat by its own peculiar whistle pitch.

"I never tired of watching the landings. As the vessel came in to the wharf, which was about 175 feet in length, with fender piling extending above the dock, a deck hand stood on the main deck with a coil of rope called the heaving line in each hand. At the end of this line, was a heavy spring line loop, called 'the Turk's head,' large enough to drop over a piling.

"Most deck hands were very adept at heaving a line. After the man on the dock had thrown the line over the piling, the deck hand hauled in the slack and fastened the line to the heavy cleat on the deck. When the procedure had been repeated at the stern end, he called to the Captain, 'All fast, sir!'

and the crew was ready to unload freight and to take on wood
and water. When the 'All clear, sir!' sounded, the big wheel
commenced its turning again and the boat pulled away from
the wharf."

There was no store on the Island during the steamboat era
nor for a long time afterward. Between rare shopping trips to
the mainland for supplies, Islanders from both McNeil and
Anderson shopped on board the steamboats that had been
fitted up as stores. One of these floating stores, as they were
called, was the *Otter*, a stern-wheeler.

Fitted out in 1892 by Captain Roscoe G. Brown and his
cousin, C. A. Brown, the *Otter* stopped at McNeil one day each
week and anchored in a quiet cove on the south side. Members
of the crew donned aprons and became store clerks. Island
farmers brought produce by row boat and exchanged it for
cotton goods, oilcloth, pins, needles, thread, bandannas, shoes,
socks, hardware.

"The shelves on the *Otter* were boxed in at the front,"
Bessie remembers, "to keep the contents from sliding out when
the boat was in motion. A lot of joshing went on between the
crew and the Islanders, who knew them all well. One day, one
of the clerks, named Frank Brown . . . wore a red flannel under-
shirt to wait on trade. Everyone who came in gave him a bad
time. It was a long time before I found out what they were
laughing about. The shirt, which he had borrowed from his
wife, had openings in the front for breast feeding.

"I don't think much money changed hands on the *Otter*.
Islanders had little cash and none of it went for nonessentials,
unless you'd call snuff nonessential and I guess it wasn't for a
Scandinavian. Men supported families on as little as fifteen
dollars a week, and lived well enough. But they didn't have any
extra to throw around. For all that steamboat fare into Tacoma
was only fifty cents, few Islanders went in merely for shopping.
When they had a need to go, they thought nothing, even the
womenfolk, of striking out by rowboat to save the fifty cents."

An early-day Islander, Nella Warner Higgins, who lived

on the Island as a girl, tells of such a trip, taken with her mother when Nella was around seventeen. The distance was probably five or six miles from where the Warners lived, on the north end of the Island. This is the way Nella tells the story.

"One day in late summer, Mother and I decided to row across to the town of Steilacoom to buy outing flannel to make our winter nightgowns. The water was calm enough when we set out, and we made pretty good time with the oars. But then the wind came up suddenly, the way it does sometimes, and we were surrounded by whitecaps and rollers. The boat, which seemed sturdy enough normally, was tossed about like a peanut shell. To add to our difficulties, the going was so slow that the tide turned against us before we were half way across.

"I was never so scared in my life. The waves looked mountainous as they bore down upon our little boat. My arms felt as though they were being pulled from the sockets with each stroke. We didn't dare change places because the boat was heaving and pitching like a piece of drift. Most of the time we seemed to make no headway at all. We were drenched to the skin by wave after crashing wave, that seemed bent on foundering us. Our teeth chattered and we shook with cold inside our wet clothing.

"I still don't know how we made it. But we did, finally. I can't tell you how good that Steilacoom dock looked to me. I don't think I could have taken another half dozen strokes. The thought of rowing back to the Island filled me with terror.

"But we were in luck that day. Glen Elder's launch, the *Eagle,* was coming this way, and the skipper tied the skiff on behind and took us on as passengers. I was so tired I slept all the way across."

One of the boats Islanders remember best was the stern-wheeler *Multnomah,* that stopped in regularly at Johnson's Landing. "Most of the steamers, when you came to know them, had a kind of individuality," Bessie recalls. "We could hear the *Multnomah* coming from a long way off. It was always a thrill to see her come around the bend and head for the Landing."

The *Multnomah*, a river boat, had been built by the Willamette Steamship Company of Portland for the Oregon City run on the Willamette River. She was 143 feet long and her beam was twenty-eight feet, with a five-foot, three-inch hold. She had operated on the Columbia and the Willamette up to 1889, when Washington Territory became a state. Then, the Wiley Steam Navigation Company of Olympia bought her and brought her up the coast to Puget Sound to go on the Olympia-Seattle run, and so she fueled regularly at the Island.

She was considered one of the most economically operated steamers for her size at the time of her launching. "We could hear the *Multnomah*'s exhaust and hear the sound of the waterfall surging and splashing over and through her paddle wheel as soon as she rounded Penitentiary Point on the way from Tacoma to Olympia. We always ran down to the Landing to watch her come in."

On most of the early steamers, the texas, or officers' stateroom, stood just behind and joined to the pilot house. But in the case of the *Multnomah*, the pilot house was above the texas and had a decorative border, giving her a majestic look. The passenger deck was divided into three main compartments. The foremost cabin was the men's cabin, where the men could smoke and spit tobacco juice into the numerous spittoons.

The sternmost cabin was for the ladies. Men were permitted to enter there, but no smoking was allowed. The floor of the men's cabin was covered by linoleum. But the ladies walked on a thick red carpet. The cushioned seat formed a semicircle around the cabin and was upholstered in red plush. There were comfortable easy chairs and a big library table. A wide carpeted stairway led to the lower or main deck.

"Between the ladies' and the men's cabins was the diner. The tables were covered by spotless white linen, and there were real linen napkins and a white-coated steward with a white towel over his left arm. The prepared dishes came from the galley on the main deck by dumb waiter. The food was delicious."

Bessie recalls that flowers from Anna Johnson's yard often graced the center of each table in the *Multnomah* dining room. "One of our more pleasant chores was to race down the hill with bouquets of fresh flowers when we heard the long-drawn whistle that heralded the coming of the boat. In return, the steward tossed to the wharf a current copy of the Tacoma *Ledger* or perhaps a Seattle newspaper.

"We didn't go into town often. But when we did, we generally took the *Multnomah*. As children, we loved to race on the promenade deck. If the steamer had come from Olympia and was bound for Tacoma or Seattle, she usually carried sacks of the tiny Olympia oysters that have since become famous the world over, and cases of Olympia beer. We came to know the members of the crew. One I remember especially, because he always waved to us children, was a chief engineer by the name of Staley, who went about with a long-spouted can oiling the mechanism of the big water wheel at the stern."

When steamers going the same way got up a race, the fireman was the busiest man aboard, throwing in the best of the wood supply in order to keep the steam at high pitch. When a steamer won a race, a broom was tied to the jackmast to indicate that she had "swept the field." A steamer that raced often was the side-wheeler *T. J. Potter*, a fine vessel, with roomy, elegantly furnished cabins. Her owners, the Oregon Railway and Navigation Company, boasted that she was the fastest side-wheeler west of the Mississippi. She was challenged, at different times, by the *Multnomah*, the *Bailey Gatzert*, and the side-wheeler, *City of Seattle*. (The *Bailey Gatzert*, named for a Seattle mayor, was considered the grandest paddlewagon of her day.)

When the *Potter* returned to the Columbia River in 1891, having finished her work Up Sound, she took on a hundred cords of wood, Bessie remembers, a record for the Landing.

"I rode on the *Potter* once after she left our waters, and it was like meeting an old friend. That was in 1905. I was nineteen years of age and teaching in Cowlitz River country. I rode the *Potter* from Ladu, Washington, to Kalama, to attend a teachers' meeting there."

Another fast boat that stopped in at Island woodyards was the stern-wheeler *Greyhound*. "The Pup" was 139 feet long, with an eighteen-foot beam. Her skipper, Captain Wilson, brought her into the Landing often for wood and water and passengers during the early nineties. True to her name, The Pup was both swift and skinny, with a whistle that could be heard for miles. She had other nicknames, "The Wheel and Whistle," or "The Hound." It was said that when she raced the *Bailey Gatzert* once, over a twenty-five mile course, the crews had such fires going that sticks of wood shot out of both funnels like clinkers out of an erupting volcano. The Pup finished three minutes ahead and wore the broom triumphantly on her jackmast. In 1907, she was converted from wood to oil. She wound up her years of service as a landing float at the Foss Launch and Tug Company moorings.

"Once," Bessie remembers, "an exciting thing happened at the Landing. Captain John T. Shroll, who was known as 'hellroarin' Jack,' was bringing his stern-wheeler, the *Capitol City*, in for a landing at the wharf. The tide was running hard, just starting its ebb after a full high, when Jack lost control. Moments before he hit the wharf, he yelled, 'Look out! I'm a comin' in!' The wharf began to quiver as though in anticipation of the blow, and all of the bystanders ran to safety. Lizzie Peterson, a neighbor of ours who had come down with two boxes of wild huckleberries, grabbed her freight and flew off the approach just as the steamer struck.

"If the tide had been at its low ebb, it would have been disastrous for *The City*. As it was, the bow stem hit the cap on top of the piling, which prevented the boat from running underneath the wharf. . . . The boat company sent a pile driver and a crew from Olympia to repair the damage, and they roomed and boarded with us. I must have been about fourteen at the time. Papa had bought a little Burdette organ, and for want of better entertainment the crew would ask me to play for them of evenings. I couldn't play much, of course, but I had had a few lessons, at twenty-five cents a lesson, from a teacher on McNeil Island, and I knew 'Nita Juanita' and a few of the other popular songs of the day.

"One day, a while after the repair crew had returned to Olympia, a package arrived for me by steamer, along with a note of thanks for the 'entertainment.' Five yards of blue wool serge, with buttons and thread for a new dress!"

Among other stern-wheelers Islanders remember were the *Fairhaven*, the *Emma Hayward*, and *The State of Washington*, built in 1889, the year Washington Territory became a state. A side-wheeler seen often was the *Politofsky*. Built in Sitka, Alaska, as a gunboat for the czar when that territory was Russian owned, she was taken over by private parties when Alaska was purchased by the United States in 1867. Following several years of towing logs for the Port Blakeley Mill Company, she was converted into a barge and wound up in Alaska again. During her run as a towboat in the Sound, she passed through Balch Passage often. It seemed a bit of an anomaly, Islanders say, to see a former gunboat of the czar of Russia trailing a tow of logs, but she always moved with a regal air, as though unaware of her tow or determined to ignore it.

The cordwood era did not end all at once, but gradually, with the coming in of the new gas-rigged craft. As these underbid the old woodburners on freight cargo rates, the old-timers began to convert to oil fuel for power. A few boats still burned wood for a long time, because conversion was expensive and wood was cheap fuel and in plentiful supply. But eventually the woodyards were obliged to go out of business. The new and smaller boats that met the need for communication between the Islands and the mainland were powered by gasoline engines. "Naphtha burners," they were called. Several Island residents had their own gas-powered launches, and a few commercial boats stopped in on their rounds.

"But the fact that the boats were smaller now did not mean that the water would calm down to accommodate them," Bessie said. "I well remember being out once in my brother Gunnard's small open gas boat, the *Betzita*. We had crossed to Steilacoom to take a couple of passengers and were on the way back when a storm came up. Maybe it wasn't a storm, really, but just a stiff wind that whipped the water into a fury, the way a wind can do in a few minutes sometimes.

"The *Betzita*, an eighteen footer, would give a lurch, throwing the stern up with the propeller out of the water. This caused the engine to speed up too rapidly. Gunnard sat in the stern, to control the motor. My duty was to keep the rudder steady as we tried to clear Penitentiary Point. In order to keep the waves from washing in, we had to face the craft into them. With the wind on the side, this was no easy job. We did have one thing in our favor, it was still daylight. But I can tell you I was never so glad to see anything as I was to see Johnson's Landing come into view."

One of the smaller craft that served the Island commercially after the end of the steamboat era was the little gas-powered *Eagle* that stopped in at the Island each morning en route from her home port at Longbranch on the Peninsula to the city of Steilacoom and again in the evening on her return trip.

The *Eagle,* a forty-nine footer, was powered by a twenty-horsepower engine. Operated by Glen Elder, who was well-known among the islands, she cruised along the shore and picked up passengers from floats or rowboats wherever she found them waiting. These stops were called flag stops. People rowed out into deep water and climbed aboard, or they signaled from some private float and the *Eagle* swung in and picked them up.

"One dark winter night my brother Ben went out in his skiff to meet the *Eagle,* because he thought my sister Augusta might be aboard. As it happened, she wasn't. But four men who had come to work at the Babcock Logging Company, set up temporarily on the Island, were. While Ben was talking to Captain Elder at the pilot house door, these four climbed down into the skiff from the stern.

"Ben let go of the *Eagle,* which set directly off into the dark. The skiff began to take water from the overload in the stern, and went down. Ben called to the men to grab their blanket rolls and start swimming. Blanket rolls served very well as life preservers when the need arose. It was too dark to see the shore, but Ben kept calling to the men to follow him in.

"He and three of the loggers made shore all right, after being carried a considerable distance by the strong ebb tide. Our neighbor, Walter Larson, took his rowboat out and searched, as did some of the other Islanders. But neither the fourth man nor any of his belongings was ever seen again. If he had a family, I suppose they were at a loss to know what became of him. The skiff was picked up several days later, when the wind blew it ashore off Cole Point. But there was nothing in that to identify the missing man, and so far as we knew, no inquiry was ever made."

Nearly everyone who lived along the waterfront on the Island owned a boat of some sort, just as everyone does now, even if only a rowboat or an outboard for fishing or gathering bark. The few who lived back from the waterfront mostly owned boats, too, and moored them at their neighbors' beaches. Some of these, like the *Betzita,* were of the round-bottomed type, which rowed much easier and faster. But the sixteen and eighteen-foot skiffs were more serviceable, because they carried more freight and were considered safer for family use.

"One of the things that was impressed on us children was what to do if a boat capsized. Unless we were sure we could make shore by swimming, we were told to hang onto the overturned boat if possible until help came. Even a strong swimmer can run into trouble in 40 to 50 degree water and in the kind of tides that run through these narrow channels.

"They used to tell a story about Matt the Hunchback. One day, Matt and two other men, Henry Halvorson and Ernest Luhr, were off Otso Point, in a sailboat Matt had rigged for carrying the mail, when the wind changed suddenly and the water roughened to a dangerous chop. In spite of all the men could do, the craft upset, and they were obliged to straddle the keel in order to save themselves.

"As they clung there, shouting for help, one of them overheard Matt plead, 'Oh, Lord, if you will help us, I will give you half of my fat hog.' 'What were you talking about, man?' one of his companions asked after the trio had been rescued. 'You *know* you *have* no hog.'

"Embarrassed over having been caught out, Matt explained sheepishly, 'Aw, I was only fooling.' "

Towboats, referred to as "workboats," stopped frequently at Island woodyards. One such boat, the forty-five-foot *Magnet,* was built at Villa Beach by Islanders Fred and Gus Carlson. Other tugs became familiar as they negotiated the passages with logs or other tows. It was said that owning even a small tug was as good as having a license to steal. Small-scale logging operations, carried on by farmers along the waterfronts, produced a constant supply of logs to be towed away to the sawmills by these independent tugs.

Often, Bessie remembers, the skippers were obliged to lie at anchor in the vicinity of Otso Point when the tide was flowing strongly through the Narrows. "If the delay was several hours, the crew came ashore. We children loved to go down and listen to their yarns."

As had the paddlewagons, the small independent workboats decreased gradually over the years, with the slow cessation of small independent logging. Of late years, towboat operations Up Sound have largely been taken over by fleet operators who maintain a schedule around the clock. One of the pleasures of living near the water, we found, lay in watching these graceful and sturdy boats trailing their big log rafts upon which hundreds of gulls settle for a free ride. As in earlier times, the crews wait out the tides off shore.

On foggy nights, we heard the intermittent hoarse voices of the tugs and the hammer of their engines as they sounded their way cautiously through the channel. Some of them passed quietly or far out, and we only knew they had gone by when the waves began to strike the shore in soft rhythmic series that diminished as they moved away toward Sandy Point or Eagle Island. One morning shortly after our arrival on the Island, we were startled to see a Foss Launch and Tugboat Company boat coming in toward shore with our small outboard in tow. The crew had been well along in Balch Passage, the skipper explained, when they discovered the boat. Under cover of darkness, the skiff, anchored and tied to a float, had become entangled somehow in the tow as it passed the house. Having left the tow in slack water, the crew was about returning the boat to us.

We were grateful but puzzled. With boats tied out all around the lower Sound as they passed, how had they known where this one belonged? We had yet to learn that boatmen, both active and retired, are imbued with a special mental marine registry. "No two boats look alike," they tell you, "nor sound alike. There's always *some* little difference." Most male adults on the Island have worked on boats in some capacity at one time or another and most have an uncanny ability for distinguishing passing boats by the sound of their engines.

An independent workboat skipper on Island shore leave was asked once how he knew so well which boat was passing. "Well, I don't always," he admitted. "But you can always tell if it's one of those Tugboat Annie jobs. They've somehow got the engines set to whisper, '*Henry Foss . . . Henry Foss . . . Henry Foss,*' and you can hear it plain as day if you listen close."

13

THE STORE BOATS

During the years following the *Otter* and other store boats, several ambitious boatmen tried floating-store routes Up Sound. For a time a Captain Green made the circuit in a small boat, the *Argosy,* carrying freight to and from Rozzini's General Merchandise and Feed Store at Vaughn Bay on the peninsula, and stopped in at the Island en route. He carried a supply of groceries and dry goods and took produce from the Islanders in exchange. The little gas boat could be heard for miles, the "putt, putt" of his engine heralding his coming far in advance of his appearance to barter from the farmers' landing floats and docks.

Ernie Ehricke, skipper of the floating store the *Vaughn*, which Islanders remember best both because Ernie was an Islander and Anderson was the boat's home port, came West from Chicago as a young man, in 1905. He did not "discover" the Island at once, but took a job with Foss Launch and Tug Company and then went on to skipper the *Bertha,* a boat also owned by Rozzini of Vaughn Bay.

Ernie and the *Bertha* were on their way to the store from Tacoma one day with a load of freight when he encountered a strong wind with high waves off Vashon Island. When he realized that the boat was doomed, he dived overboard and swam the rough cold water to Gig Harbor, waded ashore and walked the several miles to Vaughn Bay to report to his boss.

Having come to the conclusion that he liked the floating-store business, and undaunted by his drenching, Ernie set out in search of a boat of his own. When he came across a boat builder by the unlikely name of Seabury L. Mastick, who had a boat nearing completion, he looked the boat over, liked what he saw, and bought her. He christened her the *Vaughn,* equipped her with a thirty-two-horsepower engine, and set out on a route of his own.

Islanders who remember her talk about the *Vaughn* as though she had been a possession, and in a way she was. She was a good-looking craft, they say; and, like judges in a beauty contest, they name her dimensions—44.8 by 13, with a depth of 4.1 and a tonnage of 10 net, 14 gross. Ernie continued to carry freight for Rozzini for a time, but the area was too far-reaching. And so he established quarters of his own and gave the *Vaughn* a home port, Oro Bay on Anderson Island. In 1912, he built a warehouse and then a shop at Johnson's Landing, and he kept store there between trips. Having completed her years of service as a store boat, the *Vaughn* was sold in 1941. Ferry service to the Island had been established, and she was no longer needed.

For a long time now I have been trying to persuade Ernie's

widow, Ellen, who came to the Island in 1917, to write her
memoirs of the floating-store route.

"I couldn't do it," she says, her electric-blue eyes kindling.
"The best of the stories couldn't be told and the rest of it
would make dull reading."

But Ellen, who is Norwegian and who also hails from
Chicago, talks about the *Vaughn* often. For a number of years,
even when Bob was a small boy, the Ehrickes made their way
back and forth through the rough fast-running waters of the
Narrows on a regular run from the storehouse at Johnson's
Landing to the Port of Tacoma in Commencement Bay. Out-
going cargo, picked up from floats and docks about the Island,
consisted of cases of eggs, crates of chickens, boxes of apples,
and huckleberries, every manner of Island produce. The
Vaughn made the home trip with bags of flour, sugar, and
feed, rakes, hoes, brooms, kerosene (called "pearl oil"), case
lots of canned goods, all carried on board and carried off
again, frequently up long flights of beach stairs to some
Islander's farmstead.

Between trips, Ellen kept house and tended store. Still
sturdy after more than fifty years, and picturesque as well, the
combination store and living quarters wears its original roof
of oiled cedar shakes, moss-grown now, but almost as sound as
on the day of their application.

Ernie died in August of our first full year here, and is
buried in the Island cemetery. His was the first death I had
heard of here, and I was impressed, as I have been at the time
of each and every death since, by the general feeling of common loss evident all over the Island. Ernie had been ailing for
some time, though he had kept at work in the shop and on
the house, which he was about remodeling. He died in a
Seattle hospital, where he had gone to undergo an operation
for a malignancy.

When Earle boarded the ferry that evening for the last run
of the day to the Island, he heard the same words spoken over
and over again by a member of the crew, relating the news to

the boarding passengers, "Ernie didn't make it." By the time
the boat was tied up on the Island side, several of the passengers and both members of the crew were a trifle drunk, from
the bottle that had gone the rounds as respectfully and as
sorrowfully as had the news, in a trans-voyage farewell toast
to a fellow Islander who had "gone over," a man who had
contributed more, probably, than he knew to the little world
he left behind him.

On a still evening the following summer, we went by for
Ellen and cruised slowly along the east shore of the Island,
from Yoman Point to Sandy Point, in our small outboard. I
suppose each Islander has his favorite bit of shore line. The
east shore, with its quiet coves and wooded banks draped with
maidenhair ferns, with its cascading springs that furrow the
beach in wet weather, is the shore I like best in any season.

When we first came, you could walk from Yoman Point,
where the Island perimeter turns approximately east from
approximately north, around Sandy Point and Cole Point and
well into East Oro Bay, a distance of several miles, without
seeing a single human habitation. For such a walk, the tide
had better be at an extreme low, or headed in that direction.
For the bank, in long stretches, arises one hundred feet or
more above average high-tide flow.

During almost any season, the east shore is a blend of rich
color. On a quiet evening with a clear sky overhead, the firs
and the madroñas, many of which grow from the cliff side in a
horizontal position, are mirrored in the water. In early spring,
the banks are carpeted with red currant and white sweet
coltsfoot and with the delicate pale pink flowers of Siberian
miner's lettuce. In summer, yellow mimulus blooms among
the maidenhair, and the lacy cream tips of ocean spray set off
the clusters of ripe red elderberries.

As the summer wears on, the lacquered gold of *Ranunculus*
mingles with the blue-purple of the lupine and the rich magenta of the fireweed. In moist places, tall white and rose-pink
spikes of foxglove and a feathery border of steeplebush arise

from a tangle of sky-blue brooklime. Over and above these, spilling down the banks in July and August, are ripened salmon berries and smoky black caps, purple oso that natives call "Indian plum" or "bird cherry," bitter wild cherries and the bright orange pendants of ripening madroña, and clear scarlet vine maple.

In September and October, the dogwood trees that occur at intervals against the soft green backdrop of conifers, hung with the dark red fruits of their spring blossoming and re-splendent with the starched green-white of their second blooming, shake with feasting robins.

Because any sound seemed an intrusion that autumn evening, we cut the motor and drifted in silence among the shadows that patterned the sunset-tinted water. Down the channel, the lights of Tacoma and Steilacoom were beginning to come on along the darkened bluish hillsides. But the main-land seemed light years away.

"This is the way it was, always," I remember Ellen said. "We would come home on the *Vaughn* late and tired, and cruise in close here. And no matter how weary you were, you felt somehow restored and rested."

During the second decade of the century, after the ending of the steamboat years, the face of the Island changed more rapidly, probably, than it had during the earlier years of settlement, and it continued to change until mid-century.

Fires burned off a good deal of the remaining big timber on the high portion of the Island, and there was also clearing everywhere; as a result, wild huckleberries sprang up and bore heavily, supplying a cash crop, as had the cordwood, for open-range harvest. The harvesters used sticks to beat ripened berries off the bushes into wash tubs set to receive them, and cleaned them in handmade huckleberry cleaners, operated by a crank and equipped with fans for blowing away the leaves and with screens for the removal of the small immature green berries.

The berries were packed into boxes holding twenty-five

pounds of fruit and shipped to the mainland, many on board the *Vaughn*. Later some Islanders transported berries in their own boats across Drayton Passage to a packing shed at Longbranch. When the firs and alders gained a foothold, huckleberries began to be crowded out. Now Islanders gather them only for their own use.

It was in 1915, just prior to the entry of the United States into the First World War, that the Island acquired a *south-end* store, with the opening of Gus Carlson's on Oro Bay. Early-day "south-enders" recall how fine it was to have a store within walking distance. Roads remained little more than trails through the woods, and most Islanders counted boats as their sole means of transportation.

In the beginning, Gus was obliged to depend upon outside boats to bring in his supplies. He delivered and picked up produce over indifferent roads by horse and wagon. Early-day Islanders tell a sad story about Gus's delivery horse. "Started backing one morning without any reason. Backed Gus's rig right off the dock into deep water, and himself with it."

"Gus got his own boat finally, the *Ruby Marie*. But he had bad luck with her, too. Woke up one snowy morning at four o'clock, to see her on fire at the dock, water in the bay as red as blood. Burned clear to the water line, and not a penny of insurance on her." But Gus was sturdy Island stock, and he had good help—his wife Emma and his children. He managed to come by a bigger and older boat, the *Cosmos,* and carried on with that.

Gus and Emma are both dead now, and their son, Lyle, tends store at the old stand. Pleasure boaters come into the bay to drop anchor overnight or to buy herring from the bait boxes there, and exclaim over the picturesqueness of the ancient dock with its barnacle-encrusted pilings, the sweeping view of the mountain, and the lengthening tree shadows stretching to meet across the fingers of the bay.

14

THE GROWING YEARS

After the steamboat era ended during the first decade of the century, the Island settled down to become an agricultural community. The big poultry houses and haybarns, fallen into decay now and grown over with blackberry and wild honeysuckle, attest to the fact that it was a thriving one. The land cleared for cordwood supplied pasture and meadowland. The orchards planted by the first settlers had reached bearing age, and the growing urban communities on the mainland created a volume demand for foodstuffs. The Island population, too, was still in the growing stage. New settlers, nearly all Scandinavian, trickled in. Families increased in size. Seven, or even ten, children was considered average.

The decline in Island population, also gradual, followed the pattern of over-all decline across the nation. Farming and poultry raising had become so specialized that the little man could no longer make an adequate living. The years following the end of World War I were bad years here, as elsewhere.

The Island children grew up and left the Island because there was nothing for them to do. The older folk stayed on. The population dwindled from 141 in 1920 to 119 a decade later. By 1950, it was down to 106. By 1958, the grade school population had dropped to a half dozen, and the school was closed.

The cordwood business was still flourishing when the Island got her first and only industry, a brickyard. With building going on at a great rate on the mainland, small brickyards sprang up all about the Sound, wherever there was clay available and a good dock site.

Island brickmaking machinery was shipped out from Athens, Pennsylvania, and a man named John Koucher came out to manage the business, bringing along his son Charles. Brickmaking on the Island began, and remained, a small operation. A picture taken in 1890 shows twenty-four workmen, including a few who were little more than boys.

Nor was the plant itself elaborate. The main building was a shed, probably forty feet in length and little more than ten or twelve in height, with peeled poles for uprights. Underneath this roof stood the kiln. Some smaller buildings stood about, a few bunkhouses for outside workers, and a cookshack.

Modest in proportion though it was, the plant with its new faces and its payroll enlivened the Island. The foreman, a big stalwart Englishman named Charles Anderson, owned a high-spirited pony, which he used to ride the roads from the yard to Johnson's Landing on week ends to catch a steamer to town.

One morning, Bessie remembers, Anderson got a late start and arrived at the top of the hill above the Landing·as the steamer was easing away from the wharf. Urging his little steed, the big Britisher galloped down the hill onto the pier and gave her a command to jump. Sailing through the air over the widening expanse of water, pony and rider landed without mishap on the deck.

Anderson, a hot-blooded man, sometimes ran into trouble. Once he became involved with an Islander, Charlie Carlson, and there was a shooting scrape. A yellowed clipping, dated October 20, 1894, relates that "C. G. Carlson came to the city from Anderson Island Tuesday and surrendered himself after having shot Charles Anderson of Tacoma . . . during an altercation. The wound is dangerous but not necessarily fatal." But the affront that brought Anderson's English blood to the boiling point was when the newspaper referred to him as "the big Swede."

One of the workers, Bessie remembers, was a boy of sixteen, Alfred Engleberg, who had allegedly got into some kind of trouble "back East" and had been sent West by his father in the hope that he would straighten out. " 'Back East' was only a phrase to us children, as remote geographically as India or China. To have come from there gave Alfred an aura of glamour.

"He had acquired a pony and cart, which he drove back and forth from the Landing to the brickyard. I suppose he was lonely for young company, for he used to stop off at the schoolhouse and give us rides."

Another of the sixteen-year-old workmen was Oscar Cammon from Still Harbor on McNeil Island, later to become Bessie's husband. Oscar recalled seeing the cook level pans of batter by the simple expedient of dropping them onto the cookhouse floor; and the day two Island tomcats engaged in an altercation and fell into the brickyard well and had to be fished out, thoroughly cooled off.

Brickmaking on the Island came to an end around 1894. The buildings were torn down, the bricks hauled away. The Point grew up to trees again. But the era had left its impact. Young Charles Koucher married the eleventh Ekenstam, daughter Elva. Elva's sister Louise married a brickmaker named Ostling, and the pair remained to buy a farm and raise a family on the Island. Brickmakers Frank and Charlie Johnson settled down quietly to till Island soil, and lived out their lives and died and were buried here. And there were others. . . .Islanders like to point out the fact that the first building at Western State Hospital was made from Island bricks, many inscribed, when wet, with the names of their Island makers.

The Point is wooded over now by second growth, fir and cedar, alder and madroña. The roads that led in to the site have grown over, too. Crows roost in the trees and fly out of mornings and back home at night, like black leaves drifting across the sky. At low tide, the big blue heron comes and fishes offshore, moving quietly on his long stilts, or perches like some great gray-blue blossom on an overhanging bough.

If children come to poke among the shards of broken brick and cooking utensils, as they frequently do, the heron takes to the air with deceptive lack of grace, to rattle away toward Thompson Cove. But he is soon back again; for the east and west shores of the Point, which protrudes like an Adam's apple from the skull-like contour of the Island, are his favorite fishing grounds.

During the years following the closing of the brickyard, small "gyppo" logging outfits appeared from time to time, and portable sawmills were set up and moved from place to place. Most of the remaining virgin trees came down, giving way slowly to second growth. Deer increased in numbers.

More recently, in our time, some of these operations have come and gone, leaving barn-high heaps of sawdust, mountains of slabwood, and many root-disturbed leaners. These bothered me at first. It was as though a storm had gone through, or as though great blocks of serene Island woods had served as battlegrounds. But I was soon to learn that in this country of fast growth, nature can be a swift and benevolent healer. As the leaners sagged further and went down, salal and huckleberry and sword ferns, elder and bracken and fireweed, encouraged by sunlight, appeared literally to leap up and soften and conceal the ruin. A year, two years, wrought a kind of miracle. I remember one of these portable outfits with a certain fondness. The jerry-built equipment excited a good deal of levity among the knowledged Islanders, as did the Southwest accent of the operator-owner. One Islander who liked to poke sly fun at my pronunciation repeated with glee an exchange he had had with this particular logger.

"Wherever did you see anybody log like that?" he asked, unable to curb his wonder.

He roared with laughter over the owner's reply: "This is the way we logged back in Kansas." I explained in vain that I had seen black walnut trees three to five feet in diameter taken out of southwest Kansas river bottoms. That trees of any variety of logging size grew in Kansas was something he flatly declined to credit.

Island gardeners, myself included, still haul away the sawdust left by these enterprises to use as mulch, and cart away the slabwood. Deer found the new growth that sprang up in the sunlit clearings tender for browsing, and wild blackberries grew rampant over the stumps and the trimmings. After a few years, infant firs began to show, like miniature Christmas trees, and alder saplings stood as high as a horse's back.

Two stationary Island-owned sawmills were in operation when we first came. Burton S. Turk, a "Jenny" flier left over from World War I, ran a leisurely business on the shore of Amsterdam Bay, where mud-stranded boomsticks and logs towed in behind Island boats were sliced into useful lengths for Island construction. The Cammon Brothers logged and sawed off Otso Point. Great hands for nicknames, Islanders referred to these local enterprises as "The Thick and Thin" and "The Rough and Ready." But the product these mills turned out was "hell for stout" and had grown in Island soil, and they used a lot of it.

The mills are gone now, the Cammon mill disassembled and shipped to Alaska in boxes carefully labeled on Bessie's ancient Remington. Burton has retired to live on the north end of the Island. But the two sites, as do Johnson's Landing and Brickyard Point, and extinct Yoman and Vega, still serve the Islanders as landmarks.

Even during the agricultural heyday, the Island boasted insufficient cleared land for anything but small farming; nor is the soil, shallow and filled with stones in most places, suited to row crops. But the settlers found that in this climate, where grass remained green the year around, cattle throve and grew fat, and hay became an important commodity.

Curiosity prompted my first visit to "the swamp," a natural little world of its own that lies in the approximate center of the Island, land owned by descendants of the fourth family of settlers, the Nels Magnus Pettersons.

Coming to the terminus of the Guthrie road, which plunges sharply to intersect the Ekenstam-Johnson, I had seen the swamp many times through a screen of trees. During fall and

winter, when the deciduous growth had dropped its leaves, patches of water caught the light from the sky seen through the stripped limbs, and stunted jackpines that had died from lack of drainage stood out like bone-picked skeletons among the living green, giving the place an eerie look.

My first trespass into this Waldenesque area was induced by "Lord God Woodpecker," the big pileated bird I had heard frequently hammering away in the woods or squawking in flight but had not yet seen. That day I was on foot. Having negotiated the entire length of the Guthrie road from east to west, I was hesitating between a turn to the left or the right at the intersection when this incredible creature flashed up from a dead snag, as large as a young pheasant cock, and took off with a loud irregular "kuk, kukkuk, kuk!" over the tops of the dense underbrush.

The month was June, the trees in full leaf, and he disappeared quickly, leaving an impression of brilliant black and white and red but no real notion except that gained from Roger Tory Peterson's bird guide and the Audubon calendar as to his appearance. I did not see him again that day, though I have seen him, or his counterpart, many times since. He is a year-around resident. As I thrashed my way through highgrowing huckleberry and salal, the earth fell away and then turned boggy and unsubstantial, and I found myself on the shore of a seasonal pond, half-choked with watercrowfoot and cat-tails and surrounded by a vigorous growth of steeple bush and of rank-smelling red hedge nettle. Completely encompassed by trees, I stood in a low clearing, open only to the June sky, reflected in the stagnant water. The feeling of solitude was intense. Only the distant song of a chain saw and the lisp of a pair or a flock of invisible bushtits broke the silence.

I have visited the swamp time and again since, always with a feeling of trespass and a strong sense of gratitude toward the owners. It is a fascinating and a rewarding place at any season. After the pond has dried away, as it generally does in late summer, little opportunists—sedge and horsetail, squarestemmed self-heal, and marsh-loving water plantain—emerge to carpet the spongy bog until the rains come to drown them out again.

The swamp was once tamed as a productive meadow, drained, and with a shed of hand-hewn shakes and poles built to shelter the cattle that pastured there after the hay was taken off. The hay, which grew rank in the wet soil, was cut and raked by hand with homemade wooden peg rakes and hauled out over the stumpy road in converted wood wagons.

After the hay was gone, the meadow served as a ball park, where young people from Anderson and McNeil met for fiercely contested matched games. When the accumulated run-off froze sufficiently hard in winter, the same young people built a roaring fire and skated there.

But after a while the swamp was abandoned as meadow land. The trees grew back, and the drainage ditches became clogged with dirt and brush, and the swamp reverted to bog once more. Lately, even the trails once used by the wagons have grown thick with young alder and almost impenetrable. Fighting my way through on a Sunday morning last fall, I met a disgruntled deer hunter, who declared he had been sitting for hours on a fallen log without having seen a sign of life.

The secret, I have found, is to sit unmoving until I am accepted as a part of the growth. Deer come to drink or to browse. Long-tailed mice and chipmunks and shrews emerge on various errands that have to do with feeding or storing. Birds, ranging upward from the smallest rufous hummer (in summer) to the big colorful pileated, go about their business.

The pileated woodpeckers work in pairs generally. In habit, they do not differ greatly from others of their family, *Picidae*. It is their size and their brilliance of color that makes them spectacular. A shining black, with bright red crest and pure white underwing, they move about the tree boles, chopping away with their chisel bills to strip off bark in search of grubs, ant colonies, or tree-boring insects. Drilling the elongated holes they use as nest entrances, they hold their tails stiff against the tree bole, while their heads move with the rapidity of jack hammers and with an equivalent racket. The pileated young, fed by regurgitation of the parent birds, remain in the nest until full-fledged, necessitating a constant remodeling by enlargement of the nesting hole. I came across these holes sometimes, running vertically with the tree's growth, usually in some dead snag, with a telltale untidy heap of stripped bark at the base.

Understandably shy, conspicuous by their size and color, these big birds avoid the clutter accumulated by man and even his clearings. I glimpsed one (probably the same each time) on several occasions among the fruiting madroñas above Higgins Cove. Disturbed by my arrival, he betrayed his position and scared me half out of my wits by exploding like a rocket from among the foliage and setting off on a noisy undulating flight to disappear in a dense growth of conifers.

I surprised a pair of pileateds in the orchard once, less than a dozen yards from the house, or they surprised me. Aware of a passing shadow on the shade, I stepped to the kitchen window and watched the male alight on a limb, cleave an apple neatly in half with his swordlike bill, and share the treat with his exotic mate.

Even before the steamships stopped coming, shrimp fishing became an important Island enterprise. In the year 1895, Albert McCay and his sons launched an oar-propelled skiff from Villa Beach on the northwest corner of the Island, fitted with a trawl and a hand-powered winch. The following year, the McCays were joined by Frank Brown, with his little steamer, the *Marion A.*

Shrimping by hand methods, in unpredictable waters, was hard work. Without refrigeration, the catch must of necessity be cooked quickly, and "prospecting" might go on for days before a bed of the little crustaceans was located. But the going price was four and one half cents per pound, there were no restrictions, and men accustomed to being out on the water liked the life.

Shrimp taken were of four varieties, called, respectively, "spots," "coon stripes," "side stripes," and "pinks." Of these, the pinks were preferred because of their more delicate flavor. Trawls, or nets, of very fine mesh, were attached, bag-like, to a heavy iron frame, oblong in shape and with an opening approximately four by ten, giving forty square feet of trap space. The net was protected from sharp stones at the bottom of the channel by heavy canvas.

Each time a drag was made, the fishermen took land bearings from both the bow and the stern of the boat, using some rock or tree on shore as a landmark. If a fisherman hit pay when another shrimper's boat was in sight, he took his mental bearings and dropped his trawl again as though nothing had materialized. If the boat were of sufficient size, the shrimp were cooked on board, using salt water with salt added. This kind of small-scale shrimp fishing went on for more than a quarter of a century, from a variety of little boats that included the *Zebeta,* the *Trio,* the *Viola,* the *Starling,* the *Rover,* the *Violet,* and the *Anna B.* The last of the Island shrimp fishermen was Walter Larson, who had purchased his little steamer *Orlou* from the Seattle Fish and Oyster Company in 1916 and used it until 1931.

Of the dozen or more Islanders who made their livings by shrimping in Island waters and went on to other vocations after the beds were depleted, two (both retired) remain. Paul Camus, who fished from the *Trio,* lives on Amsterdam Bay not far from the site of Christian Christensen's woodyard. Bengt Johnson's youngest son Otto, who shrimped for Victor Brolin of the *Orlou,* looks out toward Eagle Island from the house he has built between Otso Point and his birthplace at the Landing.

Young people who had grown up on the Island took naturally to boats. But few remained away permanently. When their working years were finished, they returned, many to live on the land that had stayed in the family. You can live better for less here, they declare stoutly, but that is only a part of it. You live *longer.* And there is something about Island living that gives you a happier outlook as well.

15

THE LITTLE ISLAND

In 1887 Bengt Johnson was named by the Department of Commerce in Washington, D.C., to tend the stake light on tiny Eagle Island, that lay like a stepping stone in Balch Passage, less than a quarter mile offshore from Johnson's Landing. He kept the job until his death in 1917.

To the Johnson children fell the task of rowing out at dusk to light the light and back in the morning to extinguish the flame; they were also to keep the lamp clean and filled with coal oil, to trim and renew the wick when needed. "I was only a year old at the time he took the job," Bessie said. "But later, as soon as I was old enough, the responsibility often fell to me. One thing that was impressed upon us was the importance of seeing that the light was kept burning. There was not much of a parallel, to be sure, between me and the storied lighthouse keeper's daughter. But when I went out alone, that was the way I saw it."

As had Luark in his diary, the Islanders referred to Eagle as "the little island." Seen from the house above the Landing, nothing marked the island save the big trees, which seemed to grow out of the water. But at low tide it was surrounded by a pale beach fringed with white foam, like white lace around a green doily.

"In the beginning, the light was located on the north end, to mark the reef, which extended a good way out. But then it was moved to the south end, so that we could watch to see that it didn't go out, and so that we wouldn't have so far to go in order to tend it. Orders, relayed from Washington to the district office in Portland, were that we were to put the light out in the morning, in order to save fuel, and light it again in the evening. In this day of free spending, this kind of economy seems a trifle ridiculous. But born to thrift ourselves, we thought nothing of it, and did as we were told.

"Arriving at the light, I did each thing in order, so as not to forget any of it. The lamp, which was in a heavy brass frame, had a chimney of thick ridged glass. The fuel container had to be filled every twenty-four hours. The filling and the cleaning of the chimney were done of an evening, when the globe was cool, before the lamp was lighted. To do this, it was necessary to lower the big lantern on its rope, fasten the rope to a cleat, and remove the container. When I had filled the container with coal oil, which was called 'mineral oil,' I adjusted the wick and cleaned it, lighted the lantern, unwound the rope, hoisted the lantern back into place, and secured it there.

"For cleaning the globe, we were provided with crash towels sent out on the lighthouse tender *Mazanita* along with other supplies, such as the oil and matches. I can remember how fine I felt as I rowed back to the Landing, to see the lantern burning and to think it might save some boat from destruction. Actually, the worst that could have happened was that a boat might have run aground on the reef, and at high tide it would certainly have floated free again."

Once, a long time later, after the light had become automatic, the *Texada* did run aground on Eagle Reef. It was at night, and the dark shadows from McNeil must have looked foreboding. In any case, the skipper got over a bit too far

and hung up in the sand. As a result, a red light that could be
seen as a boat approached from the north was installed.

But the little island was *useful* to boats, too. In times of fog,
pilots habitually sounded their whistles at frequent intervals
as they groped through the narrow channels. An experienced
skipper could tell from listening to the echo just how close he
was to shore and in which direction the land lay. The big
trees on Eagle, like the trees on Anderson, served as a buffer
against which the sound was bounced.

The tender *Manzanita* called in once each quarter. "She
had a special signal," Bessie said, "and I think our ears were
always attuned to it. The signal was one short blast followed
by two longs and another short, 'Boop, booop, booop, boop!'
When we heard it, we hurried down to the Landing, got out
the rowboat and set out as fast as we could to receive the
supplies." The big item, of course, was the mineral oil. The
amount left was fifty gallons, and it had to last until the
Manzanita returned again. Other items were matches and
soap, cotton waste, towels, wicks, Manila rope, burners.

Bengt served as lamplighter for thirty years. For this work
he received, for the first sixteen years, the sum of twelve dollars a month. In 1903 he asked for a three-dollar-a-month
raise.

There followed a month of correspondence between the
Lighthouse Inspector of the Thirteenth District at Portland,
to whom he had made application, and the Lighthouse Board
in Washington. The Honorable Francis W. Cushman of the
House of Representatives wrote that he would do everything
in his power to increase the compensation, because he felt
that Bengt had been "unusually faithful in the performance
of his duties."

At long last a letter arrived from Portland, enclosing a note
to Representative Cushman from Captain Hutchins of the
United States Navy stating that the Portland Inspector had
looked into the matter and had found himself able to grant
the increase from twelve to fifteen dollars. "I have to state

that your compensation will be increased to $15.00 per month," the letter read, as though the Department had acted under pressure and with considerable reluctance.

Some time after 1917, an order came to the effect that the light was to be left burning twenty-four hours a day. Later still, an Edison battery light was installed, and tended every six months. The tender *Manzanita,* no longer needed, was converted to a towboat and rechristened the *Daniel Kern.* In a final rite, in April, 1939, after she had been thoroughly scrapped, her hull was burned on Richmond Beach. For sentiment's sake, Bengt's eldest son Gunnard (Captain G. W. Johnson of the Pioneer Sand and Gravel Company's tug, the *Anne W.*) paid one hundred dollars to save the pilot house and texas from the flames. Towed back to Anderson Island, where the boat was well-remembered, and deposited on the gravel spit at Villa Beach, the cabin stood, a landmark to Islanders and to passing boatmen, until a few years ago when it broke up.

Early-day Islanders who played on the little island as children recall having picked up beads and trinkets there, lending credence to the belief that it was, indeed, Eagle from which Michael Luark obtained the burial canoe mentioned in his diary. The island is covered now by second growth, fir and cedar and hemlock, interspersed with madroña and alder. Of the virgin trees, only a few blackened snags remain.

It was on a day some fifty years ago that the forest on the island caught on fire. Men who had come to clear and burn the brush around the stake light went away, thinking the fire was out. The fire burned for days, underground, in the layers of leaves and needles. As Anna Johnson went about her work in the house above the Landing, she could hear the big trees going down. After the last tree was gone, a pall of smoke obscured the channel.

Eagle was noted for its clam beds once. The wide, gently-sloping, soft sand beaches served as ideal breeding grounds for butter and rock clams and for the big heart-shaped cockles used for chowder. But as pleasure boating increased Up Sound, the beaches were dug out by visitors who often wasted the little ones and took more than they could use.

"The little island was our playground," Bessie recalls, "aside from the fact that we were obliged to go there to tend the stake light. I suppose we took it for granted that all children had a little island in their front yards."

Eagle came near to being a leper colony once, or at least a home for one alleged leper. This was around 1912. The man's name was John Early and he lived in Tacoma. When word got around concerning the diagnosis, Early's neighbors became alarmed and insisted that a place be found where he could be isolated. Someone thought of the little island, and

it was suggested that Early might tend the stake light to make recompense for his enforced incarceration there.

Pierce County commissioners forwarded a request to Washington State's Representative Stanton Warburton. United States Lighthouse Inspector Beck replied that the light had been kept in good condition for a quarter of a century and that it would be an injustice to relieve Bengt of the job, which by now paid the munificent sum of fifteen dollars per month. Beck suggested that the government might instead issue a revokable license to the county commissioners to permit Early to live on the north end of the island, provided he should cut very little, if any, timber, as the big trees were necessary to afford an echo for passing steamers in time of fog. At the end of five years, if necessary, the license might be renewed.

Whether John Early died or went elsewhere, or whether his ailment was diagnosed as something more sociable, nothing came of the proposal. Perhaps the prospect of being quarantined for life on an otherwise uninhabited island did not appeal to him, and he left the country. Or he may have died before the snarl of red tape was untangled and permission granted.

More lately, it has been rumored that a plan is afoot to "develop" the little island as a marine park for pleasure boaters. Islanders who put stock in the rumors view with alarm the prospect of "yacht clubbers" with their noise and rubble so close offshore. There is something virginal about this dot of uninhabited land. Whether at ebb tide or at flow, Eagle arises cleanly out of the water, bearing its burden of green. It may be brooding and dark, or fog-enshrouded, in the winter time. But in the spring the island is gay with bloom, and in the fall, vine maple and the scarlet leaves of poison oak, the orange of ripened madroña berries, the russet of big leaf maple, and the yellow of alder lend it color.

Eagle is a natural reserve for wild birds. At low tide, gulls alight on the beaches to feed. A kingfisher comes to sit on an overhanging branch for his day's fishing, or an eagle stops to rest for a time in the steepled top of one of the old snags that may have cradled a dead chief among its foliage. A great variety of small birds nest here, unwatched and unmolested by humans.

On a day last summer when the little island wore her foam-trimmed beaches like a fringed skirt, Bessie and I set out in her skiff at slack tide for a visit there. Bessie still handles a boat well, sitting tall and erect in the oarsman's seat and charting a direct course.

The tide was coming in as we pulled the boat up and tied it to an overhanging manzanita. I could not help wondering how this one had struck root here. The manzanita, for which the lighthouse tender was named, is a native of the Northwest, an ericaceous shrub (*Arctostaphylos tomentosa*), but, although I have searched diligently, I have yet to find the species on Anderson. Like its evergreen cousin the madroña, the manzanita has a liking for rocky acid soil, and its white urn-shaped flowers are similar. But it is a shrub, not a tree, a sun-lover. Its branches are gracefully misshapen, its bark of a smooth rich red-bronze shading to raspberry, the twigs covered thickly with wooly hairs. The fruit, which was prized by the Indians, consists of a reddish-black mealy berry, similar in flavor to the fruit of salal.

We walked completely around the island and even followed a faint overgrown path into the center, without finding another specimen of manzanita. The tall snags that still stand among the second growth, and tower above it, bear the blackened scars of the old burn. Their boles are pocked and pitted by woodpeckers, nesting sites for the nuthatches, the creepers and the chickadees, that flew from bough to bough that day, too high for positive identification.

A bell has been installed at the north end now to augment the automatic light in times of dense fog. The bell was out of commission that day, and we climbed up to the installation to see if we could find the reason, though on a day so bright the bell's dumbness didn't seem to matter much. Seen from there, the curving shore of Anderson presented a serene face, with her climbing bluffs of feathered trees splashed here and there along the bank with scarlet maple, mirrored in the sunlit blue and silver water.

We untied the boat and made the row back in silence

broken only by the cries of the gulls overhead and the creaking of the oars in the oarlocks. As the ruins of the Landing
receded behind us, I tried to visualize how it had been when
the log house perched on the hillside above and a stern-
wheeler came splashing up the passage. On an afternoon so
tranquil, time seemed to stand still. But I thought I knew
what my companion was thinking as she set her course for
Otso Point by the tallest tree on the little island.

16

THE HAPPY BRUSHPICKERS

If the Island can be said to lay claim to any form of industry, now that both sawmills are closed and farming has dwindled almost to a standstill, it consists of the gathering of forest greens for the florist trade. But even "brushpicking," like beachcombing, clam digging, and huckleberrying, is an individual and an independent business.

Island brush is good and fairly plentiful, but it is for Islanders. Poachers from the mainland are not welcome, nor would ferry fares make such encroachment feasible.

On the Island, when we first came, I learned to my astonishment that the gathering of wild greens could be a vocation. It seemed to me then, in my ignorance, a remarkably easy as well as delightful manner of earning a livelihood. Driving about the Island or walking along the old logging roads, I had seen signs that read No Brushpicking, and I occasionally came across mounds of huckleberry and salal, covered with fir boughs, in some clearing. I saw cars heaped with brush, sometimes, parked along the wooded roads, and caught a glimpse of a brushpicker at work in deep shade, his red or yellow hat a bright spot among the forest colors. Once, in the vicinity of the swamp, I had met a little blue-eyed gnome of a man with a bundle of sword ferns on his back.

When I set out to learn where these greens went, I was even more impressed. Brush picking, packing, and shipping constituted an industry of almost astronomical proportions, a five-million-dollar annual turnover, with customers in every state of the union who purchased greens in carload lots. In 1951 brushpickers had accounted for twelve hundred carloads, exclusive of greens that went by express, in refrigerator cars, and even by air, to fill small retail orders. As one interrogated greens shipper remarked to me with a great show of modesty, the industry could hardly be compared to Standard Oil, but it was doing all right.

And so, too, it seemed at first glance, were the brushpickers. "Every brushpicker is a little company by himself," a shipper told me. "He takes orders from no one and he owes no responsibility except to his own family. He has no capital invested save perhaps in some ancient jalopy converted to a brush carrier and designed to make its way over roads that bear no resemblance to roads, and a bit of rope for bundling his bales of brush together."

I heard fantastic stories, even from Island pickers, to the effect that a good picker could make as much as thirty dollars a day and that in some cases entire families went into the woods, realizing a tidy income indeed. All of this, I found, was true, sometimes. Indeed, I know a picker or two who has realized as much as thirty dollars for a full day's work . . . *if* the brush is plentiful, *if* it grows in the proper shape, *if* it is bright green, showing no frost damage or russet color, *if* the picker does not have to pay too high a fee to the owner of the land, *if* he can get his brush to market before it begins to deteriorate, and *if* he has access to a road of sorts, so that he need not spend more time lugging his brush out on his back than he spends in harvesting.

The russet-tinted brush that grows along the roads and in the clearings is lovely to look at, but packers reject it, I was to learn, save for a little at Christmas time. To obtain bright green brush of top quality, a picker must go deep into the woods, where it grows in shade. Frequently he must chop his way in, climb over logs, fight his way through underbrush, and fight his way out again with a mound of greens as big as a haystack on his back.

All of this may be pleasant enough in the summer, when woods are dry and days are long and the weather is mild. But if the picker is to earn his livelihood by his craft, he must pick throughout the winter, too, when walking in the woods is like wading through a cold shower. In addition to the weight of the brush, then, he must bear the weight of snag-proof rubber boots, breeches, coat, and rain hat, or risk pneumonia. He must work when days are short as well as long, gathering what he can in the daylight hours during the gloomy, overcast months of October through May, when rain drips steadily from the trees that surround him, or in an enfolding blanket of chill gray fog, in which he well may lose his bearings.

"It's not all pie in the sky," a picker, turned packer, told me. "It used to be better, when a man could stop along a road anywhere and go into the woods and start picking. But these past years, landowners who make a marginal living off their land in any case have become aware that they can come in for a share of the picker's earnings, and that's right, of course." The picker has to lease his woods by the acre, the same as if he were pasturing stock, or pay by the bundle for the greens he takes out.

Literally, salal (called "lemon") and huckleberry (known as "brush") are picked. An experienced picker knows the acceptable length and shape, and he picks in such a way as to ensure that the plant will renew itself for another season's harvest. Sword ferns, on the other hand, are cut by means of a knife arrangement worn on the picker's fingers. They are slightly frozen before shipping, whereas brush and lemon are refrigerated at a temperature a little above the freezing point. Ferns grow in abundance in Island woods and gulches, but they are rarely picked here. Most ferns are picked on the slopes of Mount Rainier and farther west, toward the ocean where rainfall is greater.

Chronologically, brushpicking is an infant vocation in the Northwest. Most packers give credit for the initial enterprise of fern packing to Sam Roake, of Castle Rock, Washington. As early as 1915, Roake was picking and packing sword ferns for local florists. Florists throughout *other* parts of the country were dependent upon what was known as "fancy ferns," a product, mainly of Vermont, that could be picked only during a short season. Roake's enterprise was small, but it was a beginning. His ferns went across the Cascades to Spokane, into Idaho, and then as far as Salt Lake City.

In 1919, G. R. Kirk of Tacoma experimented with, and then instituted, fern packing and shipping on a national scale. Sword ferns, prolific in the Northwest, had been found to work well into most floral arrangements. On the rainy slopes of the Cascades, along the Coast Range, and in the Olympic Mountains, it was found, ferns could be gathered practically the year around, insuring a constant fresh supply.

In 1926 the first refrigerator carload of ferns was dispatched to a Denver wholesaler. So enthusiastic was the reception that small independent packers sprang up everywhere, enlisting pickers who would otherwise have remained unemployed.

In 1925 Joe Evans of Bandon, Oregon, who had been shipping small lots of huckleberry to retail florists in the Midwest
since 1921, sent a case of brush by way of the Panama Canal
to New York City. There it came into the hands of Jack
Kervan of the Kervan Company, a large distributor of florists'
greens.

For years, Kervan had traveled about the western hemi-
sphere looking for new varieties of greens, and he set out for
the Northwest now to investigate. Driving along the roads, he
saw banks of flat-branched evergreen huckleberry, with its
waxy leaves and its natural grace of arrangement, and ascer-
tained that it would keep for weeks in a jar of water set in a
moderately cool place. "I felt that this type of hucklebrush
would go over," he wrote. "I had no idea that the response
would be so tremendous."

When Isaac Callison of Aberdeen, Washington (who had
been engaged, along with his brother Henry, in the cascara
bark business for the eastern drug trade for a number of
years), made a trip East and saw Northwestern huckleberry in
use, he hurried home and recruited his pickers to gather
"brush."

By the early thirties the elder Callisons and Isaac's sons
were well established in the brush-packing business, and Kirk
and his son Paul had expanded their fern enterprise to include
huckleberry. Salal came later, and it, too, caught on, for the
same reasons. There was plenty of brush for the two growing
firms as well as for the small independent packers that had
mushroomed up in the area; the demand was on the increase,
and, with the depression hovering like a cloud over the economy of the country, there was no dearth of pickers.

Before another decade had passed, more than two thousand
pickers—men, women and children—throughout the cool
damp forests of western Washington and western Oregon,
were bringing tons of greens into packing centers. After a
while, a good brushpicker who worked at his job could afford
a nice home, a good car, could send his children to college.

Some pickers did have these things, too. But largely the vocation appeared to attract those with gypsy blood, men and women who liked to be on the move, people for whom roots struck down anywhere amounted to stagnation. I still shake a little over the aftermath of an article about the greens business I wrote several years ago for a national magazine. But I think it proves something about people, that there is something of the gypsy in most of us.

I have reread the piece several times since, in print, wondering what it was that brought the (literal) deluge of communications. I had set forth the facts as they were related to me, described the wet climate, the discomfort, the work involved in hacking a way into the forest. The color photographs (some of them posed for, I learned, by professional models) *were* enticing, as were the captions (not mine) about the "$18 to $40 a day to be earned by picking ferns," and the "No bosses, no time clocks, no deductions from paychecks, and all the work you want . . . up to $400 worth a week . . . these Northwestern brushpickers have on the carefree picnics they call their jobs."

Most of the letters were not, as might be supposed, from the uneducated or the jobless. Generally, they were from literate and established men and women who wanted to be brushpickers instead of what they were. One man, a teacher, wrote that he had resigned his job on the East Coast, sold his home, traded his family car for a Jeep station wagon in which to haul brush, and was headed West, or would be by the time I received his billet-doux, in which he thanked me for changing his life.

The letters came, literally, by the handful. I answered them all by return mail, urging, begging the writers not to come. I played the coward, I enclosed no return address. I have since wondered, in dismay, how many people came, and how many returned to where they had come from, cursing me, an unknown scribbler, for their upheaval.

To my relief, the response from Northwest brushpickers

was negligible. I have a notion that if they saw the article at all, they were more amused than annoyed by the extravagant promises of the captions and by the dainty garb of the pickers and packers in the glossy photographs. The Island pickers, although amused, were charitable, and I loved them for their charity. Humbly, I clung to one deliberate omission. I had not *named* the Island. If city people fifteen miles away had never heard of it, it wasn't likely that some starry-eyed would-be brushpicker in Rhode Island would find it. I was mistaken. . . .

"There's a new family on the Island," Ellen told me one morning, with a twinkle in her blue eyes. "The woman told me they read an article about picking brush and came West to try their hands. . . ."

I winced. "You didn't tell her you knew me?"

"Wouldn't you like to meet her?"

I could only shudder.

I did come to know her, of course, as everyone here comes to know everyone else sooner or later. But meanwhile she and her husband had tried brushpicking and had turned to another enterprise. She was always cordial, too. But I was never quite able to overcome the sense of inner guilt I suffered in her presence.

Once I was given an opportunity to defend myself. The letters were still coming in distressing numbers when I chanced across an irate "letter to the editor" in a local paper, written (and well-written) by a woman picker of many years' experience. She had been especially nettled it seemed (and who could blame her?) by the words "carefree picnic" in the subhead to the boldface title THE HAPPY BRUSHPICKERS OF THE HIGH CASCADES, which, in itself, must have been a bur under the saddle blanket.

I wrote a careful reply, disclaiming responsibility for both photographs and captions, as well as title. Had I any illusion that brushpicking was a picnic, carefree or otherwise, I assured my unseen audience, I would be picking brush instead of writing, which was no picnic either.

Eventually, the letters stopped coming, and I no longer trembled when a strange car stopped in front. But if I thought all was forgotten and forgiven, I was in for a letdown. A little while ago, I came across a piece about brushpicking in a local paper. Harking back to the photographs and extravagant promises, a still-resentful picker declared that Midwesterners, and especially Oklahomans (those nasty Okies again), had come West in numbers to muscle in on the diminishing brush harvest.

17

ANY ROAD LEADS TO THE END
OF THE WORLD

A visitor who wishes to familiarize himself with Anderson roads would do well to purchase at an Island store, for twenty-five cents, a map made by Islander Jane Cammon. Roads sketched in on the skull shape resemble the division lines drawn on the manufactured cranium prepared for students in an anatomy class.

Geographically, Otso Point to the north is the bump of knowledge, Yoman Point the termination of the long sloping forehead, Sandy Point, the nose, Cole Point, the chin, Jacob's Point, the elongated Adam's apple, Amsterdam Bay, the nape. Lake Florence falls into place as a watery eye, Lake Josephine a teardrop.

To help a stranger to find his way around, there are a few landmarks—the clubhouse, Wide Awake Hollow, the post office, the swimming hole at the end of Lake Florence (privately owned but for public use), the herring boxes in Oro Bay, the county garbage pit. Even so, visitors consistently become lost among the maze of wooded roads.

The first road, known as the Ekenstam-Johnson, bisected the Island in approximate halves lengthwise, linking Thompson Cove at the south end with Johnson's Landing at the north.

Tributary trails from the farmsteads along the east and west shores fed in like the transverse veins of a leaf. Though little more than a rough narrow trail through the woods, the road would accommodate a wagon or a sled and provided a walkway to the little one-room schoolhouse, built in the center of the Island during the early eighties. Islanders still found it easier and faster to row around to the neighbors', if the tide were in the oarsman's favor. But for the farmers, the road meant that goods could be brought in and produce hauled out on the steamers.

Whether these new trails were a factor, tracts were taken up with some rapidity, either by outright purchase or by homestead or pre-emption claim. Connecting roads were not built for some time, and they came gradually as the Island settled. Generally, these roads followed the pattern set by early trails, which meandered to avoid the biggest trees and stumps, circumvented bogs, and zigzagged up the steeper hillsides.

When it proved necessary to cross a bog, the Islanders built "puncheon" roads from split cedar logs, with the face of the log roughly dressed to serve as a kind of flooring. Traces of these remain in low places, where the big yellow spathes and spadices of skunk cabbage, and "sweet-after-death" and wild lily-of-the-valley grow among the long fronds of sword fern that stay green throughout the winter.

When the county commissioners proposed building roads to terminate at the newly established ferry slip, the project met with the usual opposition. To date, many Islanders argued stubbornly, they had managed with roads built as a community project, where roads needed to be. They looked upon the influx of surveyors with suspicion, and viewed the condemnation of land as an invasion of rights as well as of privacy. Build turnpikes to accommodate visitors with fancy automobiles, and the Island would soon be swarming with speculators.

Now all of the main roads are county roads, and maintenance is an Island joke. Save for the fact that they sometimes resent seeing their hard-earned tax money wasted on a hope-

less cause, no one cares much. Barring an emergency, no
Islander hurries, really. Nor would it be safe to hurry. Because
of dense growth, most corners are blind corners, and there is
no telling when or where a deer may appear suddenly from
the underbrush.

In early autumn, before hunting season begins, when the
deer are most prevalent on the roads, Islanders set out at dusk
to make a "deer count," and they drive slowly. Tear along at
break-neck speed, and you are apt to miss the spotted twin
fawns down by Bill Peterson's place, or the albino doe that has
haunted the Guthrie road and bordering woods for a number
of years.

I saw the doe once, during an early morning walk up the
Guthrie road, and mistook her for a snow-covered stump until
she moved suddenly. The fawn beside her wore the normal
darkened coat of winter. It occurred to me to wonder how an
animal so conspicuous had escaped the hunters that grow more
numerous each year. But doe seasons are rare and brief here,
and perhaps it is her coloring that affords her protection.

Once you become familiar with the Island as a whole, you
tend to think of it as divided by the network of roads into a
variety of shapes, like a jigsaw puzzle. You think of the roads,
generally, in terms of who lives along them, of course, the way
you remember the roads of your childhood. But you tend to
think of them, too, in terms of that which grows and blooms in
changing seasons.

One of the pleasures of traveling Island roads, I found, had
to do with the changing pattern of flora according to the moisture available in light or shade, or persuaded by the thinness
or richness or by the variety of chemical composition the soil
offered to the seeking roots. Scotch broom grows thick along
some roads and is not seen along others. Oaks grow in profusion at the south end and hardly at all at the north. There are
areas where fir gives way to jackpine, and groves where alder
replaces madroña as the dominant tree.

Along ditches and fence rows where moisture holds the year

around, hardhack and mimulus grow thick. Fireweed stands in drifts in recent clearings. Trillium and wild mint, wood lilies and hedge nettle have their haunts. And there are thin dry roadsides where, in autumn, goldenrod and chamomile provide the only color among the Queen Anne's lace.

Even more intriguing was the discovery that climate and temperature varied, dividing the Island roughly into shifting zones according to wind direction and proximity to salt water. I set out from the ferry slip up the incline from Villa Beach on a mild-seeming winter day and encountered snow, suddenly, in the vicinty of the clubhouse, or on Stephans Road. Long after other roads have cleared following a bad spell, the steep curving approach to the clubhouse "Y" is apt to remain a sheet of ice, difficult to negotiate. Temperatures from Oro Bay to Otso Point may vary several degrees in any season.

Island roads are roads to stop along. Each year, below the schoolhouse and around the corner, a wild orange tiger lily emerges heads above the bracken and suspends its blossoms in a whorl, like little girls in bright skirts around a carousel. You come to expect it, but each year it is a fresh discovery. A pair of pileated woodpeckers, often heard but rarely seen, hammer away at an old snag, oblivious of passers-by. A white cat crouches like a bit of statuary at a fieldmouse run. Sunlight striking through the clear translucent scarlet of vine maple against gray-dappled alder boles brings you to a sudden halt at the foot of the cemetery turnoff.

Islanders are fond of citing the case of the driver, now deceased, who rarely shifted from second gear on any Island road. In these days of automobiles, the Island can be negotiated from end to end and from side to side in a few minutes time, less than half an hour certainly, and Island roads are no more geared to speed than are Island people. To pass a man on his way to the ferry if both are sailing is to violate an unwritten code of ethics. The *Tahoma* carries nine cars, and that might make him number ten. Few Island roads are really suited to passing in any case. More than one expeditious motorist, myself included, has landed in a ditch and been obliged to walk to the nearest telephone, which may be a mile or so away, to call Bob Ehricke.

Newcomers frequently find themselves lost on Island thoroughfares. Strangers need only remember that all roads, with the exception of the few dead ends that terminate at the water's edge, eventually lead to the ferry slip. On a few corners, unless

they have been upset by the road grader or have been lost in growth, inconspicuous arrows point to Amsterdam or to Lake Josephine, or to Yoman or Vega or Johnson's Landing, places no longer extant save in the minds of those who remember them.

Until a few years ago, when three small billboards appeared describing a real estate development, not a single advertising sign marred the landscape. Islanders are, happily, too few and too thrifty to tempt roadside advertisers, and they account for insufficient votes to persuade political aspirants. When one of the real estate signs unaccountably fell over after a day or two, an Islander paraphrased the famous line beginning, "Something there is . . ." from Robert Frost's "Mending Wall." But the developer, a friendly and industrious young man, was granted the right to promote his product, and the little billboards, modest and in good taste, were accepted, so far as I know, without further comment.

During the spasmodic spells of county roadwork, when the ferry is cluttered with machinery and the narrow roads are invaded by graders, Islanders mutter about short work days designed to coincide with ferry schedules, and grumble a little about the "taxpayer's dollar," inasmuch as the crews leave the roads little better (and frequently worse) than they found them. But generally they are philosophical about these efforts. Potholes, filled with loose gravel, are scoured out directly, and after a few weeks the ridges on "Washboard Hill" are as sharp and unrelenting as ever.

Recently, Islanders had occasion to chuckle over a letter to the editor that appeared in a Tacoma newspaper, signed by Islander Ray Weinrich. It was entitled *The Forgotten Land*, and it deserves a place in Island archives.

To the editor: The land the county commissioners forgot in regard to the right-of-way that the county commissioner calls roads is so full of bumps and hollows that it isn't safe to walk at night because one might fall in one of the many large holes and break a leg.

Any automobile company that wants to test cars for durability should bring them down here as any car they can drive from the ferry landing to the south end of the Island and back at a speed of twenty-five miles per hour if it still has four wheels on it and the engine did not fall out or any doors bounce off it, is a real strong car.

The only good part about these so-called roads is that if you are driving at night in the fog and come to a smooth place you know that you are off the road.

"But there's one thing *about* these roads," people say cheerfully. "They slow down the fast drivers." When a chuckhole appeared a few years ago in the approach to the swimming hole in Lake Florence, it was left unfilled on the theory that no speeder was going to risk a broken spring. Islanders are re-markably tolerant of summer visitors. But nothing so arouses their ire as the fast or reckless driver who stirs up a cloud of blinding dust in summer and poses a constant threat to Island children.

"Thirty-five Miles Per Hour" speed-limit signs, posted by the county at the ferry exits a few years ago, were looked upon as an infringement but with forbearance. Few Islanders drive more than thirty, even on the straight and comparatively smooth stretches, and would-be speeders were well aware that the Island was without the machinery for enforcement of such a rule.

Island automobiles, like Island people, rarely leave "the rock." Passed along from owner to owner, they chuckle over the roads until they literally fall apart. If the breakdown occurs on the road, the driver sets off on foot, leaving his defunct vehicle, often, for days, weeks, months, even for a few years in the precise spot where it gave up the ghost. Mainland drivers are prone to be unreasonable about these hazards. Island driv-ers, who know where the vehicles are, simply drive around them.

Days go by, especially in winter, when less than a dozen cars could be counted on Island roads. Although our house stands on a well-traveled thoroughfare, by Island standards, I recall a Christmas Day when not a single car passed. People still talk about a collision (one of the few Island wrecks I have heard about) that took place one winter day between a pick-up driven by the *Tahoma* deck hand and the jeep station wagon driven by the Star Route mail carrier, the only two cars, probably, abroad that day on the roads.

One of my favorite stories has to do with a beaver. Where he came from, whether he swam the salt-water channel from the mainland, looking for adventure, and so came into Oro Bay and up the creek that crosses the bog there, no one knew. When discovered, he was already comfortably established in a pond he had created by building a stout dam of alder logs and mud, and his neat little island house of sticks showed above the surface.

The news went the rounds quickly, and the calls began. The trail across the bog and through the woods became a beaten path. As the dam widened and heightened and the pond deepened, visitors were taken to see the establishment, as city guests are taken to the zoo. New growth appeared in the clearing made by the busy little logger, until it was like a miniature park dotted with tooth-marked stumps. The bank of the widening pond was carpeted with trout lilies and wood violets in the spring and, throughout the summer, with buttercups and English daisies.

When the rains began in the fall, increasing the creek's flow and so the content of the pond, the water backed into the road. But there was still room for a vehicle to negotiate, and Islanders cheerfully drove around or through the resultant shallow puddle.

I was away that winter when the villains, in the guise of a road crew, discovered the flood and sought out its source. I heard the sad story by letter from an exercised Islander. A trap was set. The dam and the beaver's home were destroyed, and the pond set to drain.

Eventually, the beaver was caught. The first time, the animal was released by a pair of indignant Islanders. Busy at his repair work, the animal was trapped a second time by an expert sent in for the purpose, and was quietly removed from the Island. Islanders still mourn his loss, and watch hopefully for his return, or for a new immigrant. The beaver was looked upon as a fellow Islander, and his work was admired; they felt deprived.

I like the story, too, about the last-day-of-school picnic. The dinner was spread (long before my time) squarely in the middle of the road because someone discovered that the guard rails of the bridge across Schoolhouse Creek were precisely the proper distance apart to serve as supports for the table planks.

The Island is one place where people walk the roads as well as drive them, and they do so for pleasure as frequently as to

reach a destination. Local motorists, who stop to ask all pedes-
trians, even strangers, whether they want a lift, nearly always
add, "Or are you out for a walk?" I recall a closed-in morning
last winter when a strange pedestrian materialized suddenly
out of the fog at the head of Oro Bay as I was proceeding slowly
along the Ekenstam-Johnson.

In response to my inquiry as to whether he wanted a lift, he
shook his head in a confused manner. "I only want to know
where I am," he told me.

Puzzled in turn, I said, "Well, you're at the head of Oro
Bay."

"Oro Bay? Where's that?" he asked.

I looked him over carefully, wondering whether I should
simply roll up the window and drive on. But he looked so
pathetic. "Well, it's at the south end of the Island," I began.

"Good Lord!" he ejaculated. "Am I on an *island*?"

Lost in the fog as he was fishing from his small outboard,
he explained, he had drifted about until he sighted land, and
had come ashore to get his bearings.

All of the roads bear names, bestowed a long time ago—
"Sam Stephans," "Sandberg," "Brandt," "Guthrie"—but these
are map names. Islanders say, "The road past Ivill's," or "south
from Rudy and Oscar's," or "down by Viv's old place." I tend
to think of the roads when I am off the Island (and I think of
them a good deal) in terms of something remembered . . . the
buck with the incredible rack of horns that I saw silhouetted
against a morning sky, the bend where I saw a half-dozen raccoons at play, rolling and cuffing each other, the midnight sight
of eleven deer crossing in lightly stepping procession from a
patch of woods into an orchard.

Along the Guthrie Road, that first winter, I observed the
phenomenon of the silver foliage. I know, now, that this is a
characteristic of Northwest wooded roads on damp winter
nights, when lights sweep the sides. But, not having experienced the sight previously, I will always think of these woods
as a sorcerer's realm, a place touched by magic. Although I

have seen a few references in botany tracts, I have yet to see any real attempt at explanation.

Enter the Guthrie Road (or any narrow wooded trail where madroña predominates as roadside growth) on a damp cold night, with lights on high beam, and you find yourself moving through a wonderland, as though the whitish undersurfaces of the broad leaves and the glowing tips of the conifer branches, freighted with moisture, had been brushed by an enchanter's wand.

To me, the most interesting roads on the Island remain the subroads, paths made by brushpickers, or those that lead in to some old logging site, where a residual mountain of sawdust or slabwood remains to keep the trails negotiable. Mostly, these roads meander, as did the early roads, to pass around big trees or stumps. Left unused for a season, they fill up with young alders. After a few such seasons, the only trace is a line of opportunist alder, obliterating ruts and little upstarts. But in shaded areas where conifers grow thick and tall, these trails remain for years sometimes, aisles carpeted with green moss and little deer and lady ferns and furnished with more varieties of fungi in graceful shapes and colors than anyone save a mycologist can name.

To learn the roads and subroads, and finally know them, is to feel that you have the entire Island in your pocket. You know where you will go, come spring, to look for morels, and along which roads, in autumn, the big pale huckleberries with the frost-blue bloom will appear. They become an excursion in the mind, a memory of paths where long cream tips of ocean spray hang like lace curtains, paths that lead to a hidden pond in which red-bellied salamanders lie like something primordial in the moss-coated shallows. Then, it is easy to cherish the illusion, along with the Islanders, that this world will remain unchanged, because this is the way you want it to remain.

18

THE GOOD SHIP TAHOMA

Although she is privately owned and operated (on lease to the county), Islanders look upon the ferry *Tahoma* as peculiarly their own. They may refer to her sometimes, affectionately, as "the bottleneck," but they set their clocks by her comings and goings, and they are quick to point out to those who poke sly fun at her size and shape that in the quarter of a century since her maiden voyage she has made some forty thousand crossings without mishap.

They tell a story here, with satisfaction, about a time several years ago when the *Tahoma* was loaned to Fox Island, the larger ferry having gone dead in the water. Anderson commuters, being fewer in number, cheerfully used their stand-by, the *Pioneer,* and felt quite virtuous over the exchange.

Overhearing a group of Fox students laughing merrily about the "funny little ferry we rode to school this morning," young Islander Janice James burst out hotly, "That's our *very best* ferry you're talking about! And there's *nothing funny about her!*"

The *Tahoma* was *built* for the Anderson run, with McNeil as a way stop, and so Islanders feel they have every right to claim her. They cherish the issue of *Pacific Motorboat* that describes her construction as they would prize a family record. Designed by naval architect Leigh Coolidge, she was built in 1939 by Western Boat Building Company, for Olson Ferries. "Under the sixty-five-foot limit, with a 31.6 beam, powered by a 135-hp Atlas Imperial diesel," she was declared "one of the fastest of her size in the Northwest."

The *Tahoma* was not the first ferry to touch in at Island shores, but she was the first to call Anderson her home port. The dock at Anderson's Villa Beach was built in 1918, the slip added three years later. Just as with every other major change in Island affairs, the building of the slip met with opposition. Islanders grumbled that it was a needless expense, that only two or three vehicles a day would make use of it. And there was the old bugaboo: Suppose it should result in a raft of unwanted outsiders?

When ferry service began, Anderson was only a way stop. Beginning on April Fool's Day, 1922 (a date some Islanders felt was significant), a reconverted fish carrier, the *Elk*, with a regularly scheduled run from Longbranch to Steilacoom, initiated a stop at Anderson.

Contrary to die-hard predictions, by 1924 a larger ferry became necessary to handle the traffic, and the newly built *City of Steilacoom* was put on the run. When the doomed Narrows Bridge (to become famous as "Galloping Gertie") was opened for traffic, the *Elk* discontinued her run, and Anderson acquired the *Tahoma*.

Down Sounders, accustomed to seagoing ferries, tend to find the *Tahoma* hilarious. Seen from the shore as she approaches, or broadside, she has a pudgy rather than a streamlined appearance, and she does buck a bit in troubled water. But Islanders, whom she has served faithfully for more than a quarter of a century, are satisfied with both her appearance and her performance. She has an endearing quality usually reserved for the animate. Watching her go down the Narrows last fall on her way to major surgery in drydock, I found myself running foolishly from window to window of our mainland apartment. Seen from high above the channel, glistening white in the sun, her familiar lines reduced to miniature, she looked sturdy but defenseless, like a first-grader trudging off to school on opening day.

And, whatever she may lack in elegance, she *is* undeniably sturdy, and her quarter of a century of service, Islanders say, proves the fact. Her deck was built to accommodate ten automobiles. Actually, Deck-hand Ivill Kelbaugh is sometimes hard-pressed to load nine. It isn't that the *Tahoma* has shrunk; it's the size cars they're building now.

Even adult Islanders become as possessive about the *Tahoma* as they do about their hills, beaches, and gulches. She is a projection, an extrusion of the Island itself, the drawbridge by which they come and go to and from their little autonomy in the water. Islanders generally regard the ferry in much the same way most men regard their wives. She may be no *Queen Mary*, but she is an old shoe and a comfortable one. She serves, but she can upon occasion dominate.

During the more than twenty years of Olson ownership, the *Tahoma* was berthed at the Island slip when night fell. When she changed hands several years ago, from Olson to Tokarczyk ownership, some Islanders heard with dismay that she would henceforth be tied at the mainland dock. But the change went relatively unnoticed. In case of an emergency, the *Tahoma* arrives within minutes following a call across. On one occasion, when an expectant Island mother became a trifle nervous, the skipper obligingly slept aboard the boat for two or three weeks on the Island side. The throb of the *Tahoma*'s engines at night is an uneasy sound. Hearing them, we get out of bed and peer through the windows at the mast lights moving across the water, and our thoughts go combing about the Island among the aged and the ailing. . . .

A few old-timers still grumble about having to pay fares. Mainlanders do not pay tolls to ride over county bridges, they reason, so why should Islanders be penalized. For a time after ferry service was inaugurated, some did ride free, as foot passengers. One Islander, even in our time, crossed over each warm summer day on the afternoon run to purchase an ice cream cone, a delicacy unavailable at Island stores.

But, by and large, Islanders look upon ferry fares as a not unmixed blessing. "Keeps a few people off," they say cheerfully. "That's worth *something*." They are inclined to say the same about the line-up of week-enders on the mainland side on Friday nights in summer and on the Island side on Sunday. Visitors obliged to wait two to three hours for a turn may think twice about coming back, or settling here. By the same token, most Islanders view with scant enthusiasm the occasional talk of a larger ferry on the run.

They are invariably amused by week-enders who drive onto the ferry laden with more belongings than they could make use of in a month and who depart even more burdened with Island loot, cars piled high with driftwood or Christmas trees, with firewood or fir boughs or fruit. "Once the mainlanders get off on a Sunday night in apple time," Peter James was wont to say, "the Island sets six inches higher in the water."

These past years, save for an occasional day when the wind is blowing hard and the tide is running fast, the crossings of the *Tahoma* are "as steady as she goes." But earlier runs were not without their peculiar hazards.

"I've seen the skipper crawl up the ladder to the pilot house so under the influence he didn't know whether he was on a boat or a bicycle," one old-time Islander related. "But we never worried. As long as he could hold onto the wheel, they didn't come any better. Sometimes he'd all but beach her trying to slip her into the slot. But he always made it.

"Except once. It was on a Friday night and we were all in a Friday night mood in the cabin, and every little while somebody would run up the ladder to pour one for the captain. We were going along at a pretty good clip when John looked out the window and yelled that we'd passed the slip and were headed for the reef.

"We knew right away what had happened. Sure enough, the

skipper was out cold on the floor of the pilot house. None of us knew much about a boat, and we weren't any of us in very good condition, either. But somehow we managed to bring her around and stuff her into the slot. We got the captain to bed in the little shack where he lived. By morning, he was as good as ever. If he knew he didn't bring the boat in, or who did, he never mentioned it, and neither did we. He had a lot of pride and he'd have been embarrassed."

The *Tahoma* makes five trips a day, and the lives of the two-man crew are not as leisurely as they were once. On fine summer Sunday afternoons during the layover, we often watched the boat pull out of the slip and cruise along the shore while the crew and some of the other Islanders fished off the deck. Or the skipper would swing off course during a regular run, to hitch onto a floating log or to allow the passengers to have a closer look at a school of blackfish.

Prior to the establishment of the telephone cable, the crew provided a grapevine of communication to and from the

Island. Messages phoned to the mainland dock were brought across, gratis, and passed along by whichever passenger happened to be going by the home of the party for whom the message was intended. We never ceased to marvel at the fact that the deck hand always knew, to a man and car, how many mainlanders were on the Island, where they could be found, and when they expected to take their departure.

He made it his business to know, by the time he had finished his ticket rounds, both the names and the destination of any strangers aboard. If it occurred to him that they might be of use, he jotted down license numbers. Nor did he hesitate to ask questions concerning tires or car parts or junk being carted off the Island.

He took justifiable pride in his skill at loading cars close and in getting them on and off without nicked fenders, and he was especially irked by drivers who thought they knew better than he or by timid people who ignored his hand signals.

But the only time I ever saw him really angry was on an afternoon when a passenger whose car was parked close in the center of the ferry handed him a large well-filled bag and said, "Throw this overboard for me, will you?" At that time, with no garbage dump on the Island, this was frequently the method of disposal.

Pete obligingly reached for the package and tossed it overboard. As it hit the surface, it came to life, and two kittens emerged, mewing and struggling in the water. The look on Pete's face was something to see. I half expected him to haul the sometimes Islander from his car and toss him into the water with his unwanted felines. I doubt that anyone aboard would have raised a finger to stop him.

Whether it had to do with the rhythmic sound of the engines, or whether it was simply an awareness that the mainland and its cares were being left behind, there was always an air of relaxation aboard the homebound *Tahoma*. To Islanders who had been to town (all Islanders are convinced that town is ten degrees hotter in summer and ten degrees colder in winter), it meant homecoming. To us Friday nighters, it meant a week end away from cares and worries, which always seemed to remain on the mainland.

The time of crossing varies little, and it always seems leisurely. Previous to the installation of the new engines this past year, crossing required a half hour, or more, if a stop were made at McNeil. When the channel is rough, as it is sometimes in winter, the *Tahoma* rocks and rolls. Her timbers creak with effort, and the cars aboard may be drenched with salt spray. But the times she has had to remain tied at the slip because of a running sea have been few. On such occasions, the run is at the skipper's option, and you rarely see any nervousness aboard.

As unofficial wardens of Island property, the members of the *Tahoma* crew are invaluable. Were an Island car to be driven onto the ferry for the mainland crossing by a stranger, the driver would have some explaining to do, and the same would be true were he to have visible Island property of any kind aboard.

Once the deck hand's post-sailing chores are done, he generally retires to the passenger cabin to visit. One hand tells of an Island family for whom he used to perform a peculiar extra-curricular service. "The kids would come rushing on board at sailing time still in their pajamas and carrying their clothes, and I'd have to help with zippers and buttons. Old lady wasn't any different when she joined them for the early trip to town. She'd get up late and come on board half dressed and I'd have to zip her up, too."

The stand-by *Pioneer* is gone now, sold to private parties, to be converted to houseboat status. Her going leaves a vacuum. Brought here from the Deception Pass run at Whidbey Island, from Taylor Bay to Puget, she stood by for the *Tahoma* from 1939 until a few years ago, when she was condemned for even a stand-by run.

She was a pretty sight beside the dock, and she seemed to belong there. Moored to a tree on shore, she cast an irregular reflection in the water. On a bright day, when the sun was shining, you could stand on the bridge and watch the big cod and the little pogies swim about among the tall sargasso that grew around and underneath her like a submerged forest. The smallest ferry Up Sound, she was like a mascot, even to the *Tahoma.*

On January of this year, listed as "a pleasure cruiser," she was beached at Crab Point near Point Defiance, when fire erupted in the engine room and destroyed the second-deck wheelhouse. Pictured with her bow ashore and smoke pouring from her wheelhouse, she looked something less than familiar in her new guise. But she was the old *Pioneer,* and Islanders, in whose hearts she had rated second only to the *Tahoma,* knew a pang of sadness as they speculated concerning her *final* disposition.

19

THE DISTAFF SIDE

"All Island affairs," Mr. Baskett told us, early during our sojourn here, "are run and ruled by the Anderson Island Sewing Society and Cemetery Association, and they do a good job of it."

"Well, it's not quite like that," Bessie laughed. "But then, I guess it is a little bit, too. Island affairs have always been more or less run by the womenfolk. I guess the men have been too busy to bother, or else they just have a lot of confidence in us. They help out when they're asked, all right. But, mostly they leave the organization to the women."

The name isn't so far-fetched either. Originally, the Anderson Island Community Club, which is called, simply, Club, included both McNeil and Anderson. Known as the Utopian Club, it met first on one island and then on the other. Members went in the morning and stayed to dinner. If the affair were an evening one, they stayed the night. No one wanted to row home after dark.

After a while, no home was large enough to accommodate the members and their families, which included almost everyone on both islands, and so the get-togethers were held in haybarns, built snug enough and large enough for all. Because there was no one left at home to baby-sit, children were brought along and bedded down in the corners. Grown-ups danced the night away and went home in the morning.

Dances, for the most part, were "square." Accompaniment consisted of violins, called "fiddles," and an accordion or two. Occasionally, in later years, someone brought a hand-crank graphophone, the kind with a horn. There were pie and box and ice cream socials, too, along with dinners and plays and needlework auctions.

The plays were nearly all comedy or melodrama, on the theory that everyday life provided enough of grimness and tragedy. Attics and trunks were ransacked for costumes. Bedspreads and sheets provided curtains. "I expect some of the plays were pretty corny and far-fetched," Bessie says. "But we thought they were hilarious and talked about them for weeks afterward."

One thing that impressed me especially as I looked through the albums and boxes of snapshots taken at these events, was the fact that everyone dressed for them. Even at out-of-door picnics, which were legion in summer, men and boys wore white shirts, suits, ties, hats, and vests adorned by chains and watch fobs. By contrast with today's slacks, women wore long skirts, jabots, ruffles, plumed and flowered hats, elegant high-topped laced or buttoned shoes, and carried parasols.

By 1908, each island had reached a point in population sufficient to form its own group, and there was a parting of the ways. The Utopian Club disbanded. Anderson Islanders built their own hall, at Otso Point, on land donated by Helda Christensen Lindstrom's son, Daniel.

That year cultural development widened to embrace the newly formed Cemetery Association, which, to be sure, comprised the same membership—practically everybody. Islanders met around at homes, and they still came for dinner.

The cemetery had been in existence for some thirty years, but without any really organized maintenance. When a burial ground became a necessity, in October of 1883, with the death of Bengt and Anna Johnson's son Emil, the handful of Islanders agreed by common consent to appropriate two acres out of the ten acres previously donated by Peter Christensen to serve as a school site.

As it is enclosed now, the burial ground was dedicated with the erection of a stone to Emil's memory and to that of a cousin, John Martenson, who had died of the smallpox in 1881 during a Tacoma epidemic. Actually, neither lies beneath the memorial. Emil's grave, somewhere outside the enclosure, is lost now, and John Peter's body was never found. Bodies of those who died during the epidemic were often carried away quickly by public officials, sometimes in the middle of the night, and buried without any kind of identification.

So impressed were the Christensen girls, Kate and Julia, by the first burial they witnessed that they went home and undertook to bury the family cat. Catching the cat after they had dug the hole was simple enough, Kate remembered, but inducing him to stand still while they shoveled the filling in was another matter.

"Death seemed a simpler and more natural thing in those days," Bessie said, "and a funeral cost nothing at all, really. Shrouds had not come into fashion yet. The deceased was washed by the neighbors, and dressed in clean underwear, and the body was wrapped in a sheet. The casket, a simple box, usually of cedar, and homemade, was lined with a second sheet. If it was summer, the Island women brought flowers from their yards. In winter, greens from the woods sufficed. The body was hauled to the cemetery in a wood wagon. Burial was solemn and dignified without being ostentatious.

"I suppose there must have been disagreements between people then, as now. But it seems to me that the business of helping each other in times of need, such as birth and death, tended to draw people together better. Whatever we have gained by hiring help from the outside, I think we have lost something of value, too."

Although the membership rolls of Island organizations overlap, the Cemetery Association tends strictly to business. The group meets once a year, in December, at the homes of the members. Dues, until recently twenty-five cents a year, now come to a dollar. Belong for five years in good standing, and you automatically become the owner of a lot large enough to accommodate ten graves. A nonmember can buy a lot for fifteen dollars, or a single grave for five. But if you die without funds, never mind. Someone will find a place for you.

By 1910, the ladies had succeeded in raising seventy-five dollars for the cemetery, and there is a notation in old record books that ten dollars were sent to "Chinese orphans." By 1913 Club was in such good shape financially, that the members were ready to espouse another cause. Communications being still slow in bad weather, the women branched out once more, to form "The Ladies' Aid Society for the Benefit of a Telephone."

But then, before the intra-Island phone could become a reality, the name of the club was changed again, to include and embrace all good causes, and became "The Ladies' Improvement Club of Anderson Island." That year, an open "chapel," built of logs at a cost of two hundred dollars, was erected in the cemetery for funeral services in warm or rainy weather.

By 1917, the intra-Island telephone lines laced the Island, with the ladies contributing $123.00 for incorporation and franchise fees, wire, brackets, and insulators. The telephone company, a nonprofit organization consisting of the same membership as that of the Improvement Club, became the

Anderson Island Social Club, which name it still bears. Members, then as now, must be voted upon, and they often furnished poles or labor in lieu of a membership fee.

Membership of the Social Club is made up currently of everyone who has a telephone—thirty-three, on a single line. When we first came, there were two lines, red and blue, and you had only to throw a lever to switch from one to the other. A few years ago, in the interests of better service, the two lines were consolidated into one. A few subscribers complain that the lines are overloaded, impairing the efficiency of the service, and that with thirty-three different combinations of longs and shorts, phones ring overmuch.

But there is something companionable, too, Islanders think, about hearing your neighbors' rings. And after a while, they say, the only ring you are really aware of is your own.

When we first came, a "free" phone hung on the wall of the comfort station at the ferry dock, for the accommodation of the public. The story persists that when (infrequently) a sheriff's deputy or a game warden disembarked on the Island side, a member of the ferry crew stepped into the station and rang "emergency," consisting then as now of one long ring. "It wasn't that anybody here was up to anything," our informant told us with a chuckle. "It was just that our hospitality committee liked to be forewarned." When the free phone became a nuisance, it was taken out.

In 1924, as a concession to Island visitors, the ladies paid sixteen dollars for the first road signs, small directional arrows that pointed the way to Yoman and Vega, Otso Point and Amsterdam Bay and Johnson's Landing, and to guide the lost traveler back to the slip. In 1926, they erected a sign at the ferry dock that read ANDERSON ISLAND on one side and COME AGAIN on the other, to prove their own hospitality, and began to look about for a site for a clubhouse.

Islanders August Burg and Gunnard Johnson each donated an acre beside the road, a mile from the ferry. Husbands contributed the labor for the building. On March 28, 1930, the ladies filed articles of incorporation with the secretary of state and the Pierce County auditor, and became the current "Anderson Island Community Club, Devoted to Island Improvement." How could you inculcate in *any* title a clearer statement of purpose than that?

Club, as the full name implies, is the cement that holds the community together. Its activities and its accomplishments are multitudinous, and it has a finger in almost every pie. The clubhouse, a pretty shake-roofed building painted gray with red shutters, warmed from a native stone fireplace built as a memorial to Islander Nels Warner, is the center and the hub of all Island group activity, whether it be social, of a business nature, or of such solemn mien as a funeral or an occasional wedding.

It is the scene of Saturday night dances, receptions, card parties, the annual rummage sale, the October all-Island fair, Hallowe'en and New Year's parties, the Christmas program, the Island Arts and Crafts show, church dinners, periodic movies and quilting bees. It is available, by vote of membership, for "private parties," with *one* provision. Everyone on the Island must be invited. Serious considerations, weed and fire control and power meetings, take place beneath its roof. Until recently, when Anderson lost its status as a voting precinct because of the diminution of voters, the building served as voting headquarters.

This latter development created a minor tempest. Poll books on the Island date back to 1892. Islanders felt that their role as citizens had somehow been challenged. To vote by mail, as absentees, made them feel they had been relegated to second class, and they resented the implication. In this one instance, they all spoke with one voice. But they went unheard. "When we used to have the vote," they remark wryly, harking back.

Island women are not Amazons by any means, but they almost manage to give that impression. They mow the picnic site at the lake and gather up the litter left by careless picnickers and haul it off to the garbage dump. They hustle up their own wood when the menfolk are busy, haul sawdust for mulch, and collect fertilizer for their gardens. They drive nails and saw lumber, paint houses and pour concrete, split shakes and change their own tires and spade their own gardens. One young Island woman not only kills a deer for the family larder each hunting season, but loads and hauls it in.

But they are equally skilled in feminine pursuits. Their

daily garb may consist largely of breeches, boots, and sweat shirts, but they go to town as fashionably turned out as the women they meet on mainland streets. They subscribe to current magazines, read the latest books, listen to radio, watch television, and try out the latest recipes. They also own deep freezers, waffle irons, vacuum cleaners, and automatic washing and drying machines.

No Island woman, though, let it be said, makes a fetish of these. They leave their householding at the hail of a neighbor, to set out for an agate hunt on the beach or a walk through the woods and the orchards in search of berries or morels, or simply for pure pleasure.

I like to remember a day in late summer when Aggie Lindsay and her husband Lloyd shared with me a discovery Aggie had made. In a wood so dense as to be bare of undergrowth, masses of red-striped coral root had sprung up out of the thick brown carpet of needles. There they stood, great parasitic clumps of ghost flowers, as far as the eye could see.

And I like the habit Island women have of leaving their work without a backward look to set out on such excursions. I think it might well explain the fact that they seem to remain younger in face and outlook than any group of women I have seen anywhere. It isn't to say that they are not homemakers, and good ones. It would be difficult to find better all-around cooks and housekeepers, and the garments many of them turn out would do credit to a professional dressmaker. But they live close to nature, too. Their homes and their conversation reflect this.

The discovery by one of their number of a patch of rice root lily *(Fritillaria)* in a meadow, or of a single stalk of jewel weed or of pipsissewa, is enough to set them off. I recall a day in late spring when I trailed along with a threesome of Island wives (one of them alternately leading and carrying a two-year-old) half across the Island, to follow a wooded, steep-sided gulch to salt water. I forget, now, what it was they sought . . . ladies' slippers or rattlesnake plantain. I remember indelibly from that day a patch of clean spicy Canada mint with pink blossoms and a single specimen of bunchberry *(Cornus canadensis)*, a miniature dogwood not more than six inches in height, with a tiny greenish center of flowers surrounded by showy white bracts.

The shelves of books in the clubhouse, requested from county library headquarters, reflect their interests. Island women are bird watchers, wildflower collectors, gardeners, knitters, rockhounds, mushroom hunters, potters, painters, carvers, dollmakers, poets, fisherwomen, weavers. Few are college graduates. Some never finished high school. But they are, with hardly an exception, creative, with that peculiar creativity engendered by solitude and by natural surroundings.

In the outside world, save for the fortunate few, the self-taught artist is lost among his myriad fellow creators. Here, he stands out. The Island boasts two painters (which is quite a percentage), Maebelle Gordon, a grandmother, and Lucille (Billy) Hansen. Both paint familiar objects and scenes—the deer, the Island birds, the boats, the wildflowers, the picturesque old barns and boathouses and water towers.

On a day last summer when I was driving about the Island with my eight-year-old granddaughter Hollie, we passed a field in which Billy Hansen was at work, with her husband, clearing brush. We exchanged waved greetings.

"Is that Billy the famous artist?" Hollie asked me.

"Why, yes," I said. "I guess you might say that."

Hollie gave the answer a moment's thought, and then tempered the question. "But then I suppose she's not *really* as famous as Leonardo da Vinci?" Impressed by the recent furor over the Mona Lisa, she simply wanted to say the name, I suspected, but I went along.

"Well, no," I agreed, "I suppose you couldn't quite say she's all *that* famous."

As usual, Hollie had the last word, and it involved reason. "But, then," she concluded happily, "I guess she *is* on *Anderson Island*."

The Island Arts and Crafts show, inaugurated three summers ago, caught on as such a project could only in a small community. The show lasted for two days, and it was all Island work, with displays of handmade dolls, created (there was no other word for them) by Jane Cammon, a young mother of three children, and art work by adults as well as by the Island children. Everyone, even the men, helped with the show, and they turned out for it. An easel was set up, with blank sheets of newsprint and crayons, and labeled with a conspicuous sign, "Now You Try It."

Club sponsors the dances, held on alternate Saturdays during the summer, as a concession to visitors, who sometimes bring along their "country manners" and have to be bounced by a husky Islander. It is only of recent years, with the increase of summer people, that these have become considerable affairs. When we first came, dances were held less frequently, and they were more nearly Island functions, winding up, as often as not, with a poker or gin rummy party that might last until ten on Sunday morning. One evening when an insufficient number turned up to hold a dance, the gathering resolved into an impromptu hymn singing around the battered old Club piano.

If a practice duplicated again and again in a given place in a given way becomes a tradition, I reckon it might be said that the outstanding tradition on the Island is the annual making of the Club quilt and its subsequent award as a dramatic climax to the October clubhouse fair. I suppose it is a matter of record on the Club books how many quilts have been made and raffled and what their patterns were and who won them. Whether or not she can relate all of the statistics about all of the quilts, any Club member of long standing can tick off the data concerning those that have remained here.

Along about midsummer, after much deliberation, a pattern is chosen, and the colors selected. Whatever its pattern, the quilt is a subject of note from the day of its inception up to and including the breathless moment when the lucky number is drawn.

The winning of quilt, no matter what its guise, carries a prestige all out of proportion to its value, or even beauty. Following an evening of milling about, looking at the exhibits of flowers and vegetables, always impressive (for Islanders live close to the earth and take pleasure in its production), playing bingo, patronizing the needlework bazaar, following the raffle of cakes and stuffed dolls and whatever, comes the final moment, quilt. No one wants to go home until he finds out who has won it.

One function of Club is to sponsor the library, a county branch consisting of two cases of books, one for adults and one for children, available on Thursday afternoons. Anderson can hardly be said to be a reading Island, though there are the few who always show up and who send in numerous requests to headquarters. "People don't have time to read in the summer," the librarian says. "They're too busy out-of-doors then." But let winter set in, with its enforced leisure, and circulation steps up."

People smile about an early Islander of religious bent who took it upon herself to serve as a one-woman censor board. With some books, they say, she was content merely to delete objectionable passages by blacking them out with pencil lead or by removing a page or two from the text. But in one case (it occurs to me that the book was *King's Row*), she confessed to have torn the volume apart page by page, and to have consigned it to the purifying waters of the Sound. Having done her duty as she saw it, she came in and reported the act, and cheerfully paid new-book price for the tome.

But that was an isolated case and an unusual one. Generally (we came to see and to be impressed, and sometimes astonished, by the fact), the attitude is one of "live and let live." Islanders always *know*, and they frequently comment. But they show, by and large, the kind of tolerance you see exercised in a family that stands together no matter what. Affairs that at first glance seemed nearly unforgivable, so that you braced yourself for an explosion that would rock the Island, were not only forgiven but obviously forgotten by both offender and offended, who soon enough coexisted peacefully, as though nothing had happened.

20

NEIGHBOR TO THE NORTH

Whereas they are two distinct and separate islands today, growing further and further apart, McNeil and Anderson were once looked upon by their respective populations as one island, separated only by a salty liquid road called Balch Passage. The two islands were isolated together. Except for the inmates and employees of the territorial penitentiary (still called "the pen"), comprising in the beginning only twenty-seven acres walled in by a high board fence, the population of McNeil, as of Anderson, was made up largely of farmers.

Woodchoppers for the Christensen yard, for Lindstrom at Otso Point, and for Johnson's Landing, rowed to work daily, as did brickyard workers during the tenure of that plant. Church services were held on McNeil, and social life overlapped.

Sometime after the turning of the century the amoeba-like division came about. The population of both islands was on a slow increase, making them more independent of each other. Once started, the increase on McNeil was the more rapid one. The liquid road figuratively widened. There sprang up a friendly rivalry between the two.

From the beginning, it seemed, McNeil was destined for the

limelight, Anderson for comparative obscurity. Even the first
settler on McNeil, so far as is known, was to become a celebrity,
his name something of a legend.

He was Ezra Meeker, who, with his wife Eliza and his infant son, Marion, had crossed the country on the Oregon
Trail in 1851. Meeker was to become noted not only for his
writing and his hop growing, but for his enthusiastic promo-
tion of the upper Puget Sound country as a garden spot. When
Meeker returned to New York in 1870, he took along fifty-
three varieties of flowers, found in bloom in December.

Ezra Meeker's claim (if it could be called that) on McNeil
was not a donation claim. Nor does it appear to be a matter of
record whether he obtained permission to build a house and
plant a garden along side the "bight," about where the main

penitentiary compound now stands. Following a rather remarkable exhaustive tour of Sound waters by rowboat in 1853,
accompanied by his brother Oliver, Ezra settled on this spot
because of its close proximity to and yet isolation from thriving
(but somewhat wicked) Fort Steilacoom, three miles across the
channel.

The ready availability of natural foods, wild berries, venison, and clams—appears to have been a factor in his decision.

The latter, which "spouted on the beach" at each low tide, he hoped might become food for the pigs he wanted to raise. With the help of his brother, he built an eighteen by eighteen cabin there, clearing to obtain the timbers and to plant a garden. But then he followed Oliver across the mountains to assist an immigrant train of which the elder Meekers were a part.

Ezra was about planting turnips on the third of September when the three-month-old request for assistance came. He charged one Dr. Weber of Steilacoom, whom he did not much admire, to keep an eye on Eliza, her nurse and companion Mrs. Darrow, and the children. Dr. Weber assured Ezra that he could see everything that went on over there by means of his telescope. But the good doctor also sent an Indian woman with gifts twice a week, to paddle across to the little cabin to see that all was well.

When Ezra returned to McNeil in November, in company with his father (his mother had died en route) and a considerable number of other immigrants, he and Eliza were able to serve a succulent meal of garden vegetables, venison, and wild huckleberries to their guests. The Meeker boys' father praised the construction of the cabin, only seven feet in height, but with a genuine glass window and a fine "cat and clay" chimney. But he would have no part of island living. Nor did he seem to have experienced difficulty in persuading his sons to move to the mainland. After all, it was *November*.

Following a series of adventures and misadventures, including the establishment of a general store, J. R. Meeker and Sons, in Steilacoom, and the death of Oliver by drowning in 1861, the remaining Meekers wound up with donation claims in the Puyallup Valley, where Ezra was to make a name for himself. The story of Oliver's death, as related tersely by Ezra, is a sad one. Having borrowed money with which to stock the aforementioned store, the three Meekers decided that Oliver should make the trip to San Francisco to buy the goods. During a storm off Cape Mendocino, California, the ship *Northern* sank, and Oliver, and the stake, were lost.

If any Meeker is of interest to Anderson Islanders, it is Oliver rather than Ezra. Ezra's writings come to a good deal, but he devotes only a few lines to Anderson, sufficient to whet the appetite, which remains unappeased. He complained that a high rise island, Anderson, of several sections in extent and of varying elevations to a maximum of near four hundred feet (a bit of an exaggeration unless the Island has settled since) obstructed his view of Medicine Oak Council Grounds.

One fact concerning Anderson impressed Ezra. Neither he nor his visitors could understand, he wrote, how a nearby island, Anderson, could contain a lake of clear fresh water several hundred feet above tideland and that this lake should have neither inlet nor outlet. It was on the margin of this lake, nearby where Oliver had staked *his* claim, Ezra revealed, that the first deer was killed. An Indian friend, "Mowich Man," accompanied the younger men among the visitors to the lake where the first exploit of hunting bore fruit. Oddly, Ezra mentions only one lake, as though unaware of the existence of a second.

And there the trail appears to end, at least currently, so far as Oliver's claim on Anderson is concerned. A survey of the lakes was made in 1853, but no record of any kind of claim on either McNeil or Anderson for that year exists. Nor is there any record so far as I could find of any claim ever having been registered to *any* Meeker on *either* Island. It is interesting to note that Michael Luark tells in his diary, composed in the spring of 1854, of having discovered the *two* lakes and of having named them "The Twin Sisters."

In his reminiscences, Ezra mentions the fact that settlers crowded into the district to take up donation claims until the Donations Act expired by limitation in 1854, and then by "squatters' rights, which seemed as good as any." Inasmuch as the Meekers filed claims later in the Fern Hill area, and later still in the Puyallup Valley, it may be conjectured that both Ezra's claim on McNeil and Oliver's claim on Anderson fell in the squatters' category. The first recordings of land ownership on the lakes do not occur until some thirty years later, and are credited to Dahl and Alward. It is from Florence Alward that Lake Florence derived its name.

Actually, the two islands began to settle at about the same time. The "claim" on McNeil fell, in 1862, to a J. W. McCarthy. McCarthy lived there four years and sold the property to Rominus Nix. Nix was bought out by Jay Emmons Smith. In 1870, the year of Christian Christensen's arrival on Anderson, an agent for the attorney general of the United States came West in search of a site for a territorial jail and discovered McNeil.

The island appeared to him to be an ideal site. The surrounding waters were deep and cold. The tides, channeled through the Narrows, ran fast, making an escape by water virtually impossible. On the island itself an enormous spring promised an abundance of fresh water. A portion of the claim originally staked out by Meeker lay in a natural sheltered harbor facing the pioneer town of Steilacoom, and was already cleared land.

According to one report, the United States government paid one hundred dollars for the 27.27 acres. By 1873, a cell house of brick and stone had been completed, and by 1875 the new territorial jail, as it was called, opened for business.

The first prisoner was sentenced for selling liquor to the Indians, as were many of the early inmates. Several early prisoners were captains and mates of vessels, accused of brutality to their crews. In cases where mates and captains were of Chinese ancestry, jail records, meticulously kept, referred to them as "heathens."

Whereas the site continued to appear ideal for security purposes, the new jail was not without its problems. Prisoners had to be taken across by rowboat, which often meant, during the winter months, that they had to be held in Steilacoom until the waters had calmed sufficiently for a boat to cross. The island began to populate. Like the storied camel that got his nose inside the tent, the federal government increased its holdings. In 1904, sixty-one acres were added. In 1930, an additional sixteen hundred acres were gobbled up.

In 1937, Franklin Delano Roosevelt signed a bill providing the sum of three hundred thousand dollars to take over the remaining twenty-three hundred acres, and the camel was inside. Reactions of "the McNeilers," as they were called, were mixed. Much of the land had not been cleared or was reverting to forest again, and was not worth a great deal as farm land. Some of the inhabitants felt well-compensated, and left gladly. But to others the island was home, and roots went deep. To several, life on a mainland was unthinkable, and they moved across Balch Passage to Anderson.

Headlines in Tacoma and Seattle papers shouted that McNeil was about to become an "American Devil's Island." Rumors flew that prisoners past reform were to be incarcerated there. Actually, from the beginning McNeil has been considered such a "model" that men sentenced on federal charges supposedly beg to come there.

Following a visit to McNeil, the late Clarence Darrow declared it to be the finest prison he ever saw. Told that Warden Finch Archer had a standing offer of ten dollars to anyone who found a bedbug or a louse within prison confines, Darrow is said to have regretted not knowing of the offer in time to have brought a bedbug along when he came. Even Al Capone's brother Ralph, who was an enforced resident for a time, referred to it as a "model prison without walls."

Certainly the island, and the compound itself, present anything but a grim facade. Painted a pale buff, the buildings are backed by a clean meadow and a gently rising forest of evergreens, resembling more nearly a university campus than a prison. The schoolrooms inside the brightly lighted buildings, where inmates may study to receive a high school diploma, add to the illusion.

Anderson Islanders paid little attention to the penitentiary at their front door during those early years, when their children rowed across to attend school or church, pick up the mail, or merely to visit. They rarely saw prisoners, or thought much about them when they did. Because the uniforms were traditionally striped, prisoners were easy to recognize.

Occasionally an escape occurred, and then, as now, Anderson was alerted. Once, late at night, Bengt Johnson opened the door to find a half-frozen man in a striped suit standing on the porch. While Anna prepared a hot meal, Bengt helped the man to change into dry clothing and gave him a chair behind the stove. "We tried not to stare at him," Bessie recalls. "But I don't think he would have noticed if we had. He had come across on a log and was all but numb from the cold water. After he had eaten, he fell asleep. Papa sent one of the woodcutters across to McNeil to notify the warden."

In 1928 an escapee spent several hours on Anderson and was captured by Mr. Baskett and a road crew boarding at the Baskett place. Periodically, there is an escape now. But it creates little excitement here. The siren sounds at intervals, and you see the government cars moving along the McNeil roads. Mostly, it is only the recently arrived prisoners, those unfamiliar with the tides and the depth and temperature of the water, who try this escape route.

On one occasion, we awoke to find armed guards, accompanied by bloodhounds, in the front yard. Nothing came of the search, and the escapee was presumed to have drowned. I have reason to remember this particular escape. Earle was away on one of his frequent business trips, and I was staying alone on the Island. Having returned late from a visit, I was about to insert my key in the lock when I heard a sound inside.

The Ehrickes were away, and the next nearest neighbors, down the road, were long since abed. I stood on the porch for a good while, undecided. Hearing no further sound, I finally opened the door, cautiously, to be greeted by the Ehricke's dog, Tomti, whom I had inadvertently locked inside.

On Sunday afternoons in summer, the voices of the prisoners, engaged in some athletic contest among themselves or with a mainland team, carry across the water. Seen at night, the lighted compound against the dark hills resembles the skyline of a small waterfront city. The lights cast long columnar reflections like colored prisms in the water. The snow-white prison launch moves out from the dock, carrying a change of guards, the lighted mast skimming along the dark water. Of an early morning, the little valley where the compound stands catches the first rays of the sun.

Private boats no longer ply the passage between Anderson and McNeil—a distance of less than a mile—but there is still considerable rapport between the two islands, especially now that the Anderson children attend school there. Islanders cross over by ferry for school functions. And, although their number is dwindling, old-timers from both islands still get together on one summer Sunday each year for an annual reunion.

21

SOMETIMES YOU CAN'T TELL
WHICH IS PEOPLE

Until we came to know, the tendency to use nicknames on
the Island confused us about as thoroughly as did the relationships. But in a welter of Johns and Roberts, Johnsons and
Andersons and Carlsons and Petersons, nicknames, some of
them ironic and funny and a few unflattering, made sense.

There was, for example, the Croft lily grower, known as
"Bulbs." I doubt whether a half dozen ever knew his Christian
name. There was "The Fisherman," who lived for years in a
little house perched perilously on the edge of the gulch at the
head of Oro Bay, and who was found dead there. Although I
saw and heard of him often, until I saw it in the obituary
column, I had no notion of his name. If anyone calls "Uncle
Al" by his Christian name, I have not heard of it. I doubt
whether Island children know he has one.

Many ex-Islanders who have gone away or have "gone over,"
as they say of the dead, are remembered by their nicknames,
graphically apt but not unkindly meant. There was "Sea Gull"
whose speaking voice resembled that of a gull in cry, "Bare-
belly," who disdained a shirt no matter what the weather,
"Knot," who suffered a wen on his head. There was socialistic
"Commy" and talkative "Windy," "Baskerville," with his

savage Doberman, "Ivan-the-Terrible," and others. The names "Lil-Up-the-Hill" and "Lil-Down-the-Hill" serve nicely to distinguish sisters-in-law, Lillian LaRue and Lillian LaRue, and do not offend them at all.

There have been other Franks and other Charlies, but if "Frank and Charlie" are mentioned together, as these invariably were and are, the speaker refers to Frank and Charlie

Johnson, brothers who lived out their lives together and who lie together in the Island burial ground.

The bewildering custom of attaching to the names of dogs and cats (and other pets) the Christian names of their owners proved equally confusing until I became acquainted with these creatures, that were not so much pampered as simply given status. Frequently, during those first years, I had occasion to ponder a remark made by Deck-hand Peter James one Friday afternoon when a trio of loud-mouthed deer hunters drove onto the ferry with a braying donkey in the back of their truck.

"Sometimes," he remarked dryly as he stopped for my ticket, "you can't tell which is people."

"If I'm given a choice," Mr. Baskett used to observe, "I'll come back to earth as an Island dog. They're as free as the breeze and they're treated like people here." I came to agree that a canine's life was anything but the proverbial "dog's life."

Tomti Ehricke, who called in often, and who became a fast friend, was a terrier. Pete Armentrout, who bore no resemblance, was her half brother. I heard the names Lula Ward and Duchess Gordon and Babe Burg and took them to be members of the respective families. Pups, like automobiles, changed hands, but rarely departed Island shores.

Jane Cammon's monkey, Chi Chi, went everywhere with the family, sharing attention with Cockers, Slabs, and Logs, a burro, guinea pigs, chipmunks, mice, birds, kittens. Billy Hansen's mother cat, Little One, along with Nella Higgins' Freckles and Lady produced offspring in abundance for Island homes. That the supply sometimes exceeded the demand was evidenced by the bands of half-wild felines we saw in the meadow or on the roads at night.

Our Scottish Susie, who looked upon the Island as her own discovery, had died, and we missed her sadly. But we have never been without canine friends whenever we are on the Island. We were pleased to introduce Ginger, a red cocker-chow combination belonging to our city neighbors, to a new master, a lone brushpicker here. Ginger, a superior mutt, courageous, intelligent, and warm-hearted, spent many happy years here and preceded his master in death by only a few months. Probably the way both would have wanted it.

Ginger was devoted to Mac, but he returned periodically to take up brief residence with us. When his feminine friend, Babe, down the road, was in a courting mood, he dutifully traveled the length of the Island. But during that time, he snatched his forty winks on our porch, to save himself the trouble of commuting, and asked softly and politely for handouts.

When the Ehrickes left the Island for a night or two, their Tomti, as dainty and as smart a canine as I have seen, moved in with us on a voluntary basis, meeting each ferry to check for her family's return, but returning each evening to our comfortable fireside instead of to her own inhospitable porch box.

When a stout-hearted Island spaniel fell into an abandoned

reservoir and barked all night and finally drowned there, a
local ballader wrote a long narrative poem mourning the loss.
There were other tales handed down, dog talk. My own favorite had to do with a honey-colored cocker named Maverick.
When Maverick's master, Islander Neal LaRue, was obliged
to move to the mainland, taking Maverick along, the dog
grieved for his former freedom so vocally that he was taken
back to the Island to make his home with retired postmistress
Lena Christensen, at Otso Point, some three or four miles
from the ferry slip.

It was a happy arrangement all around, until Maverick
discovered one day that his mistress had gone away without
him. Unable to find her (we may suppose he searched), he set
out for the landing. Arriving just previous to sailing time, he
trotted down the ramp and took his place on the deck. When
the *Tahoma* docked on the mainland side, he disembarked on
the run.

"Didn't even say anything about a ticket," the deck hand
told. "Just scooted up the ramp and across the railroad tracks
and knocked on Neal's door, like he figured if he'd been
abandoned he could at least go back to his old diggings on the
mainland."

Because we were, for the first time since leaving Oklahoma,
surrounded by bird life, we became not only watchers but
feeders of every kind of feathered freeloader we could coax
to our feeding board, and more kinds than we could name.
Although a few of these, such as Steller's jay (which is as handsome a bird as I have seen anywhere), and the beautifully
groomed cedar waxwing, were lovely to look at, I missed the
generally brighter and more melodious songsters of the Southwest. I still do. Some of the deepest pleasures of a visit back
to home grounds have to do with the lilting "What cheer!" of
the cardinal, that we called "the red bird," the spirit-lifting
notes of the meadowlark, the whistle of the bobwhite, the
sweet evening song of the mocking bird or of the brown thrash-

er, the plaintive "coo, coo," of the turtle dove, even the lonely
night call of the "whip-poor-will." The repeated crying rise
of the nighthawk, which we called for some reason "the bull-
bat" (who lives here too, though I have never heard him), and
his whirring unseen fall remain one of the most vivid memories of childhood.

We encountered the familiar, the killdeer, well-named
Charadrius vociferus, the crows, the juncos, which we had fed
on the snow back in Kansas, the black-capped chickadee, the
little screech owl that appeared to rotate his head like an organ
stool. But, as with the flora, I was obliged to provide myself
with a western field guide.

Here, for the first time, we encountered the Oregon towhee,
the golden-crowned and the white-crowned sparrow, the Pacific varied thrush with his orange breastband and jet black
necklace, the tiny golden-crowned kinglet, the unbelievable
pileated woodpecker, and a score of others. By chance, I had
become acquainted with a woman from Sequim, Washington,
who knew an expert ornithologist, E. A. Kitchin, who, in turn,
knew the Island from having hunted there. She prevailed upon
him to mark me a check list of Island birds in his *Birds of the
State of Washington*. It has proved invaluable.

Like most amateur bird watchers, I get lost among the
sparrows. But, because of their neat striped caps, the golden-
crowned and the white-crowned (which were far more numerous) were easy. The white-crowned sings at night, or, indeed,
any time the mood suits, and his is a pleasant song, though it
ends in mid-air. The golden-crowned, with his median yellow
stripe, is a shyer bird with a shorter song, more like whistled
notes. I have seen both birds sitting in some sopping wet
bush, under the rain, singing their hearts out.

Last summer, a thing happened that led me to wonder if the
bird world, too, does not have its mental aberrations. For days,
a white crown nearly drove us distracted with his efforts to
enter the house through one and then another of the window

panes. He would start at the top of the pane and work his way down, hammering with his bill and sliding and scratching with his toenails.

It did not the slightest good to turn out the lights and sit in the darkness so that there would be no reflection. Nor could we frighten him away by rapping on the window. He simply changed to another pane and continued his assault. I do not know when nor whether he slept. We heard him in the night, scratching and pecking, and in the morning all of the panes bore scratch marks from top to bottom. This went on for days, until we were at our wits' ends, and then he vanished. I suspect that Earle did away with him, but I did not ask. We had been reduced almost to a state of nerves by his seemingly senseless performance.

We also had a peculiar experience with a pair of cinnamon-breasted barn swallows that chose one year to nest on a ledge of the front porch. Reluctant to put up with the mess we knew they would make later, when the poultry houses provided plenty of nesting sites, we removed the nest before any eggs were laid.

That night, as we sat at the table in the lighted dining room, the pair returned, not to complain on the ledge itself, but to walk slowly up and down the window sill, heads turned to gaze at us as we sat, and uttering reproaches. This kept up until the light was extinguished. Early the next morning, they began reconstruction in the identical spot from which the nest had been removed.

This new edifice was finished in much greater haste, as though haste were expedient, which I suspect it was. But they showed no gratitude for our having left them alone. From the moment they began the second nest, they looked upon the porch as their premises. If we stepped outside the door, they swooped upon us, voicing their displeasure. During the brooding, they took turns setting on the eggs, and seemed very attentive and considerate of each other. By the time the young were old enough to leave the nest, they looked larger than the adults. But all the same the entire family returned each night at dusk, and made a great to-do as they jockeyed for position.

By mid-June, the swallows are legion, and we have at least four varieties—the violet-green, the tree, the barn, and the cliff. The last-mentioned build gourd-shaped nests in colonies. When the young emerge, they line up on the television aerial like notes of music on a staff. The tree and the violet-green, sometimes difficult to distinguish from a distance, build eagerly in the houses put up for them. Once when a new house was nailed up, one of these former shot through the opening to establish claim before Earle had time to clear the ladder.

22

REMEMBER THE SABBATH

Anderson Islanders (with a few exceptions) are a moral and an upright people, but it can hardly be said that they are church-minded. On fine Sundays, too much needs doing outside, or the woods and the water are too enticing. On bad days, there is the cheerful comfort of a wood fire, or other distractions. But, come Sunday morning at 10:30, Sunday school is in session at Wide Awake Hollow. And, although the atmosphere may be somewhat cheerless, the chairs folding, and the privies outside, a faithful few disregard the weather, "to keep the Sunday school alive for the children."

In a community so closely knit, it may seem strange that the Island has never supported a church building of any kind. The first settlers, largely Lutheran, made the long trek into town to services when they attended at all. Currently, Islanders represent a variety of denominations, and the faithful talk occasionally of building. But to raise sufficient funds at present construction costs in a community with so little cash income appears a nearly insurmountable obstacle, and it is to be admitted that attendance could hardly be expected to increase much.

"People went better in the old days when it was harder to get there," old-timers say, recalling the days when they were obliged to go by rowboat. Sunne Mission on McNeil Island became a religious center, as well as a social one, for Lutherans of both islands. Services for the Christian and Missionary Alliance were held, in good weather, on a McNeil beach equipped with a treadle organ played by Martha Warner.

The couple Islanders remember best at Sunne were a woodcutter, Gustaf Nelson, and his wife, Olivia. Gustaf, a determined man, set about trying to create a choir of sorts, a capella. Olivia gathered the girls of both islands together to teach them sewing. "We loved Olivia, a gentle soul, who always fed us skorpa and coffee before we started the long trek

home," Bessie remembers. "But we respected Gustaf, and learned after a while to sense, when he stamped his foot, whether he was just beating time or whether we were off key, which we were a good deal I expect."

In the past year or so, interest and attendance have increased at the Wide Awake Hollow Sunday school, with occasional visiting ministers from the mainland and pot-luck dinners at the clubhouse. But the Sunday school, as I first knew it, was strictly an Island enterprise, and an admirable one. It occurs to me that some kind of special medal ought to be struck for Rudolph Johnson and Burton Turk and Christine Anderson, who assembled in the schoolhouse more winter Sundays than not, those days, to sit alone or with a handful of other intrepid Islanders, to keep the enterprise alive.

Burton, a bachelor, generally walked the long muddy road from Amsterdam Bay. Christine, a pretty, vivacious, hard-working Island-born woman, who makes a home for her brother Andy above Oro Bay, rarely came without a bouquet of garden flowers for the altar table. Hens and cows remain unaware of Sunday, and so Rudy, the superintendent, sometimes arrived at the last minute, to start the session. Because the room was draughty in cold weather, we occasionally went in boots and breeches. The children played on the swings until they were called in, and raced back outside as soon as the service was over. The swings and slides, stoutly made at Ehrickes' shop, were an inducement and an integral part of the program.

Once on a week day, when I was driving past the schoolhouse with my three-year-old granddaughter, Lael, she said, "Please, Hazel, could we stop and slide down the Sunday school?"

Charming things happened sometimes. One Sunday Burton came without his spectacles. At a loss to conduct the lesson, he tried on all of the bifocals present. Finding that Rudy's glasses served best, the two men shared, passing the spectacles back and forth as the service proceeded.

I am afraid that I did not attend as frequently as I might have done, but when I did go I always felt rewarded. The service made little gesture to creed and was hardly formal, or even consistently spiritual in flavor. Discussions, sometimes lively, were apt to wander from Biblical history, in which

Burton at least was well-versed, to current Island problems, the depredations of deer (and of summer people), the control of slugs, road conditions, the state of the world outside. But we repeated the Lord's Prayer and the Apostles' Creed, and we read the day's lesson. We also sang, lustily a capella if no pianist put in an appearance. Once when a summer boy, a very young member of a mainland combo, came, he was asked whether he could accompany. He might, he said, if the hymns we chose were not too slow, and if we would sing a few bars to get him started. Our "Throw Out the Lifeline" would have outdone that of a genuinely shipwrecked sailor. Immediately the last "amen" was said, the kids converged around the piano for a rock and roll session.

But the times we ran out of talk and sat quiet and looked into the woods outside the windows were rewarding times, too. I knew a woman who said she went to church to show which side she was on. We sat together as neighbors for a little while, lined up on the side of right as we saw it, and came away stronger and more courageous, I think, for having taken the trouble.

I remember warmly a Sunday when the talk turned to the insignificance of the ordinary individual in the great over-all scheme. Rudy, a man of few words, put in dryly that when his own life had come to an end, it would be as though a finger had been inserted in water and then withdrawn, leaving no trace.

Several Islanders were present that day, and I like to recall the vehement and spontaneous round of protest and denial. During all of their working years, which have come to a good many, the first concern of Rudy and his brother Oscar has been the production of clean wholesome milk and farm-fresh eggs for Island consumption. I am sure it would be difficult to find two men anywhere more dedicated to this self-appointed responsibility, nor two more universally liked and respected by their fellows.

The Island's first venture into publishing its own newspaper for the dissemination of local happenings originated during the middle fifties at Wide Awake Sunday school as recreation and busy work for the young people. The *Island Gazette* lived for two years, and served its purpose admirably. Most of us, I imagine, still hold onto every copy that rolled off the mimeograph. I refer to mine often.

Staffed by the teen-aged members of Bessie's Sunday school class, the paper was stencil-cut on her ancient Remington. Within a few weeks of its inauguration, the *Gazette* boasted 132 subscribers, more than half of them mainlanders, and carried Island news half around the globe, to ex-Islanders and service families overseas.

The sole qualification for staff membership was church school attendance, but the *Gazette* was no Sunday school paper. Strictly Island and a trifle folksy it may have been, but that was the way the subscribers liked it. Editorials, frankly worded, called attention to potholes in the roads, dangerous brush-obscured corners, peeling paint on the ferry bridge, and the need of a public garbage dump. Issues were mailed, gratis, to the county commissioners.

Perhaps the little flurry of attention accorded the Island that first winter was coincidental, but to the young members of the staff it was gratifying. Potholes were filled, road ditches were cleaned of years of accumulation. Directional signs were renewed. The ferry bridge received a fresh coat of paint. Presently, a garbage pit appeared on county property in a brushy area in center Island.

Following the first few staff-composed issues, the *Gazette* became an outlet for adult essayists and poets and letter writers. But, aside from the page of Island history contributed by the sponsor and avidly read and talked about, the contents were the work of the young people, who ran the papers off on a mimeograph purchased out of profits, and who were in charge of mailing and distribution.

However slight, the news was reported. Not only were birthday dates, and *ages*, recounted, but readers learned how many puffs were required to extinguish the candles. The staff wished the honoree a HAPPY BIRTHDAY in capital letters. Partly, the *Gazette's* charm lay in the fact that little concession was made to newspaper style in the usual parlance. Surprise endings were more fun, and so the who, what, when, and where were saved until last.

If a new telephone pole went up, we learned when and where and by whom. Readers heard that Bones Skelton was pouring the basement of his new house, and that Murph Bond, having failed to reach water on his first four attempts, was about to start a fifth well. He was wished success.

Mary Johnson's amaryllis came into bloom with four flowers to a stem. Club selected the pattern for the quilt. Visiting Boy Scouts from the mainland, having done their good deed for the day, set fire to the schoolhouse. A tugboat ran aground. This was all pertinent stuff, and the Islanders as well as those homesick for Island shores loved every word of it.

The *Gazette* was a going enterprise, and it suspended publication with its debts paid and money in the bank. The dozen young people who had written and edited and printed and illustrated it closed their books and went away to school and married and joined the Navy and the Coast Guard.

This past autumn a new and more streamlined monthly, *The Anderson Island VIP*, emerged, under the sponsorship of a comparative newcomer, Mrs. Irene Goss. With its talk of power outages and wishful thinking about oiled roads, the *VIP* reflects the changing times. But history does not change (only the interpretation of it does), and this one, too, devotes a page each issue to Bessie Cammon's Island, largely reprinted from the old *Gazette*.

23

"NOT SNOW NOR RAIN . . ."

In Otto Johnson's front room, which is on the water side
of the house (the back door is the one through which guests
enter), stands the first Anderson Island post office, a small
breakfront desk with a hinged lid that opens back to serve as
a writing table. Behind the lid are the pigeon holes where the
mail and the money order forms were kept.

The desk really did double duty. It served as a secretary
for Bengt's wood accounts, and as post office for the entire
Island. For the Johnson children, it was a touch-me-not piece.
They were given to understand that the handling of the
United States mail was a sacred trust, and were obliged to keep
their distance when it was being sorted.

The certificate of Bengt's appointment as postmaster is dated January 21, 1890, and bears the signature of Postmaster General John Wanamaker of "Washington City." Up to that time, the Islanders, taking turns, had been obliged to row or sail to Steilacoom for the mail, a ten-mile round trip that took the better part of a day, even in good weather. Even after Bengt's appointment, the mail continued to be brought across by skiff. But now it came in sealed bags, and for the first time, Islanders had a post office of their own, with an Island address, Vega, Washington.

The bags were brought in, sometimes sopping wet if the crossing had been rough, and the contents were dumped out on the sitting room floor and sorted. The total proceeds for the sale of stamps for the quarter ending December 31, 1890, came to $6.27. This was considered the best quarter of the year, because of Christmas, when a few Islanders dispatched Christmas mail to relatives and friends on the mainland. Of the nine remaining copies of receipts, the quarterly average of business comes to $5.69.

The postmaster served without compensation, as did the men who made the long row to the mainland. In December, 1892, Vega was discontinued, the Islanders took turns rowing across to Filuce Bay on the Peninsula for their mail. But Vega, which appears now as a town on Island maps, was reincarnated after a few years at August Lindstrom's woodyard at Otso Point. After Lindstrom took his own life in 1897, his widow Helda was appointed postmistress, and she moved Vega, bag and baggage, across to her old home at New Amsterdam.

But Vega failed to survive for long there, either. With the increasing Island population, being postmaster involved a good deal of paper work as well as responsibility, for the dubious honor of bearing the title. When next the Island ran out of postmaster material, Islanders were obliged to cross Balch Passage to Bee post office on McNeil. Bessie remembers that she made the trip frequently for the north siders, tying the boat where the ferry landing is now, and walking the beach trail along the high board fence that then surrounded the twenty-seven acres of penitentiary.

For whatever reason, Vega was reborn in 1904, at Lyle Point, with James W. Youk as postmaster. In 1908, a second Island post office, Yoman, came into being at Yoman Point, and Alfred Willard was named postmaster. The following year, Vega moved to Oro Bay, where Islander Sidor Johnson kept post office for twenty-four years, until his death in 1933, when his widow, Gerda, was named to succeed him. Yoman continued to prowl for a while, moving north to August Burg's place when it was little more than a yearling, and then west by north to Nels Warner's, where his wife Martha kept post office and store hard by the beach, selling candy and soft drinks to her customers.

When Yoman settled down, finally, in March of 1918, to leave the name on the map, it was a good way from Yoman Point and "less than a holler" from Otso Point, where Vega had started. Islanders regard with amusement the efforts of visiting strangers to find the "towns" Yoman and Vega, prominently marked on Department of the Interior maps of the Anderson Island quadrangle. The tiny building that was Vega, at Oro Bay, is gone now, leaving no trace. At Otso Point, the little red-roofed structure with its homegrown flagpole is used as a storehouse by its last postmistress, Lena Christensen, Helda's daughter-in-law, now retired.

As of late years, Islanders have one common address, Anderson Island, and one postmistress, Gerda Johnson, the granddaughter of the fourth settler, Nels Magnus Petterson. Incoming mail is brought across from the mainland six days a week by ferry, and delivered by a Star Route carrier to Island boxes, along with a lot of good will and sometimes odds and ends of unmailed items.

On July 1, 1938, the late Star Route carrier, Simon Westby, who was to become an institution on the Island, began to bring the mail to Yoman and Vega in his boat, the *Roald*. The *Roald* was a thirty-two footer, powered by a fourteen-horsepower engine, and it took Simon six and one half hours to make the twenty-six mile round trip from Steilacoom to Longbranch on the Olympic Peninsula and back again to the Tacoma dock. Anderson was a way stop. Even after the first Narrows Bridge became a reality, eliminating the Longbranch run, Simon continued to supply the Island. When ferry service was inaugurated in 1942 with the *Tahoma,* Simon could come by automobile, and Islanders at last knew the luxury of daily delivery to their rural boxes.

Although he never made his home here, Simon belonged to the Island, as his son Rang, who succeeded him, is looked upon as an Islander, now. Simon, who died recently at the age of nearly ninety, is a man difficult to get down on paper. "Westby Pere" we called him after Rang began to relieve him certain days on the route. The son of a Norwegian ship captain, he was every inch a Norwegian. He had been a California real estate man, a railroader, and a North Dakota farmer. He had served as a county clerk (in Pierce County, North Dakota) and as a railroad and warehouse commissioner. Carrying mail by boat, after he came to Washington in 1928, was a retirement job.

The run from Steilacoom across the channel was frequently a stormy one. On November 7, 1940, the day the ill-fated first Narrows Bridge went down, Simon and the *Roald* braved a forty-mile-per-hour wind that churned the Upper Sound to a froth.

For four years, Simon made the rounds in the *Roald* without missing a trip, and it was a challenge. But the daily crossing on the *Tahoma* and the leisurely run around the Island to deliver mail to those he had come to know suited him even better. He came across on the eleven ferry and returned on the three, which gave him ample time to visit with his patrons. He nearly always had a story to tell, and he was possessed of a charming accent that enhanced the telling. His favorite stories were about Norwegians and Swedes, and invariably the Swedes got the worst of it.

I asked Simon one day why it was that the Norwegians always diminished the Swedes, and vice versa, whereas the Finns and the Danes obviously looked upon each other as equals. Although Swedes and Norwegians get along all right on the Island, and even occasionally intermarry, I have found that you had better not mistake one for the other.

Simon thumbed slowly through the letters I had handed him and turned to stuff them into a pigeonhole at the back of his jeep. "I'm darned if I know," he admitted. "I reckon it's because everybody has got to feel superior to somebody, and the Swedes are right there handy."

He had eased his foot off the brake to resume his descent down the long hill when he became aware, obviously, that my "vice versa" had gone unchallenged. The brake took hold again, abruptly, and his remarkably sharp, intelligent eyes assumed a look of simulated incredulity.

"You mean to say," he roared, "that some Swede has had the unmitigated gall to belittle a Norwegian? Just tell me his name, and I'll see he *eats* his innuendoes!"

Simon read all of the postal cards. He was a great reader in any case, with plenty of time on his hands during the long slow crossings and the waits between runs, and this helped to keep him in touch with the affairs of his patrons. As often as not, he gave you the gist of the message as he reached for the card.

"You're supposed to go to a meeting in town on Friday," he would say. Or, "You've got a card from your sister-in-law back in Kansas, and she says the corn's burned to a crackling."

One day, as I hurried down the path to the box, he waved a picture post card from Jim, who had gone on leave from his station in Heidelberg to the island of Corsica. "Card from Jim," he said. "Tell him I acknowledge his greetings and reciprocate." Knowing how important communications from overseas were to us, he usually came up the road tooting the horn on these occasions. I was halfway through the closely written text of the card when I came across the message, buried deliberately, I was sure, for Simon's discovery. "Give my regards to Mr. Westby."

I am not familiar with the law pertaining to the use to which a rural mailbox must *not* be put, if one exists. But Island mailboxes, I found, came to a good deal more than mere repositories for mail. Besides being guideposts that directed a stranger to the owner, they served as catch-alls for messages, notes, gifts, invitations delivered, obligingly, by the carrier or dropped off by a passer-by. An overdue library book, left in the box with a note, found its way to the box of Violet Ward, the librarian.

Occasionally, Simon himself was the recipient. For as long as he drove the route, following the death of his wife, whose grave he visited regularly, he found a bucket of fresh flowers on the same day each week beside the box of an Island gardener. Sometimes he found a passenger waiting to ride the rounds, or to catch a lift to the store, or simply in need of a visit.

I suppose if the cost per piece of mail delivered or picked up on the Island were to be calculated, the result would be appalling. "Government would be money ahead," I heard a disgruntled taxpayer say, once, "to just buy the Island and evacuate it."

But there are a few days each year when mail comes to a good deal, days in March or April when the Westby jeep is piled high with cheeping baby chicks consigned to Island farms. And there are days in spring and again in autumn when the spring-summer and autumn-winter catalogues arrive. Both Sears Roebuck and Montgomery Ward, as well as a number of lesser houses, discovered the Island a long time ago, and they do a good brisk business.

So, in a smaller way, does L. L. Bean of Freeport, Maine. If there is such a person as Mr. Bean, I would like to express to him my personal gratitude, and that of a good share of the Island population—men, women, and children—for his Maine hunting shoe, a combination of featherweight leather upper, waterproof lower, sheepskin inner sole, and tread so well indented as to give comfort, warmth, and dryness, as well as security, in even the coldest, wettest weather.

For either beach or woods walking, over slippery wet pebbles or moss-coated or algae-strewn beach, I have never seen its equal. So popular is this boot on Island that a local poet and an Island artist, who collaborate periodically in an amateur enterprise they call Fantastic Cards Incorporated, use Bean boots to identify their faceless people as Anderson Islanders. If Mr. L. L. Bean were ever to visit the Island, which is unlikely, I have no doubt he would be accorded a benefactor's reception.

For the solitary and the lonely, indeed for all, the daily exchange of greetings with Simon was something to anticipate. One elderly Islander whose mailbox stood a quarter of a mile from his woods-surrounded house, as many of them do, constructed a rustic wooden bench upon which he sat each morning to wait.

We often speak, since Simon's death, of his peculiar stiff-armed wave, a kind of salute, and of the way he pronounced the name "Bergen," as though it were "bear gun," and the way he spaced out the word "Min-ne-so-ta," in syllables like water falling. There are not so many Scandinavians among these later generations whose speech is marked by that peculiar euphony. "The Scandinavians worked at it," I heard an Englishman say once, with a trace of envy maybe. "They learned English all right. But if they didn't like the blunt way we pronounced a word, they'd twist it deliberately to make it come out liquid."

"Anderson Islanders are the best people in the world," Simon told a news reporter at the time of his last Star Route contract award, when he was eighty-six. I am sure he knew the feeling was mutual.

When I first came, I was puzzled by the fact that Island mailboxes so far outnumbered Island residents, until it occurred to me that the explanation lay in the fact that no one bothered to take them down. All up and down the roads, mailboxes stand as monuments. They have stood for years, some of them, so that the names have faded into illegibility and the boxes are laced shut with the webs of spiders.

Lizzie Larson's box, like that of the Freess boys, fell off the post, finally. It lies rusting on the ground hard by the grown-over path down which she came for the day's mail and the exchange with Simon. I stopped along the road and peered inside a half-opened box once. Having been warned as a child that a neighbor's mailbox was never on any account to be opened, I knew a sense of guilt. I don't know, really, what I expected to find, an unclaimed letter, perhaps, or an ancient newspaper. The box harbored a barn swallow's nest, packed to the mud walls with gaping fledglings.

As on Rural Route 2 back in Kansas, I found, civil servants on the Island lived up to the name. Whether or not he had mail for me, Simon always took the trouble to drive up the hill to see whether I had anything to go. A friend tells a story about the time she regretted aloud having dispatched a letter to me by ordinary mail, to a distant town and state where I was to stop briefly. "Don't you worry," Simon assured her. "I knew when I picked it up the letter wouldn't make it. So I put on an air stamp." Nor was this kind of super-service confined to the Westbys. When I mailed a typewriter, once, and foolishly neglected to insure the package, the Island postmaster obligingly filled out the forms and paid the fee, and sent me a note to that effect. The typewriter arrived at its destination in a shambles.

24

THE SUMMER PEOPLE

About the time I begin to think of myself as a full-fledged Islander, because I want to be thought of as such, I am brought up short by the memory of a *New Yorker* cartoon I saw once, nailed to the wall of an Island garage. The cartoon depicts a minister in a small country church, exhorting his flock of parishioners: "Let us strive together to be tolerant of *all* our fellow creatures. And that *includes* the summer people."

Summer people, like ferry service and electric power, are a comparatively recent acquisition. They came along with the package. Only with the inauguration of regular ferry service, in 1942, did summer people begin to come in in any numbers. Previously, there had been a few, of course. But they were genuine "summer people" mostly, not summer weekenders, as now.

The first summer folk to set foot on the Island, if they could be termed that, arrived around 1905 on Glen Elder's launch, the *Eagle*. This was the family of United States Marshal Charles B. Hopkins. The family still holds title to the wooded acres bordering on both lakes and lying between the two.

"We don't exactly consider ourselves summer people on

Anderson Island," Marshal Hopkins' daughter, Carrie Hopkins Matthews, told me. "We have owned our place there for about sixty years, and Father and Mother spent most of their weekends on the place until Father's death in 1920."

Early-day Islanders recall that Marshal Hopkins brought the first automobile to Island shores, an ancient Ford ambulance left over from World War I, with an engine too small to power the body and chassis. The car was brought in on a steamer bound for Olympia and unloaded on the dock. With the help of Islander August Burg, whose descendants own a considerable strip of Island shore today, Hopkins managed to get the ambulance as far as the road going into the lakes place.

There it broke down. And there it could stay as far as he was concerned, the Marshal swore. By the time another summer had come, however, he relented, and the family made use of the car to go to the Yoman post office for the mail. "But that was nearly all down hill. We always got out and *walked* up the hills," Carrie remembers.

"The Hopkins Ranch," as the name appears on the mailbox, is a peaceful spot, located on one of the highest portions of the Island, shut in by water and by trees. Whether or not the clear, cold, spring-fed lakes were first discovered by Michael Luark in the spring of 1854, as he believed, or earlier by Ezra Meeker's brother Oliver, at least two families, the Dahls and the Alwards lived there before the turning of the century.

But the area was unoccupied when Marshal Hopkins first visited it, around 1905, in company with the penitentiary doctor from McNeil. Hopkins, who hailed from Spokane, had held the title of marshal since 1902. But about that time, because of the growth in population on the west side, the state jurisdiction was divided into two districts, and Hopkins was assigned to the Seattle area. In 1905, his wife Josephine (for whom Lake Josephine is named) and his two daughters, Carrie and Eva, followed.

As west side marshal, Hopkins was responsible for man-

aging the finances of McNeil Island Penitentiary, which consisted of only one cell building at that time. Many of the
inmates were tubercular Indians from Alaska, who needed
care. Hopkins set about attempting to secure a full-time
doctor, and was finally successful.

In company with this doctor he first visited Anderson
Island. No road led to the lake, and so the two men were
obliged to walk an old log flume. Ducks were thick on the
lower of the two lakes, which was "very wild-looking." Hopkins, who loved to hunt, made arrangements in 1905 to buy
the place. A house had stood between the two lakes earlier,
but at the time only a stable remained standing. The stable
became the first Island summer home.

The upper lake appeared, then, as Lake Florence on county
maps. The lower lake, called Fish Lake or Eagle Lake by the
Islanders, bore no official name. The lake appears for the first
time on maps printed in 1909 as "Lake Josephine." That
year Marshal Hopkins was put in charge of the government
building that housed the fish exhibit at the Alaska-Yukon-
Pacific Exposition in Seattle. When the fair ended, he was
given a thousand large-mouth black bass. These he brought
to the Island and put into Lake Josephine.

"When we first came to the Island," Carrie Matthews remembers, "Mr. Burg, who was very strong, carried our beds
up from the landing on his back. We always kept a rowboat
on the shore of Lake Florence, and rowed across to the house
after the walk up from the landing. Only ten acres of the
original homestead had been cleared. There, a cottage, which
later burned, was built." Hopkins, who had introduced the
first telephone system into eastern Washington, strung the
first Anderson Island telephone line, to carry messages back
and forth between the ranch and August Burg's place at
Yoman Point.

To Marshal Hopkins, also, goes credit for obtaining the
original ferry dock plans, from an engineer going out of office.
If used, the engineer decreed, the plans were not to be altered

in any way. And so the dock was built high in the air, with only a ladder for access, until the present approach was made.

Except for the caretaker, Islander Harvey Miller, and occasional summer visits on the part of Mrs. Matthews, the lakes place has been largely untenanted these late years. But Charles' widow, Josephine, who died recently in Spokane, retained her nostalgia for the Island, and her almost fierce desire to see it remain unchanged. Islanders heartily approved her stubborn refusal to tolerate any mode of transportation that sounded louder than dipping oars or paddles on the considerable portion of the lakes she controlled. And they chuckle approvingly about an incident that allegedly occurred during one of Josephine's recent summer sojourns here.

Waited upon by an official with a proposition to incorporate the wooded acres, or a portion of them, into a public recreation area, Josephine is said to have shown the gentleman the door. "Old lady all but threw him out single-handed," they report with satisfaction, remembering the despoiling of roads and beaches by the visiting public, and fires left burning by pleasure boaters camped on Island shores.

Regrettably, the entire shores of both lakes are privately owned, so that there is no public access, even for Islanders. But at the extreme west end of Lake Florence, a small clearing, owned by Lenard Engvall, a public-minded grandson of Nels Petterson, is used as a picnic and swimming area.

On summer afternoons, especially on week ends, the "swimming hole" throngs with visitors, who sometimes, alas, abuse the privilege by littering the floor of the lake and the little park with broken glass and beer cans. Each spring, Islanders hold a clean-up, and mow, pick up the debris, empty the trash barrel, and fume over the broken glass in the wading area. Recently, a considerable share of the perimeter of Lake Josephine changed hands; a rumor is afoot that development will soon begin in earnest. "Well, that's progress, I guess," an elderly Islander said sadly. "But I really don't want to live to see it."

Coming upon one of the lakes suddenly, out of the woods, you can hardly believe your eyesight. Given a good right arm, you could probably stand on the shore of Lake Josephine and throw a stone and hear it splash into the still, clear water of Lake Florence. Yet they differ from each other. Whereas Florence is like a flawless oval mirror, reflecting the sky overhead and the overhanging boughs of madroña and fir and hemlock and cedar, huckleberry and salal and hardhack that grow like a fringe around the edge, Josephine is more open, and generally shallower.

Along the edges of Lake Josephine and advancing far out into the body, islands of wild iris and yellow pond lilies bloom among the big floating lily pads, and cattails grow tall. Concealed among this tangle of growth, hoarse-voiced bull-frogs make deep orchestral music throughout the spring and summer nights. Large-mouth bass, descendants of that long-ago Alaska-Yukon-Pacific Exposition, swim about undis-turbed, and ducks and geese in migration drop down to rest and to feed before they resume their journey.

In Florence, where Islanders go to swim, schools and swarms of minnows maneuver endlessly, competing for the mos-quitoes and the water skates with the violet-green swallows that dip and skim and rise without ruffling the surface. On hot summer days, gauze-winged dragon flies catch the sun, and deer come out of the woods to drink, casting moving reflec-tions in the water. Unwilling to believe that any of this can be ephemeral, we have come to take these gifts for granted I suppose. It takes a stranger to bring them to our attention.

A few summers ago, I stood on the orchard-meadow be-tween the lakes with an editor from New York, a woman who had commuted for years into the city from her home on crowded Long Island.

"What is it I smell?" she asked suddenly. "What wonderful fragrance is that?"

It was early August. I looked about to see what was in bloom, but could see nothing except the rosy hardhack steeples along the lake shore and the bright yellow lacquered faces of the buttercups in the little drainage canal that connects the two.

"I *know* what it is," she concluded, before I could answer. "It's fresh air! I'd simply forgotten how wonderful it could be."

It was well after the inauguration of ferry service that summer people began to increase, and they remained for the most part summer week-enders, family people who had contrived to pick up a bit of waterfront upon which to build a cabin of sorts or to set a trailer. A few subdivisions appeared, but the Island was still too remote and too inaccessible for commuting, and plenty of waterfront remained on the main-

land. More than this, the greater perimeter of the Island, as well as the interior, remained the property of long-time Islanders, who simply did not want to see an influx, no matter how profitable, that was certain to mean change.

I recall a conversation I had last summer with an Islander in his sixties, born here and living on a choice piece of waterfront inherited from his father. There had been a death recently, and we were talking of the diminishing population. "What do you think will be the future of the Island?" I asked him.

"It's plain," he said dourly. "It will fill up with summer people."

"I can't see that happening soon," I said. "Most of the waterfront is still in the hands of long-time owners, with no disposition to sell. Take your own place here. You have more space than you need. But I notice you're not selling."

"I know," he said. "I've thought about it. And I could use the money, too. But the truth is I like to step outside and pee if I've a mind to, without the feeling I'm being watched by a neighbor."

I hope the time may never come when any Islander is dependent for his livelihood upon outsiders. Certainly, such is not the case now. No public overnight facilities are offered for rent, and, except at some function of Club, you cannot so much as buy a cup of coffee. Even there, you are likely to find a dish simply set out for a freewill offering. Islanders are a hospitable people, and their attitude toward summer and week-end guests is as cordial and as warm as one could wish, as long as visitors behave themselves. But they remain unaffected by such guests and independent of them, and that is the way it should be.

Summer, for Islanders, is a seasonal not-so-quiet interlude in their year-around lives. The advent of the summer people is an interruption, sometimes a nuisance. Visitors may upset the ecology by affecting the milk supply, but their coming creates as little disturbance as does their departure. There is a social intermingling, to be sure. Sunday school attendance increases by a few. The clubhouse is opened for a dance every second Saturday. You see more customers in the store, more cars on the roads. The mailbags may be a trifle heavier. Library circulation increases a little. The swimming hole at the lake may be crowded these late years.

But, come September, the Island returns to normal and the lives of the Islanders remain unruffled by the summer change. This summer, as summers henceforth can be expected to do, has brought more visitors to its shores than has any previous summer season. But now they have gone away, and the Islanders take up the interrupted threads of their lives again. There will be less mail and more milk. Fewer books will be taken from the library and Sunday school attendance will dwindle. Except for special occasions, there will be no Saturday night dances. The swimming raft in Lake Florence floats high and empty. The quiet water reflects the clouds that drift overhead and the trees that grow down to the shoreline, an occasional flock of crows straggling across the sky, the slow circling of a solitary hawk or eagle, a resting flock of ducks in migration.

The dust settles and the deer reappear on the roads. The children who walk the beaches belong here. The community is a solid entity again. Islanders reach out to each other more during the winter months. Even though they may not get out so much, they call each other, and there's solace in knowing a neighbor is down the road, past the empty summer houses. There is a renewed feeling that they live in a world apart, and that they are responsible for one another.

"You can't even stop off somewhere on the way home," one Islander says ruefully, "without someone's calling along the line or out looking for your car in the gulches. Stay out all night, and you come home to find half the Island's been combing the woods for you." But he admits, readily enough, that the search would be sparked by genuine concern and that he couldn't be pried off the Island.

More daytime visitors have come these past years, strangers who looked across from the mainland on a clear day and saw the wooded hills and clean-washed beaches. They come to picnic or to water ski, or to hike to the lake, with transistors turned to loud volume as though they were intimidated by silence. Or they fish for cod from the dock, where the water is deep and clear and uncontaminated. One horrible Sunday, a horde of motorcyclists, appropriately called "Hell's Angels," invaded. Recently, a trio of soldiers confessed to have crossed because it was rumored that girls in topless suits bathed in the Sound near the ferry bridge. The rumor was true, they found; but the girls were, respectively, four and seven.

These intrusions ruffle the surface, but the Islanders shrug them off good-naturedly, and wait for Monday, or for September. The second generation of natives, who have grown up and gone away, view with alarm and dismay these strangers pouring off the *Tahoma* on a Sunday. Who are they? Where are they headed, this invading army, strewing candy wrappers and beer cans along the sacrosanct roads of childhood? "When we were growing up here," they complain, " 'No Trespass' signs were unknown." Reluctantly, now, they admit the necessity, but they are shocked by these admonitions to "keep off" that which was once open range for kids as well as for cattle.

25

WHEN THE TIDE'S OUT

Whatever their other motives for putting down roots on the Island, the early settlers must have been aware that here was a well-stocked cupboard—game and wild fruit on the land, the surrounding shores and the waters teeming with edible marine life.

For thrifty Islanders, many of whom subsist comfortably on retirement incomes of one sort or another, natural foods are a major consideration. Except for the absence of grouse, once plentiful, the Island is even more productive now. Clearing brought the deer in greater numbers and opened the way for wild fruits and berries. These in turn attracted the birds, band-tailed pigeons, grouse, and pheasants. There were always ducks and geese in early winter, and presently, when they were old enough to bear, the orchards planted by the settlers provided more fruit than could be used, sold, or even given away.

I remember a conversational exchange between Earle and Bill Baskett, once, shortly after we came, when the abundance of food for the taking seemed an almost too-kind benefaction. As he did frequently when the tide was low, Mr. Baskett had brought us a bucket of clams from the beach, and had accepted our invitation to share them with us. We had teetered on the brink of a decision to return to the Southwest all during the four years prior to our acquisition of the Island place, but I am sure that neither of us entertained a notion, after that summer, of settling down "for the long haul" anywhere else.

"I reckon," Earle said, "you wouldn't have much trouble retiring here on around a hundred a month, say? If you did a little hustling?"

"No, you wouldn't," Mr. Baskett said. "And that's a fact. I know some that live, and live well, on a good deal less here." I suspect that he himself did.

"I reckon," Earle pursued the thought, "you could live a little bit like a king on the two hundred you read about in the annuity ads?"

Mr. Baskett shook his head. "No, you couldn't," he said emphatically. "You'd have a hundred a month left over to spend for whiskey. And you couldn't drink all that much."

To be sure, good clam beds are difficult to find these late years. Like the shrimps, which were once plentiful, they have not been able to keep pace. Natural enemies, such as the moon snail and the starfish, the raccoon and the seagull, have taken their toll. But, of late years, the increase of oysters in protected areas has done much to make up for the loss.

There are various theories as to why the oysters have reappeared in such numbers. Biologists say the larvae have been drifting about all along and that the closing down of certain industries around the Sound that were pumping waste into the waters has given them the impetus to settle, attach themselves, and grow, or that Puget Sound waters were simply too cold for spawning, and over the years the bivalves have adapted themselves to the temperature and have commenced to multiply.

Following the Columbus Day blow of 1962, when surf of near-oceanic proportions rolled up on Island shores, literally thousands of oysters were broken from the cobble-sized rocks to which they had attached themselves and were left stranded high on the beaches, to die or to fall prey to gulls and other shore marauders. But on protected beaches, an ample supply remains, and will doubtless continue to propagate if care is used in the taking. On Island shores, generally free of contamination by waste, these are uncommonly good eating during any month of the year.

Some Islanders, I am told, make a chowder from the flesh of the blue mussels that cluster in numbers on the pilings at the ferry slip, and, indeed, on any tideline rocks and logs to which they can attach themselves. For the bit of flesh they contain, this would seem a tedious process, but at least they are always available.

For those who know where to find them, the shores nurture several kinds of clams. Besides the butter, or "Washington" clams, as they are sometimes called, there are the little necks, the big rock cockles, which, being coarser, are generally used for chowder instead of steaming, horse clams, found only at extreme low tide, and that unbelievable bivalve, *Panope generosa*, spelled, variously, "geoduck," "goeduck," "gweduc," or "geoduc," but always pronounced "gooey duck."

If there is a creature of the seas, the earth, or the air that looks either as ludicrous or as incredible as does the geoduck, common to the Pacific Northwest and found almost nowhere else on earth, I have not seen it. I recall a day, several years ago, when Harry Truman, then president, paid a visit to

Tacoma, in company with Mon Walgren, who was running for re-election to the office of governor of the state of Washington.

A temporary platform, from which the two men were to make speeches, had been erected at the corner of Ninth and Broadway. The Governor spoke first, and boasted about the abundant natural resources of the state, among which he included an edible shore-line life so extensive and so prolific, on both Sound and ocean, that the phrase, "When the tide's out, the table's set," coined, I think, by a Seattle restaurateur, was a literality.

Following the President's speech, in which he lauded politely the evergreen landscape, majestic Mount Rainier, and the sparkling waters of the Sound, which lay just below, a Northwest Indian appeared suddenly, in tribal costume, and presented Mr. Truman with a large dripping geoduck. Mr. Truman regarded the animal in disbelief, as though he thought he were being made the butt of some joke, while the crowd rocked with laughter. But, after a moment, with his characteristic grin, the President gingerly accepted the gift, and handed it quickly to an attendant.

Geoducks are not plentiful on Island beaches, or properly, underneath them, though, protected now, they are said to be on the increase. Natural law as well as conservation law gives them a fighting chance. Daylight tides sufficiently low for geoduck digging occur so infrequently during any one year that they are known as "geoduck tides." A lesser ebb than minus three will rarely suffice. And, although he is unable to move his body (as does the razor clam), and can only extend and retract his siphon, the geoduck often wins the contest, which may well match the speed of the digger against the incoming tide.

One factor in the geoduck's favor is that he is apt not to show at all until the tide has completed its slack and the flow has begun. A geoduck may weigh as much as six pounds. The average is something less than this. His ludicrous look comes from the fact that his almost-square shell lacks a good deal of containing his bulk, and from the fact that his united siphons, when extended, may reach to a length of two or three feet. This tapering proboscis, rough and wrinkled on the surface, is remindful of an elephant's trunk.

Geoduck hunting, as much as digging, is an absorbing pastime. The only visible part of the clam, when he does show, is the tip of his siphon, which may or may not protrude an inch or so above the sand, a roughish round knob, with an intake and a vent, through which he may (but probably won't) eject a fountain of water, thus betraying his position. If he fails to spurt, it requires a sharp eye to find him among the seaweed and other debris left by the receding tide. Disturbed, he retracts his siphon quickly, leaving only a faint round depression to mark his withdrawal.

Practiced diggers generally sink a tubular can, without ends, around the spot where the siphon disappeared, and dig inside the device, to keep the entire beach from caving into the excavation. The animal may not have retracted his siphon all at once, but may pull it in gradually, so that you might touch it occasionally. But don't try to pull him out by the siphon, even if you can get a grip on it, which is unlikely. He is probably too deeply and firmly embedded to remove in this manner, and the siphon is likely to break off in your hands.

A one-pound coffee tin, the wide kind, makes a good receptacle for dipping the sand and the water that comes flooding up into the cylinder. The cylinder itself, which should be provided with two hand holds, can be pushed down as you go. When you can feel the shell, finally, embedded an arm's length or so beneath the surface, slip your hand underneath the animal and persuade him gently until you can work him loose from his resting place and bring him to light.

Now comes the moment of truth, when you can believe you have not been engaged in a snipe hunt. It would be difficult to explain why a man will work at top speed for a half hour or more to unearth a pound or so of meat that is no better, certainly, than that of the butter clam and not half so tasty as that of the razor clam, which it more nearly resembles.

I recall a remark made by a visiting Kansas State University student who went out alone one summer and came back with a perfect specimen. "When I started to dig," she said, "I asked myself why. I didn't care for the taste, and there were a hundred things lying about the exposed beach that I wanted to investigate before the tide came in. But once I had started, I had to have him."

The flesh of the geoduck, sweet and tender, is usually sliced and fried, or chopped and mixed with eggs and flour or pancake flour to make fritters or patties. The siphons may be skinned by dipping them into scalding water and peeling off the skin in one piece (as you would peel a peach or a tomato), then chopped and made into chowder.

Chowder, no matter what the clam, is made in various ways, and Islanders eat a lot of it. Some use tomatoes. Others shudder at the thought. Most cooks try out bacon or salt pork, add minced onions, diced potatoes (along with the water in which they have been cooked until tender), the chopped clams—the more the better—and whole milk. Some thicken the dish slightly with flour or rolled cracker crumbs. I know a woman who adds a bit of diced celery and carrot for color and flavor.

"Throw in a pair of old shoes," I heard an Islander say once. "There's nothing you can add to make a *bad* kettle of clam chowder, as long as you've got plenty of clams."

How the geoduck begins, how he spends his life, eats, reproduces his kind, deep underground, is a tale so fascinating that I could not resist the temptation to attempt to write it, following my first expedition. It was never published, for a peculiar reason. Shortly after the Truman episode, I wrote an article about the geoduck as a regional character. We had unearthed a few on the Island that summer. But the tide table showed that the animal was safe for another season, so there was no opportunity for pictures.

Nonetheless, I sent the article to the editor of a national

magazine, which was then running a color camera series depicting out-of-the-way places and unusual earthly inhabitants. The editor responded that he would like to hold the manuscript until he could see some photographs.

By great good fortune, I thought, I knew a photographer who knew an aquarium keeper, who, wonder of wonders, would loan us a geoduck. We set the scene elaborately and, we hoped, convincingly, on a sandy beach, by preparing a careful excavation. The photographer's wife, a photogenic blonde, came along, wearing new yellow "clam-diggers," to pose in the act of drawing the animal from the opening.

As I stood to one side, holding the geoduck firmly by the neck, he ejected a sudden stream of water up my sleeve. Startled, I let go. When I picked him up, his delicate shell was broken.

I was dismayed, and terribly embarrassed. My companions were secretly delighted. Presented with the now-defunct geoduck, they bore him back to the studio. Suspended from a drying-line, his weight stretched the siphons to full length. The photographer took photograph after photograph, in full color, while I nursed my chagrin over the accident.

Confident that the enlarged pictures would create a sensation in the editorial offices, we sent them off. They came back promptly, along with the manuscript. The editors were sorry to have put us to so much trouble. They wished us luck elsewhere. The pictures, the editor regretted to say, had proved "just too phallic for our nice family magazine." Which describes the geoduck about as well as anyone, in more delicate language, can describe it.

The Island not only claims one of the best salmon grounds in this area; it also boasts some superb fishermen. It is true that the "bow and arrow" tactics of some of these might well amuse most sportsmen. But these are meat fishermen.

To an Islander who takes his fishing seriously as meat getting, a tide chart on his wall is as essential as a clock, and more essential than a calendar. He may fish as he gardens, according to the moon's phase, and guard his secrets like a miser. But he keeps his larder well-filled with food that would do justice to a king's table. One of these fishermen, I am told, eats fish three times a day. When he has caught a salmon, he bakes it whole in his wood-heated oven. Having eaten the last of it, he sets out for his fishing grounds again.

Islanders take big ling and rock cod, too, when they want

them, and sometimes sole or flounder, known as "bottom fish." They have a system for catching cod off the ferry slip or off the ferry itself if it is tied between runs. They attach a bit of mussel meat to a tiny hook to catch a pogie, and attach the pogie to a bigger hook to take a cod. On a still day, when the water is clear, you can even select your own cod, as he swims about, deep under water around the pilings.

To be sure, catching him may be another matter. People were wont to say that Peter James very nearly knew the secret. I saw it demonstrated once. Having fished for hours without a nibble, employing every kind of bait from pile worms to herring, an Island visitor laid down his pole in exasperation.

"How big a one you want?" Pete asked him casually, taking up the abandoned rod.

Within minutes, two cod, weighing four or five pounds apiece, lay on the deck. "You see, there's nothing to it," Peter said, handing the pole back.

During the days of long waits between ferry runs, Pete was rarely without a line or two in the water, and he hardly ever went home for the night without a codfish or two in his pickup truck. Stopping by his house above Oro Bay one evening, I found his wife Ruth frying cod livers. "They're for Frank and Charlie," she told me. "I've practically worn a path carrying livers down the hill." Convinced of their therapeutic value, the two ailing elderly brothers, neighbors of the Jameses, all but subsisted upon this redolent delicacy during their final weeks on the Island.

I like to remember a summer when Earle and I went out each evening in our eight-foot dinghy to drift and fish off-shore for whatever we could catch—sole, perch, trout, cod, or sea bass, for breakfast. A true salmon fisherman will hardly allow any one of these in his boat, unless it be for bait. But whatever we took we found delicious. Brought up to eat bull-heads and crappie from muddy ponds, and catfish and carp (which we called "buffalo") from the tepid waters of the equally roily Verdigris, we found these little saltwater denizens from the icy Sound an unmixed blessing. Because we knew we could repeat the performance the following evening, we took only as much as we needed. Taken from fifty-two-degree water and cooked a few hours later, they were both sweet and odorless, and we never tired of them.

The most rewarding feature of those evenings, though, was not the meat we took, but the pleasure of drifting along the shore, watching the reflections in the water and the late evening life of the birds and the animals. That was a wet summer, and springs descended the steep banks at frequent intervals. The long pale green fronds of the maidenhair fern overlapped like tiered curtains, and the pale fragile blossoms of the blue speedwell and of the Siberian miner's lettuce dotted the edges of the miniature waterfalls.

Sometimes a buck deer or a doe and a fawn emerged from the woods high above, at the top of the bluff, and descended to the beach, stepping as lightly as dancers. Or we watched a belted kingfisher swoop from his perch to the water and rise again with his flapping prize. Often of evenings we saw flocks of young Bonaparte's gulls milling about, dancing the peculiar ballet steps with which they arouse the sand fleas and other insects that comprise their supper, or floating about like spilled petals on the water.

Once, when Earle was casting with a spoon, a little farther out, there was a jerk on the line, and he began to reel in, while

I rested oars. The line slacked and tightened and slacked again. Overhead, gulls came and began to circle the boat, screaming, and increased in number, appearing to come from nowhere.

We became aware, suddenly, that the line was not in the water, but in the air, that it was not a fish he had hooked, but a circling gull, that had plucked the spoon from the water, and was being followed round and round by its sympathetic and very vocal companions. Reeled in, slowly, the gull flew in smaller and smaller circles, topped by a circling, crying canopy that almost literally shut out the sky, and dropped, finally, into the water.

When Earle lifted him, he made no resistance. He eyed us cautiously, but he did not seem afraid. He sat quietly while the hook was removed from his bill. Nor did he flutter so much as a wing when I took him into my hands preparatory to settling him back on the water.

He was a big gull, a glaucous-wing, but I was amazed at his lightness. His skeleton, beneath the bulk of feathers, felt as delicate as one of the toy balsa planes children assemble. When I set him on the surface, he swam a little way, making no sound, and then took flight. In a moment, he was unidentifiable among his companions. And in a few moments more, the sky was empty again.

Although I felt, after a time, at home in the woods where I had come to know commonly accepted if not scientific names, the countless specimens of in-between, shore-line life remained an almost total enigma for a long time. And although I go down frequently at low tide, armed with guides, I still feel like the student who stood in her first big library fighting back tears because she could never live long enough to read all of the books she saw on the shelves. At the opposite pole from the practical consideration of food getting, the rhythmic adaptability of tidelands life is awe-inspiring.

To go down to the beach during a low tide, when leathery giant chitons, sea cucumbers, nudibranchs, medusae, and a variety of "stars" litter the sand and stones, is to feel you have had a private showing. For a few hours, strange forms generally shrouded and protected lie exposed, and bubbles and spurts betray the presence of innumerable lives beneath the surface. This is a crowded world, and its unveiling is an ordeal that counts its toll. Although I look forward to the few extreme lows each year as times of revelation, I like to return to view the full flow that follows. Standing on the narrow line of the sandspit between the filled cove and the outer water, I know a small feeling of relief that "all's right" with this world once more.

26

THE TABLE'S SET

One of the facts impressed upon me early, partly, I suppose, because I found a parallel to the small community in Kansas where I grew up, concerned the Island habit of sharing. There was no such thing as charity in the modern parlance. Clothing was passed along and handed down from family to family, and all kinds of surpluses were shared. But this was sharing, not giving. For a people addicted to thrift, it is a form of sin to discard garments not worn out, only out-grown, and to throw away that which can be used, or eaten, by others.

People gave of themselves, too, and we were frequently the recipients. Debts of gratitude for service were paid in homely gifts—venison, oysters, clams, filberts, garden plants, fish, fruit, vegetables, pies, cakes, cinnamon rolls, light breads . . . or in the coin of service. Islanders cut each others' hair. Women gave each other permanent waves. Those who owned automobiles hauled passengers, groceries, garbage for those who did not. One Islander, whose hours without the pain of arthritis, it was said, were few, kept all of the Island clocks going, gratis. His tidy house, which he occupied alone, with its ticking, striking, chiming clocks, was a joy to visit.

"The beauty of the country," Louise Ekenstam Ostling

wrote, "was that we had all the food we could possibly eat or use. . . ." Each year sees a surplus of huckleberries, far beyond the requirements of the human and animal and feathered population. When the first rains have fallen in autumn, the leathery evergreen leaves of the huckleberry are washed clean, and its fruit is sweet and plump, nor do the first light frosts, when they come, affect the flavor.

But, as with the fish and the blackberries, the fruit is only half the reward. The women, and sometimes the men, go out with the awareness that sunshine will be at a premium soon, to absorb the color and the fragrance of autumn before the winter overcast.

Some refer to the huckleberries as "whortleberries." Early Northwest Indians called them "shotberries" or "shotoolalie." The Island, with its thin rocky soil, is especially adapted to their growth. No matter how the year runs, wet or dry, cold or hot, you never see a failure in their fruiting. In pies or jellies, in pancake batter, or simply as a sauce, they have a wild smoky flavor, remindful of the blue elderberries (*Sambucus glauca*) we gathered along the streams back in Kansas, but which we rarely bother with here.

Indians visited the Island each year, Bessie recalls, to camp on the beach and gather berries. "We liked to go down and visit them. We had no language communication, but the Indians were always friendly and kind to us children. We ourselves gathered a great many, which Mama canned. We ate the sauce ladled over hot cakes in the winter."

Before fresh vegetables were shipped in and available the year around, wild greens were gathered in the spring as a pick-up or tonic. Edible plants include tender young bracken, and fireweed, stinging nettle (in an early stage), miner's lettuce, rice root, salmon berry and thimbleberry shoots, sour dock, and dandelion. Not all of these were eaten. But the salmon berry shoots, especially, taken very young, before the thorns hardened, were especially prized by the children. Crisp and tender, these taste like young celery.

Walking through the woods during different seasons those first years, I played a game of being lost or in hiding, obliged to depend upon nature for sustenance. I thought I had never seen a place where survival could be more readily accomplished. I gathered Himalaya blackberries as late as Christmas or into February if winters were mild. Huckleberries lasted well into spring sometimes, as did the big vitamin C-rich rose hips. (A few years ago, a plane-wrecked pair in the wilds of British Columbia proved the efficacy of these latter.) Summer saw a succession of ripening, from wild currants, oso berries, red elderberries (generally the first to come) through trailing wild blacks, gooseberries, blackcaps, thimbleberries, service berries, blue elderberries, salmon berries, salal, mahonia, even wild hazel nuts, if you could beat the jays and chipmunks to the harvest.

Some of the above "edible roses" were not used, but their fruits had been or could be put to use, and I tried them all. Several times, I had seen from the road a blossoming bush covered thickly with white flowers, and had thought it might be a western chokecherry (which I have never found in this wet climate). It proved to be a service berry (*Amelanchier*) and fairly common in open woods. The fragrant blossoms of the service cover the bush from top to bottom, all but obscuring the rounded leaves with their characteristic notches around the top perimeter.

Service, which is probably a corruption of "sorbus," is only one of the several names this shrub bears in different localities. The Canadians call it "saskatoon." In New England, it is the "shadbush." Here, the sweet black seedy berries do not ripen before August, but in areas where they ripen in June, it is known as "the June berry." My first taste of it was as a child in Iowa, where it was called, locally at least, "the sarvis berry." The fruit was used by early Northwest Indians (and probably in other areas where it grows) in the making of pemmican cakes of dried meat, fat, and fruit pounded together. The wood was used, also, for arrow shafts.

Legends handed down would indicate it was prevalent, and prized by Northwest tribes, as well as by Lewis and Clark, who made a bread from the berries combined with other wild plants. I have never come across a record of their having used the oso berry, which also grows in abundance here, but they may have. For the berries, rather insipid but safely edible, are referred to as "Indian plum." At least they feed the soul. I have never seen anything prettier than one of these bushes in late July, when the ripening pinkish-orange berries hang like coral beads from each separate cluster of leaves.

Thimbleberries and salmon berries are lovers of damp ground. The former, with its five-lobed maple-like leaves and paper-white flowers, is a pretty plant in bloom or in berry. But it can turn into an all but impenetrable jungle, springing up overnight after it has been cut down. Its round red berries in no wise resemble thimbles, and they are quite tasteless. But the birds like them, so they must be nourishing.

I like the salmon berries better, and they are a spectacular sight, in either bloom or fruit, with their golden stems that shine like satin and their peculiar coral-red papery flowers, followed by hairy salmon-colored fruits. No one seems to know precisely how this shrub came by its name. The bark is said to be an aid to digestion, and may have been used to settle stomachs too delicate to tolerate the rich flesh of the salmon, or the name may have come, merely, from the color of the berries, or from the fact that the shoots of the shrub, when young, served as a relish to accompany salmon roe.

The two nature-produced foods prized above all others are probably the trailing wild blackberries *(Rubus macropetalus)*, the only blackberry considered worthy of the name, and the morel, a mushroom so sought after and so elusive that patches are kept a closely-guarded secret.

The wild blacks ripen in July, and last but a few weeks. Small and tedious to pick, as compared to the big Himalaya and evergreen escapees, they are competed for by humans, deer, raccoons, birds, and a variety of rodents. The vines of *macropetalus* overrun the Island, coming in quickly after a forest is logged or burned over, but comparatively few of them bear. Generally, they grow close to the ground, running and sprawling at the base of young alders, among nettle or over old fences, to a length of ten to fifteen feet or better. Clingers and climbers, they have an especial affinity for decaying stumps and abandoned buildings. They bloom in June. Male and female flowers are borne on separate plants, the male flowers, as much as an inch and a half in diameter, about twice as large as the female of the species.

The little berries, when they can be bought, sell upward from three dollars a gallon, reasonable enough, considering the time and energy consumed and the scratches endured in the gathering. They make wonderful pies and cobblers, and superb jellies and jams, rich in color and delicate in flavor. But these are only a part of the reward.

Excursions begin around five in the morning, and at that time of day there are many and delightful distractions. The deer have not yet retired into the woods for the day, and wander, unafraid, in the roads and the sidepaths. Eyes of dew glisten in the big spider doilies that stretch from bough to bough like lace on a drying frame. The early birds, shy and hidden through the day, are up and about, and the air is sweet and fresh. If it is not quite light yet, we sit on a log by the roadside and drink coffee from a thermos.

By mid-July, goldenrod and pearly everlasting, wide-awake purple asters and Queen Anne's lace are in bloom together along the roadsides, and bright orange tiger lilies and red hedge-nettle stand tall above the bracken. In the cutover areas and along the fence rows, fireweed still makes magenta patches of bloom, and everywhere there is the heady smell, when the sun warms, of field chamomile and gumweed.

The blue-berried elder is in creamy bloom. The red-berried elder is in scarlet fruit, and swarms with wild pigeons. Wrens move and scold, invisible, among the salal and the mountain balm. As you work, the sun comes up and the dew dries. The deer fade away silently into the woods. It is hard work, and tedious, and you often return home with little to show for your labors.

"Why do we do this?" I asked a companion, once, as we emerged into the open. Her back, like mine, ached from hours of stooping, and her legs and arms bore a network of scratches. "Is it simply that we were born to thrift and these are free for the taking?"

"It's more than that," she said. "With me, it's a sort of religion. Here are nature's gifts, as a kind of trust. If I were to let them all go, I would feel guilty of neglect and ingratitude."

Several varieties of edible mushrooms grow on the Island, both in the woods and in the open, and Anderson boasts at least two expert mycologists, William and Betty Knowles, in addition to Sammy Tokarczyk of the *Tahoma*, an Islander by adoption. Probably because it is relatively easy to recognize, the morel is the edible fungus most used and sought after. Morels, which resemble stalked sponges or little misshapen pine cones, spring up when the earth has warmed in the spring but is still sufficiently moist for their liking. If they can be said to have a preference of habitat, it is for old barn lots or orchards, where they are difficult to distinguish from last year's apples. But they are temperamental in their appearance, and likely to vanish completely from some area where they have been gathered for years, or to appear suddenly in numbers where they have never been seen before.

But, even with all of the natural bounty at hand, first thoughts among the early settlers had to be given to producing and putting away as much food as possible. Families were large, and men who worked out of doors ate heartily, three full meals a day. As the land was cleared, fruit trees were planted, and the farms were stocked with beef and dairy cattle, with chickens, geese, ducks for meat and eggs, and with sheep for wool for making clothing.

There is nothing so persistent in its blooming and its bearing as an ancient pear or apple tree. Each year takes its toll, of course. But some of these abandoned, moss-grown orchards bloom each spring in clouds of pink and white splendor, and bear each summer. The fruit is gnarled and wormy some years and many of the limbs are dead and broken. But at other times the trees outdo themselves, and the fruit is as fine as you could want.

But the Island is knee-deep and wading in fruit of one kind or another any year. And the variety of life in these old orchards makes them an engrossing study. Wild grass and daisies, bracken and Queen Anne's lace grow thick and tall among the broken trees and provide cover for the wildlife that comes to feast there. The deer browse the leaves off the lower limbs in early summer and return in the fall to eat the dropped fruit. Islanders declare they shake the trees, but I have never seen this. Raccoons quarrel and bicker as they feast through late summer nights. Finches, which Islanders call "cherry birds," work the blossoms in early spring, spilling discarded petals like popcorn escaping from a popper, until the earth is carpeted, to get at the beginning fruit.

The trees, with their thick foliage and their neglected branches, are favorite nesting sites for the robins. These birds flock into the orchards as the fruit ripens, along with the other winter stayers, the towhees and the varied thrushes, the flickers and the rusty sparrows. Ancient boles, from top to bottom, are ringed with necklaces of "cribbage" holes, drilled by an industrious little tree surgeon, the downy woodpecker. Beneath the grasses, the earth is crisscrossed with field-mouse tunnels, leading to tiny cupboard shelves stocked with apple seeds. Finally come the slugs, the most humble and slow-moving of the lot, to clean up the remnants.

Of all these, it is the raccoons that are the connoisseurs. We play a game each year, the 'coons and I, in the old hemmed-in orchard above the nameless creek that flows into Higgins Cove. This was a fine orchard, once, kept pruned and sprayed. Now the tall grass is dotted with deer beds and crisscrossed by trailways of both deer and 'coon, that come and go down the steep banks through a jungle of almost every kind of wild growth the Island affords—thimbleberry and service, currant and elder and hazel among them. Walled away from the rarely occupied house by a broken tangle of once domestic black-berries that serve to conceal all save the tops of the trees, the orchard is a banquet hall.

The apples are not much good any more, though the trees still bear heavily; and I am willing enough to leave them

alone. But both the 'coons and I prize the plums that ripen each September. Long ago, the Higginses ringed the boles of the trees with tin cut in strips and with necklaces of cans, to discourage the marauders, and we have added to these. How-ever, when the fruit begins to ripen, we take turns. Visiting the orchard, I find toothprints in the ripening fruit, as though its sweetness were being periodically tested.

This year, I was sure I had won, that we had finally suc-ceeded in building the barrier sufficiently wide to deter their climbing. But on a warm September morning, I arrived with my ladder and my pails to find that all three trees—Petite, Hungarian, Italian—had been stripped in the night. The trampled grass was littered with evidence, twigs, leaves, seeds.

At the outermost tip of a branch, I found my share, *five* ripe plums.

As I stood with my empty pails in hand, scanning the wall of overhanging fir boughs along the gulch where the little masked robbers sleep off their glut, I could fancy they were peering out in triumph. "Just you wait until next year," I muttered. "I'll pitch a tent and sleep in the orchard."

"Only thing to do is plant enough for everybody," Islanders say philosophically. "Robins, 'coons, deer. Or be satisfied to take them a little *under-ripe*."

As with the deer, 'coons have no enemies here. Occasionally, hunters come in, with their dogs, from the mainland. But I have known few Islanders to hunt them. They may grumble that the animals take more than their fair share, make a mess in the orchard, or disturb sleep with their bickering. But the 'coons' curious cunning, like their charming robber faces, is difficult to resist. The game, as with the deer, is to outwit if possible, rather than to kill. An Islander may take a deer, for meat, but it would never occur to him to kill for revenge or for the pleasure of killing.

Even so, the meat-getters are apt to do their stalking away from their own premises. "I could have shot a buck from my back porch, the day the season opened," one hunter told me, as he set off beyond the mountains in search of his annual venison. "This one had lived off the garden all summer, too. But he just stood there looking at me when I opened the door, his eyes full of trust, and I didn't have the heart to shoot him."

This year, the deer were more destructive than during any year I can remember. They came in at night and mowed the lettuce, the carrots, the green onions, peas, beans, beets, even the bearing raspberry canes. In desperation, finally, Island gardeners petitioned the state game department, which sent out deer repellent. This was only partially successful. The repellent washed away in the rain or underneath the sprinklers. Even the dew diluted it. The deer continued their depredations, ate squash, green tomatoes, chard, roses, fuschias.

Trellises hung heavy with peas disappeared, vines and all, in a night, the fruit precisely at the canning stage.

Petitioned again, the department advised cautiously that an animal or two, caught in the act, might be shot, providing the game department was notified to come for the carcass. But even the most bedeviled of the Islanders could not bring themselves to this extreme. A deer emboldened to come into your garden on a summer night to nibble the rose buds is one thing. An animal that has taken to the woods for the duration of hunting season and that must be outwitted is quite another.

All sorts of ruses were tried. One man constructed a ten-foot mesh fence, and awoke one morning to find that a yearling had crept underneath and was feasting on his cabbages. One installed a revolving red and green light, which only aroused the animals' curiosity. Another created an animated scarecrow that did practically everything save to say, "Get gone, you rascals." The deer flocked in like children to a circus.

A gardener from the Big Sur country wrote that he had solved his problem *there* by the simple expedient of a low fence draped with the nets discarded by salt water fishermen. For some reason, the deer declined to cross these nets. "But I felt a little ashamed," he confessed, "and wound up by tossing the *cabbages* over the fence. I had more than I could use in any case."

I myself fell victim to one booby trap, at Billy and Harold Hansen's place, on the west side of the Island. Stopping by after dark one evening and eliciting no answer to my knock at the back door, I went barging around to the front, and ran into a network of waist-high nylon fishing lines, with buckets attached at strategic points that came tumbling and banging at a touch. Exasperated over the nightly pruning of their choice fuschia baskets, the Hansens had hit upon the idea for intimidating their tormentors. Whatever the results so far as the deer were concerned, I can testify as to its efficacy in my case. I stood, literally frozen with terror.

There is a saying that when Himalaya and evergreen blackberries (not really wild, but escapees) ripen in waste places in the Northwest, you can stand inside a tub and pick a tub full; I found this to be almost literally true. That first year, to the amusement of the natives, I gathered and preserved and canned far more than I could use. Seeing that I could not even make a dent in the supply, I wanted to sit down and howl over the remembered sweltering hours of picking, the miles walked over the Kansas hills, and the chiggers endured in an effort to see that no fruit went to waste.

During our first year on the Baskett place, I looked at the carpet of softening windfalls and prevailed upon Mr. Baskett to join me in a cider making. Using a borrowed homemade press of the "brute strength and awkwardness" variety, we worked from dawn until dark, stung so many times by the hornets that swarmed over the pulp that we developed a kind of immunity to the pain. Earle, who would have no part in our enterprise, worked happily away at his remodeling.

By the end of the day, we had eleven gallon jugs of lovely amber raw apple juice. Better still, the grass underneath the tree was gratifyingly free of windfalls. Here, at least, I had found the answer to waste. Mr. Baskett departed for his chicken coop, and we drove down the hill to the ferry. Stung and aching, I promptly piled onto the back seat for a nap.

I was awakened abruptly by Earle, who was leaning over me with a suspicious expression. "You didn't, by any chance, screw the *tops* onto your cider jugs, did you?"

"As tight as they would go," I admitted.

"Judas Priest, woman," he roared. "Don't you know you've got enough potential there to blow the roof off the house?"

As often happened, obliging Peter James came to our rescue, took the key to the house, and promised to disarm the "bombs." The product turned to vinegar, and we never tried making cider again. But I continued to gather the apples each autumn and to store them in boxes underneath the house, where most of them quietly rotted. Pausing beside me as he staggered out with a box of these one winter day, to spread on the ground for the varied thrushes, Earle suggested that an easier solution might be to simply leave the windfalls underneath the trees where they fell, so that the deer and the birds could enjoy them in *good* condition.

On a day in late November during the first autumn, we stood at the window and watched our neighbor Ernie Ehricke maneuver his tractor in and out among the trees in the Ehricke orchard, scraping apples into an excavation he had made. Back in Kansas, each autumn, we had buried turnips in a straw-lined pit to keep them from freezing, but it seemed hardly likely that *apples* would keep in this fashion. Nor do we have hard, deep ground freezes in this area.

Ernie looked astonished at Earle's question. "But I've no *intention* of *keeping* them, man, I only wanted to get them off the ground, before they rotted there."

Few Islanders produce their own milk and eggs now. Most of them buy chipped eggs, called "chex," from Rudy's and Oscar's farm, for a good deal less than they would pay for the standard variety. When I asked an Island woman, once, how it was that there were always enough "chex" for the Islanders, she gave me a knowing smile.

"Well, they say the boys chip a few now and then, for Island trade," she said, "if they're in short supply. Of course, I don't believe it. . . ."

Most Islanders decline to eat an egg that came from anywhere except the Johnson farm. "Yolks don't stand up right," they say. "It's the way Rudy and Oscar feed their hens."

I have a theory that the high percentage of superior cooks among Island women derives somehow from the quality of the eggs they use, and from the fact that they can afford to use them lavishly.

Recently, a small tempest was whirled up here on the Island by the rumor that the Johnsons had been notified that if they wished to continue to sell milk they must pasteurize their product and install certain other up-to-date equipment. Islanders were outraged. The price of bottled milk from the

Johnson farm bore no relation to the price paid for the pasteurized and homogenized product on the mainland. To Islanders who live, comfortably, on astonishingly small incomes, milk from the Johnson farm had been an essential and considerable part of their diet.

Milk from Rudy's and Oscar's cows, regularly tested, they pointed out, had nourished nearly two generations of healthy Island children. Furthermore, it was so bacteria-free that it would hardly turn sour, no matter *where* you left it. The thick yellow top cream, which reaches half down the bottle, might seem too rich to the cholesterol-conscious and other faddists. But that was the way the Islanders liked it, and they felt they had a right to it.

If a small independent farmer wished to sell milk (or any other product) to his neighbors at his own set price, they argued logically enough, and the neighbors wished to buy it, why shouldn't they be allowed to do so? To Islanders, who lost their status as a polling place and who are threatened with losing their school district identity after more than eighty years, the threatened curtailment of their privilege to drink raw spring-cooled milk if they so choose is one more indignity.

"Cardboard milk," as they refer to the kind that comes in waxed bottles, was only sold here, prior to this notice, as a concession to summer people, who, Islanders believed, were simply "picky," or who didn't know good milk when they tasted it.

27

HIGGINS COVE

Surrounded as we were by all of this lavish natural bounty, we felt, during those first years, like that other (fictional) California-bound Okie who dreamed of grape juice "squishing up" between his toes. For those with meager incomes, the Island appeared to provide an answer. But we came to know Islanders, too, who looked upon self-reliant living as a game and a challenge.

Two of these we especially admired, because of their young approach to life, were retired railroaders Frank Armentrout and Bob Higgins, who, with their wives Mart and Nella (pretty, fun-loving women), gardened and clammed, fished, got up wood, picked berries, and hunted for wild mushrooms.

Earle still speaks with awe of the time these two men, both well into their seventies, raised the Higgins house and installed concrete-block basement walls and foundation. Until just prior to his death a year or so ago, Frank remained active in his flower and vegetable gardens, both show places, and took his venison each year.

Bob Higgins, for whom Higgins Cove at the north end of the Island was named, had served as a cavalryman in Cuba during the Battle of San Juan Hill in the Spanish-American War. During World War I, he was with the American Railway Battalion in Siberia. Following his retirement as an engineer for the Northern Pacific Railroad, he spent eighteen years on the Island, where he met and married Nella Warner.

Forced from the Island by failing eyesight seven years ago, he declared stoutly, but with a break in his voice, "These have been the best years of my life." He died on May 2, 1966, at the age of eighty-nine. During his last months, he remembered the Island and the Islanders only vaguely, as a place and a people he once knew.

The small house where the Higginses lived, unoccupied since their departure, stands high above the cove, facing toward Filuce Bay on Longbranch Peninsula and beyond to the Olympic mountain range. Surrounded by native trees, fir and cedar, madroña and dogwood and maple and alder, and by trees the Higginses planted, the house stands in a clearing at the end of a wooded road that parallels the waterfront, in a setting of secluded natural beauty.

Bob was in his seventies when we first came to know the Higginses well, his vision already commencing to betray him. But he could still make his way down the long steep trail to the creek and the old-fashioned ram that lifted the water to the house above. The clear cold water that supplied the house and garden and that caused the ram to function came from a spring on the hillside beyond the creek. For every gallon released into the lift pipe, Bob explained on that first visit, six gallons went to waste, down the creek and into the cove and so out to sea. Recalling dry Kansas summers when we used and reused water hauled in barrels to fill the cistern, or brought a muddy product from the Verdigris River to settle out and soften in pails and tubs in a lye solution, I was appalled by this profligacy.

To me, and, I suspect, to the menfolk who like to appear knowledged, a hydraulic ram is an enigma. Perhaps no Islander depends upon one, now that power has come, but several did during our first years here. At our own place, water still reaches the house by the simple expedient of gravitational flow, and I can understand that.

The first time I saw the ram at the head of the cove and heard the drum sound of its "heartbeat" in the standpipe a little way up the creek toward the settling barrel, I could scarcely believe that the lift power came from the flow of the water itself. That day Bob Higgins gave us a demonstration of how he started the ram going again when it stopped, as it periodically did.

Removing a short length of wire from the cap-like head of the contrivance, he probed about in a tiny hole he termed "the spitter." At each stroke, when the ram is functioning, a jet of water ejects from this opening. Having shut off the flow from the spring, he opened a valve at the side to free the lift pipe of "the core," a stream of murky brown water which gradually turned crystal clear.

Having performed these mysterious operations, he renewed the flow from the spring until the moss-covered box at the base of the ram had filled, poked underneath with his finger for a moment, and the ram was off, spitting and pumping for dear life, the one saved gallon starting on its 250-foot climb to the storage tank in the woodshed and the lost six going overside into the creek, and so, through cove and sound, and strait, to the mighty Pacific.

"If she stops again," he said, "you just haul off and give her a good hard kick, and she'll start."

I learned, later, when the ram was my responsibility, that

this latter method was about as efficacious as the other two. As I knelt to clear the spitter and remove the core, or drew back for the kick (it was partly the sylvan setting, I suppose), I always had the feeling that something elfin waited in the shadows, to crown or to decline to crown my efforts, and that if I only knew the proper abracadabra, he would cooperate. I never learned the secret; but the contraption did start sometimes, and it was a wonderful feeling.

When I sought for an explanation of *how* the ram did what it did, I began to suspect that even the menfolk did not know, really. A tall pipe stood on the roof of the woodshed that held the storage tank, but it made no sound, as did the musical pipe on the bank of the creek. "And what is the purpose of *this* pipe?" I asked Bob Higgins, as he stood one day with his hand cupped behind his ear to listen for the beat of the ram far below.

"Why, it has to be there to make the system work," he said. Which answer seemed about as logical as any other explanation to which I was treated.

Once when Earle was away and the ram stopped, I approached Bob Ehricke, the engineering genius, and made an effort to appear intelligent by asking a question or two, in technical language learned from my mentors, about the ram's function.

"You mean," he interrupted with a grin, "the God damned ram's stopped again."

Whether or not a nymph were lurking somewhere in the shadows, the prehistoric-seeming, orange-bellied salamanders that inhabited the path between the ram and the settling barrel lent credibility to the illusion that there was something mythical about the place, as did certain other aspects of the gulch down which the creek flowed to the cove.

The first time I descended to the creek, I thought (and I still think) that I had never, anywhere on earth, seen a lovelier spot. During earlier years, the Higginses had been at pains to set a series of wooden steps into the steeper portions of the trail at the lower end. But the slope of the upper part, from which you could look down into the cove through a screen of ivy-covered alders, and fir and cedar and hemlock and hazel, was gradual.

Here Nella had strewn the seeds of wild bleeding heart, and its delicate fringed foliage lined the trail on the cove side, dripping pale rose hearts throughout May and June. On the other side, where the bank from which the trail had been cut arose, large heart-shaped leaves of wild ginger formed

solid mats. In order to find the curious pixie red-brown flower of the ginger, you must part the leaves and search at the nodes of the hairy stems that lie next the ground.

In early spring, the three-petaled, three-sepaled, three-leaved, starched white blossoms of western trillium (wake-robin) emerged from the thick carpet of fallen leaves and needles, even in the middle of the trail itself, turned slowly from pink to purple, dropped their petals, and set seed, only to disappear completely by late summer. Arching over the trail, the many-stemmed hazel bushes were decorated during February and March with long yellow catkins. By mid-summer, the green husks that held the nuts hung from the slight twigs with perfect protective coloration.

I was puzzled by these husks, for I had mistaken the hazel for young red alder which it strongly resembles except for its

shrub-like habit of growing in clusters. The third member of
the trio I came to think of as "the three sisters," cascara, confused me, too, because of its mottled gray alder-like bark. But
cascara leaves are more like cherry leaves, finely toothed, with
prominent parallel veins, and with a tendency to bunch together.

In fruit, the three differ widely from each other, and they
attract different customers. The alders bear little clusters of
brownish cones upon which the siskins feed in winter. The
stockinged husks of the hazel secrete small round nuts favored
and competed for by jays and chipmunks. The seedy blue-
black berries of cascara, sparse on the Island, serve as hors
d'oeuvres for wild band-tailed pigeons until the fruits of the
madroña ripen.

Cascara bark, for making the drug cascara sagrada, used as a
cathartic, was taken in small quantities for a time from Island
trees. An Islander in search of these trees one day approached
a picker and made inquiry. The picker appeared puzzled over
the name "cascara," and then brightened. "Oh," he said, "you
mean the shittim tree? Sure, there's a few up the trail yonder."

There *is* a tree of that name. The Ark of the Covenant and
various parts of the Jewish tabernacle were made from its
wood in Old Testament times, as Moses was instructed on
Mount Sinai. "And they shall make an ark of shittim wood"
(Exodus 25:10). But this Hebrew word, left untranslated in
the authorized version of the Bible, is translated in the revised
version as "acacia," a spiny tree adapted for an arid desert
country, whereas cascara is a species of buckthorn.

Because of the moisture and the richness from the accumulation of leaf mold, which is knee-deep in places along the
creek, growth crowds in each year, so that every spring the
trail must be cleared anew. I recall my initial trip, on a day
in June, accompanied by Nella Higgins. We were in search
of a large fossil-marked stone she had told me about. We descended to the ram and followed the path that paralleled the
creek, and then crossed over and ascended to the spring on

the other side. From the spring, we were obliged to fight our way through dense undergrowth, and so we had taken along a machete. We stopped often, for she knew the place well and there was much that she wanted to point out to me.

In patches where the sun struck through for a portion of the day, airy, lace-white masses of foam flower *(Tiarella)* and cream-flowered alumroot *(Heuchera)* climbed the steep sloping banks. At first glance, because of the similarity of the lobed leaves and of the affinity of both for shade and moisture, these two are look-alikes, as are the two varieties of *Pteridophyta* that nudge each other for position there. Along this trail, not that day but later, I learned to distinguish between lady fern and bracken. Like twins in a family, these two look nothing alike once you come to know them.

Bracken is the proletariat of the ferns, if you discount their allied "poor relation," the horsetail *(Equisetum)*, not so much fern as scouring rush. An ex-Vermonter tells a story about a native of her state who corrected her when she referred to *bracken* as "fern." "Them ain't ferns," he advised dourly. "Them's brakes."

"Brake" or fern, bracken was the first of the *Pteridophyta* I became aware of in the Northwest, and its lush abundance amazed and delighted me. "Any moment," I wrote back to my friends on the plains, "I expect to see a pterodactyl break from cover." A sun rather than a shade-lover, this luxuriant plant *(Pteridium aquilinum pubescens)* decorates the roadsides from early spring, when the first of its fiddleheads emerge, until cold weather, when its crisp, bluish-green, starched and ironed fronds turn brown and collapse in a protective tangle. "I like a year when the bracken dies early," I heard a transplanted Nebraskan say, once. "I wouldn't go back to shoveling snow, of course. But I get a little tired of this everlasting green sometimes."

Lady fern *(Athyrium filex-femina)* remains green the year around, and the fronds, less coarse and more graceful, as befits the name, cluster from a compact base instead of branching. This one is a woodsy shade-lover. The fronds are fat in the middle and taper at both ends and arise from a compact base instead of branching, as does bracken.

Other ferns grow thick in the gulch. One bank we climbed that day was festooned with maidenhair. Deer fern, with its ladder-like fronds, grows in moist shade, nestled against fallen logs or at the edge of the stream, the terminal pinnules set in motion by the moving water, and sends up fertile, spore-bearing fronds that later disappear. Sword ferns grow everywhere, on both sides of the gulch, like great green spraying fountains.

I first saw the one I like best here that day, the licorice fern, or polypody. At the foot of the steeper portion of the trail, beside the ram, a tier of ancient moss-grown logs, obviously the remnants of an old dam, crosses the creek. Through the mat of mosses that clothes these logs and climbs the big leaf maple on the bank, to spread out along the limbs, the scattered fronds of polypody emerge from an embedded licorice-flavored rootstock, to create an aerial garden. At the base of the maple bole grow the only specimens of twisted stalk (*Streptopus*) I have found on the Island.

We did not find the rock Nella sought that day, as it happened, though we did find a smaller one later, studded with ancient impressions of clams and mussels. But I have thought, since, each time I walked the trail swinging my own machete, of a remark Nella made as we skirted the salmon berry, the currant and the blackcaps, and made our way upward through elder and salal and huckleberry to the road above.

"I always bring a knife or a sickle when I come," she said. "But, except for the nettle, it's all so pretty as it leans in across the path that I can't bear to cut any of it."

Stopping once beside the creek to admire a red huckleberry in fruit, growing out of a stump that divided the water, we saw fresh deer tracks, and discovered a worn trail leading up the bank through the curtain of thimbleberry into the old orchard. In the deeper woods, where the smell of leaf mold was rich and pungent, we found a cluster of snow-white oyster mushrooms at the base of a decaying log, and a dozen other varieties with caps in shades of red and russet and yellow, that made me resolve to return with a mushroom guide. But I never have.

I left the gulch as I left the beach, with an unhappy awareness of my own lack of knowledge. Here were layers and layers of tomes that it would require half a hundred lifetimes of intensive study to master.

The trail we took most often followed the cove in the opposite direction, to its open end, where a long sandspit all but made of the inlet a landlocked lagoon. The migrating wild fowl came across this spit in stormy weather to rest and feed; whether, at flow tide, when it was filled to the brim, or at ebb, when the meandering course of the fresh-water creek was clearly discernible across the salty mud floor to the narrow channel at one end and out over the graveled beach into Drayton Passage.

The fowl like it both ways. Walking down this trail, screened by growth in late autumn, you can hear the ducks talking together in the gentle, agreeable-sounding way ducks have, as they maneuver about in the water or in the tidepools left by the outflow. In the center of the sandspit, on stilts, stands an old boathouse, with a window facing onto the cove. In this building, Nella told me, hunters used to wait for the ducks to come in and settle.

"It bothered me to have them killed there, where they had come to rest," she said. "So, when I heard the ducks and knew the hunters were in the house I'd go down the trail singing at the top of my lungs, to flush the ducks out. Whatever the ducks may have thought, I expect the hunters thought I had taken leave of my senses."

At the foot of this trail, on a high bank of diatomaceous earth, Indian paintbrush grows in drifts, the leaf-like bracts shading from deep orange through a bright crimson. Nella told me about the diatomaceous earth one day. Idling along the beach, I had picked up a saucer-sized piece broken away from the bank. After feeling the peculiar abrasive quality, like Bon Ami, between my fingers, and testing its surprising lightness, I tossed the fragment into the water. To my amazement, it floated.

Having made the same discovery, Nella told me, she had sent a specimen to a geologist. "He reported back that it was diatomaceous earth, made up of tiny fossils, and mined commercially in some areas as an abrasive." Investigating on my own, I learned that there are more than five thousand species of the little algae called diatoms, and that hundreds of diatoms, including many different species, might be contained in a spoonful of muck taken from the floor of the Sound.

Seen under a microscope, these tiny algae are as beautiful as snowflakes and as intricate in design. Silicified cell walls of these organisms, laid down in fossilized layers throughout the centuries, have built this shoreline cliff. In addition to being used as an abrasive, diatomaceous earth is useful as a filter, a heat insulator, or in the making of lightweight cement. As much as nine tenths of the food in the ocean, consumed by a variety of creatures, consists of diatoms. Poking through a book, I came across the interesting if useless information that ten thousand pounds of diatoms devoured by copepods which are eaten in turn by smelt, that nourish mackerel, which serve as food for tuna, eaten by man, may go to make up one tenth of a pound of man's body weight, a continuing story of ingestive drama. I never open a can of tuna, now, but that I think of this.

As I stood one day, looking up at this bank of microscopic cell skeletons, a bright black and white pigeon guillemot with red feet exploded from one of the holes high above my head and took off across the water with a wheezing whistle. I remember also the flash of the kingfisher down to the water from one side of the cove and up on the other in a V-pattern; the lonely cry of a great blue heron one evening there; and the sight of a little masked 'coon-face that peered out at me from his nest in a fir bough reflected in the still water. Like the incredible, bullet-fast flight of the guillemot, these were the kind of experiences that will take me back down the trail to the cove, for as long as I am able to navigate.

The years at the cove had gone fast for the Higginses, and they had been filled with activity. Bob had constructed a kind of weir, once, he told us, to bridge the little channel at the end of the sandspit, and had fashioned a spear with which he snagged the bottom fish that enter the cove at flow tide and leave with the ebb. The little house in which he smoked the fish, on wire racks, stands above the cove. I go down frequently these late years to watch the fish come in. As the water deepens and swiftens, the big flounders and the little sole (essentially a small flounder) play a kind of cheese-it game of dash, stop, dash, near the bottom, and the others travel in schools, as fast as jets, in the clear water.

Like Mrs. Baskett, Nella planted bulbs and seeds to spill over the banks and down the trails' edges. Each fall, she looped the long trailing new growth of wild blackberries that surrounded the clearing up over the stumps and the huckleberry bushes, so she would not be obliged to stoop to pick the fruit the following summer. The Higginses made their own wine, which was delicious, and Nella canned and dried and preserved, and baked big crusty loaves of bread in her old wood stove.

"One year we went into the hog business," Nella laughed. "We got tired of fish and chicken, the only fresh meat available. Bob bought a suckling pig and we raised it to butchering size. Neither of us knew much about how to dress a pig, but we got along all right until it came to the scraping. We tried all the kinds of knives we had in the house. But nothing worked, until I thought of a couple of safety razors we had in the medicine cabinet."

Once, after Bob's eyesight had begun to fail, Nella undertook to clear the all but perpendicular bank in front of the house of the tangle of service berries and wild roses, young alders and brush, that had grown there. She donned a pair of Bob's overalls and set to work. Busy at her chopping, she got so far down that she could not climb back up again. So she let go and slid, leaving a good deal of skin and most of the overalls on the bushes during the swift descent. Like Robert Frost's "Brown," she came home by way of the beach, the

long way 'round, she reported. But the overalls were hardly fit raiment for the scarecrow.

I have wished, since, that I had taken a picture of the scarecrows (not one, but four) that stood in a line below Bob's and Nella's garden. Rigged out outlandishly, they reflected as well as anything could, Nella's puckish imagination. Asked what the figures were designed to scare, she was at a loss to explain. Neither the birds nor the deer nor the raccoons paid the slightest attention to them. But they were picturesque and personable, and the garden seemed somehow unfurnished after they had disintegrated.

We asked Bob about the little cannon mounted in a wooden framework that stood on the bluff in front of the house. It was a "life-saving cannon," he said, but he did not know where it had been used, or when, only that it was old. The cannon had been given to him by an Island widow, whose husband had come by it years before. Bob explained its use.

The first shot from shore, he said, was a projectile with an "eye" through which a light line had been strung. This shot had to be carefully placed so as to reach the vessel in distress but do no damage. To this first line, a second and heavier line bearing the breeches buoy (an instrument hung by pulleys), was fastened. After the rescue was effected, a device was dispatched along the same line to the ship to cut the hawser free so that it could be brought back to shore again.

The Higgins cats, Freckles and Lady, mother and daughter, stayed on at the cove after their owners left. Nella didn't intend to leave them, though she knew they were not town cats, and she had no place for them. She tried at first to do away with them in a humane fashion by putting a lethal and painless drug into their food. "I said as I set it down, 'If I were you I wouldn't eat this,' " she told me ruefully, "and they wouldn't touch it." Nella would have tried the Pound, then. But with that peculiar instinctive knowledge animals often appear to possess, the pair disappeared on moving day and was not to be found.

We watched for them, as we had promised. Finding them there one day, Earle mercifully did away with Freckles, who was ancient and ailing. Lady, a fine hunter, kept house underneath the woodshed for a long time, producing litter after litter, and keeping the kittens and herself fat on mice and birds and chipmunks. She was an outdoor cat, big and homely and self-reliant. She came to accept our offerings after a while, and even responded cautiously to our gestures of friendship. But she kept her reserve and her dignity.

She never came to meet us, but she was always there when we drove into the yard, seated on the back porch or stretched out in the sun, tending her kittens. After we removed the first litter, she became cagey about her offspring. She gave birth in the woods somewhere and brought the kittens out when they were several weeks old, to teach them to drink from the pans of milk we set out. We managed to tame a few of the kittens, and to find homes for them. But most remained as elusive and mistrustful as wild animals and learned to shift for themselves. One Friday, Lady was not there when we drove in, and we called in vain. We never saw her again.

28

TIME AND TIDE

During those first years, we came to like winter best of the four seasons. The beaches, clean in any season, seemed uncommonly so during the winter months. The water, pushed higher and harder, cleared out the crevices and ledges, and there was something moving and exciting, lonely and yet companionable about the sight of white caps far out, the cries of the gulls as they wheeled and circled, and the sound of the turning and churning of the gravel.

Although I felt more at home in the woods those years, and would still rather be among growing things, I found the strange, cold, in-between world peopled by creatures that spent half of their lives waiting for the tide to come in, of endless fascination.

I remember especially a morning spent on the beach that first winter. Early that day, as I went about my morning chores, I had heard the eerie falsetto "laugh" of a loon, not frequently heard, and had hurried to the window to peer out into the fog. But I had not seen him. As soon as the fog lifted, I went down.

The tide stood at a minus one. The water was quiet, with

an unusual molten look. All of the lower section of the beach was covered by a blanket of kelp. A big red sunflower starfish lay stranded a good way back from the water's edge, and the still-wet stones were dotted with blobs of clear jelly, so transparent that the markings on the rocks underneath were visible. Sand fleas hopped about, and the piled seaweed, like long ricks of hay, was alive with little shore crabs.

At the water's edge, hermit crabs in their protective canopies of borrowed shells, scurried about like busy housemovers.

A tell-tale hump of sand disclosed a moonsnail at its work of smothering and ingesting a hapless butter clam. A giant chiton, the color of mud, lay on the sand like an abandoned shoe sole. A circling gull eyed a red sea cucumber. Only the drab color of the water, reflecting the gray sky, and the notable scarcity of moonsnail egg case "collars" denoted that it was winter on this seasonless strip.

In an effort to save the clam, I unearthed the moonsnail, too late. The flesh of the clam had already been drawn through the neatly drilled hole in his shell, which the moonsnail still clasped with his great "hoof." The snail was a big fellow, some four inches across. Prior to dispatching him by cracking his shell with a stone (for the sake of the clams and oysters he would later smother), I held him at arm's length to watch him draw his enormous foot, incredibly, into the shell, as you would squeeze water from a mop, and close his tortoise shell door.

The door, or operculum, which completely closed the opening, was delicate, in contrast to the vulgarity of the mass of flesh. A pale amber, semitransparent and gracefully ribbed and whorled, the operculum was not attached to the shell, but to the foot itself. When drawn snugly into place, it completely shut out the outside world. I have several of these opercula, shading from a pale to a deep amber. They contrast oddly with the gross appearance of the smothering foot, as the translucent white butterfly-shaped plates of the big chiton, hidden in the leathery flesh, seem antithetic to the sluggish appearance of the animal to which they form the skeleton.

A little way down the beach, a boulder stood exposed, and I stopped to count the varieties of life attached to its irregular surface. It is a small world, this boulder, where animals and plants cling neighbor by neighbor and help to sustain each other. Here were various shapes and sizes and colors of limpets, encrusted with algae, tiny snails, each with his own horny door for closing out the world, little blue mussels massed together in profusion and piled up, tiny sponge-like creatures, little anemones with poisonous tentacles, mossy chitons, their plates decorated by intricate drawings, and more head-down barnacles than I could possibly estimate.

These latter had the appearance of set stone forts, long abandoned. But they were filled with living creatures that would kick open the door, when the tide turned, to fish with their feet. When they die, finally, the forts will crumble into shell sand, which lies in drifts high on the beach, giving the appearance of silver when the sun shines and forming a loose bulk into which the sand fleas burrow for protection. This is a dog-eat-dog world, but so ordered that not a single life or skeleton goes to waste, a universe controlled by the ebb and flow of the tides, as life in the interior of the island, where nothing goes to waste, either, is ordered by the ebb and flow of the seasons.

Fog often lies thick over the channel in winter, shutting away the mainland and the neighboring islands behind a gray curtain. The workboats and the *Tahoma,* when they emerge, look distorted and out of proportion, as in a mirage. At times such as this, there is a special feeling of isolation here. As I watched, the tide turned, and, although there was no drift, the line was distinctly discernible in the water. I saw a ripple, far out, and the head of a hair seal emerged, like a round, dark-brown water ball. A lone grebe dived and surfaced nearby and paid no attention. I did not see the loon. It was as though the Island had been absolved of time, or had its own timing system, with prolonged minutes and hours and days, such as those remembered from childhood.

We speak of this sensation that time is not passing or is passing at a slug's pace, which leads us into expending it in foolish or useless enterprises, in a search for driftwood or of stones to sprinkle on the garden paths. But then, we tell ourselves, a good deal that passes for enterprise in the outside world is foolish, too.

I think people really do have a different conception of time on the Island. One Islander who thought of moving his house across the road to higher ground went so far as to remove the porch steps and put the house on skids, where it stood ten years later. He had forgotten by then, probably, what impulse had led him to decide to move it, and was quite content with it as it was. The house stood in a pasture. With the steps away, he explained, with a grin, the cows found it impossible to enter.

The tide had started its flow by the time I reached the cove, but was still well out. So I waded across the slippery surface of kelp to have a look at the sand dollar bed, in protected water. The deep purple, soft-spined sand dollars stood at an angle, leaning one way, as children stand dominoes in a knock-down game. On the beach outside the spit, a few of these disk-like sea

urchins still lay in the shallow creek channel that flattened
out to nothing at all, and the beach was strewn with greenish
or bleached white skeletons, ranging from rounds no wider
than a pencil top to small saucer size.

The toll of breakage of these skeletons is high, for the shell
is delicate and soft. Island children, who call them "sea
cookies," and who write their names with the inky excretion,
gather the entire dollars and color the flower pattern on the
dorsal side that marks the position of the animal's "feet," or
break them open to retrieve the tiny brittle "birds" or "angels"
to be found inside.

That the beach is a place for renewal is more than fancy,
and I wonder why we contrive reasons such as clam-digging or
oyster-picking for going there. A wise child I know announces
simply, "I'm going down to see how in (or out) the tide is."

"How fortunate you are," a city woman remarked last summer to an Islander, "to be able to run down to the beach every
afternoon, or two or three times a day if you like!"

"I didn't tell her," the Islander said, "that I hadn't taken
the time to go down to the beach for a week. But, then, I
thought, why not, and took my hands right out of the dish
water and went down and spent an hour looking for agates. I

felt like a new woman, and resolved then and there to spend at least a half hour down there every day, whether or not I had a reason to go."

A true beachcomber checks the beach after each incoming tide, on the theory that the last flow may have brought in something of interest or value, and that the ebb may take it out again—a special piece of drift, an entire Triton shell, a sawed-off round of fir or cedar smooth enough to make an outdoor table. I know a man who once found a fine piece of monkeypod wood, drifted thousands of miles, probably from the Hawaiian Islands!

One contribution brings Islanders down to the beach in droves, and that is a "bark tide." I have never heard an explanation of this. Perhaps there is none that would hold consistently true. Perhaps it is merely an accumulation that sets out when circumstances are just right and comes to rest when they are equally favorable. I have seen a few of these, and I know they follow a run of high tides, when the water has carried a good deal of drift of one sort and another. A tide flow unexpectedly brings in an immense harvest of accumulated bark, to lie on the beach in a solid windrow. Nothing makes better or hotter fuel than big thick slabs of dried-out bark. Opportunists walk along the row and throw the select pieces out of reach of high tide, for later harvest, or come in pick-ups and reap half a winter's supply.

In addition to the practical ("lagniappe," as we used to say in the Southwest), the windrow is rife with interesting flotsam and jetsam, kelp and wrack and bladder leaf, crabs and sand fleas and starfish, a treasure trove that would lead you half around the Island but for the turning tide that might well catch you in a position where you would be obliged to scale a bluff to avoid a drenching.

29

MY ISLAND

On a spring evening this year, the old Baskett house caught
fire. The Island boasts no fire district. Several Islanders own
extinguishers, as we do. But our water pressure, powered by
gravity from the hillside reservoir, produces a flow too feeble
to activate a sprinkler, let alone to reach the high-pitched roof.

Typically, the first thought, and shouted admonition, was
to "Get Bob!"

The next hour assumes, now, the proportions of a poorly
remembered nightmare, fragmented with painfully vivid recalls, of a dash upstairs with the extinguisher, of attempting,
all thumbs, to couple hoses, of the woefully inadequate stream

of water, of my sister-in-law Hazel almost literally flying over the barbed wire fence between our places to connect a hose to their new water system, powered by an electric pump. Meanwhile, the interior of the house had plunged into darkness. The yard was eerily lighted by flames from the roof.

How many times had we said, blindly, "If this old house would burn down, we could build a new one"? Certain that it was beyond saving, I ran inside and stood, numb, in the darkness, surrounded by an accumulation, carried in over sixteen years, of cherished and irreplaceable possessions—the spinning wheel, an album of pictures Jim took in the Antarctic, fossils, a madstone found in Kansas, my mother's first geography, a bull whip from a train that crossed on the Oregon Trail, a Spanish-American War rifle, my dad's ancient muzzle loader, a century-old wolf hide, a worn ox yoke used on the Island by brothers Frank and Charlie Johnson, one of a chain of floats that served to rescue a crew of Japanese fishermen from their stranded boat, Earle's prized cranberry thumbprint chandelier.

The latter might be cut down, it occurred. But even if I could get the heavy ox yoke detached from its high hook, it was unlikely that I could carry it outside. And the menfolk were busy on the roof. In an agony of indecision, I rushed from room to room, not so much salvaging as counting the loss.

As I emerged from the front door with a beloved blue pottery jar, I became aware of car lights, converging from either direction. Men, women, and big boys poured through the front gates and over the rockery, bringing ladders, extinguishers, axes, even buckets, and set immediately to work. Relaxed in a warm tub following a hard day's work, Bob had shouted to his wife Sylvia, already at the telephone, to "Ring emergency!"

Within the hour, the fire was out, the Islanders calling for rags to mop up the surplus water and brooms to sweep away the debris. It seemed then, and seems now, nothing short of a miracle of teamwork. Outside, I looked about at the familiar faces, and counted twenty-seven. There may well have been more.

Voices were gay by then, filled with banter about the summons, the flying trip over rough roads, the near-collisions, the usual extravagant exchange whenever Islanders get together. I couldn't find words. But for their quick reaction, the house and all of its contents would unquestionably have been a total loss; and yet they acted as though they had done nothing extraordinary. When I did manage, somehow, awkwardly, to blurt out something, they appeared surprised.

"This is the way we always do," a long-time resident reminded me. It was as though he reproved me gently for thinking they might have acted otherwise.

Now the October of our fifteenth year on the Island has passed. In October, more than in any other month, I think, I look ahead to the time when we will be in truth Islanders.

But that too, of course, is only an illusion. We will be only Johnny-come-latelys, summer people who have gained a foothold, carpetbaggers. Our house will continue to be (and rightly so) the Baskett house. The cove we count as ours, because we are the paper owners, will remain Higgins Cove. As I walk down the wooded trail to the now-silent ram, I experience a feeling of trespass.

Nor, really, can I say that, after fifteen years, I know the Island. I am being constantly surprised by new discoveries, either made on my own or pointed out to me. Only last summer a pair of Islanders, as excited as children, stopped by to tell me they had found, off an old logging road, a specimen of pipsissewa (*Chimaphila*), a delicate little broadleaf no one had suspected of growing here.

Then there are the seasonal changes. You may know a thing in bloom, but do you know it in bud, or in its winter habit? The land and the surrounding waters are in an endless state of flux. Water that is blue today will be gray tomorrow and green on Wednesday. The tide will take out the old drift and clear the beaches and bring in new.

Each year, I am more reluctant to move back to town for the winter months. Each spring, I look forward eagerly to return. For six months we will be week-enders only. This is the season of rapid change, when five days away renders one alien and out of touch. The streamlined swallows that netted the air and the white-crowned sparrows have vanished. Ellen's grandchildren, Cindy and Nancy, come up the hill and collect the swallows' nests from underneath the overhang of the poultry house and fill them with pebble eggs and set them in the apple trees.

The house, when I enter it, smells musty and unlived-in. The bird feeders are bare, the chickadees and the finches gone off in the belief that we have abandoned them. A musky smell of mink permeates the wood closet. Raccoon tracks, like baby handprints, decorate the kitchen windows, and the neat heart-shaped spoor of deer surround the doorway. But this house spells "home," as did the farmhouse back in Kansas that was my birthplace. I hurry to the beach to see what the tides have brought or taken away, and down the hill to hear what news has accumulated. The outside world and its enterprises have been left behind.

Not much has transpired. A mainland 'coon hunter lost his dog; the dog showed up later at Amsterdam Bay. The county bookmobile has been out with a fresh supply for Island shelves. A record number of chances have been sold on the quilt for the Fair. There may be more serious news, an accident with a chain saw, necessitating a special ferry run, an illness, a death even. But these are items we would have heard during the crossing from the ferry crew.

Summers, when I rarely leave the Island, I come to take the freshness of the air for granted. But now I cannot get enough of it, a heady blend of sea and shore, the smell of salt and sargasso, of leaf mold and pitch and algae, the cider smell of bruised and rotting apples beneath the orchard trees. . . . The winter robins and the varied thrushes have come to feast among the windfalls. The black-shawled juncos, which we have not seen all summer, have descended in droves from their mountain nesting sites. One lone chipmunk remains. The rest have vanished into the foundation, where the cache of a summer's harvest is stored.

The face of the land is changing, too. It has been a dry summer, and the leaf fall has begun, and the roads through the woods are carpeted with brown from the needle drop. There is more color everywhere now, along the shore line and along the roadsides. Scarlet rose hips and white snowberries hang in heavy clusters, and the vine maple is bright against the mottled gray of the alder boles. The bigleaf maple has turned russet, and the alders, the cottonwoods and the willows have yellowed. Band-tailed pigeons settle and rise in clouds among the foliage of the madroña, and cedar waxwings and robins are busy in the mountain ash and in the dogwood trees.

If I were a painter, I would put the map of the Island on canvas, an ecology of color and arrested motion, the units separate but flowing together in a kind of rhythm. On a windless day, the trees are still and the tide creeps in and out with scarcely a ripple. Then the surrounding waters are like a mirror reflecting the trees and the sky.

To give a true account, though, you would need four canvases, one for each season, or better yet a dozen; to show vine maple at its brightest scarlet and hardhack and skunk cabbage and trillium at their peak of blooming. After you have come to know where to look for the rarely found, for pale shell-shaped oyster mushrooms and coral root, for wild gooseberries and delicate twinflower and the strange little speckled rice root lilies (*Fritillaria*), this small circumscribed world begins truly to seem like a possession.

Should a time and a circumstance come (as it has come for those with far more claim than I) when I can no longer visit the Island, I think my mind will go combing these roads and gulches. Memory holds so much in the way of discovery—a drift of blue chicory on a wind-blown meadow, an aromatic bed of peppermint in a shaded bog, a solitary stalk of cream-tipped rattlesnake plantain, a tiny gold-eyed owl on a limb of the apricot tree.

Each low of the ebb tide exposes clams or oysters, each flow brings firewood. In all of the years since the first Islanders came, these have not failed. Nor has any spring failed to produce, in succession, the oso, the wild currant, the elder, the blackberry, the huckleberry, the fawn. Take any year, and the wild fowl come and the water teems with fish.

By October, the trunks of the madroña are almost through with their exfoliation and the tender new green that showed in patches all through late August has turned to a pinkish cinnamon tone. All through the winter, the satin-smooth boughs will keep a rich red that contrasts strikingly with the shining green of the long leaves. The madroña is an untidy tree, dropping its old dry leaves in fits and starts instead of all at once, as deciduous trees do, but it is a great reliever of gloom in the winter woods among the conifers.

The year has been dry, and the brown tones of the dead bracken along the roadside are restful-seeming. Along the wood edges, big ripe salal berries, mealy to the taste, lend their fragrance to the peculiar smells of autumn, the spicy scent of field chamomile and of goldenrod, the pungency of gumweed, the aroma of sticky laurel and the smell of ripening apples, blended, when the road swings toward the shore line, with the faintly iodine odor that comes from the water.

The fireweed, as showy now as when it was in magenta bloom, has gone to seed in masses. Disturb a clump of it and airborne seeds, each with its tiny silken parachute, set sail on the still air. The dogwood trees, in their second blooming, stand like fruit and flower bouquets, the button clusters of red berries hanging thick among the paper-white sepals, backed by the purple-red of turning foliage.

In the open fields the changing season is even more apparent. In the pastures and the meadows, and underneath the broken trees of the abandoned orchards, the oxeye daisies that bloomed in July have given place to the little wild carrot we call Queen Anne's lace. For more than a month the clouds of Queen Anne's have covered the fields like a lace counterpane. Where the blossoms have dropped, the tightly curled "nests" cup to catch the fireweed and the thistle seeds.

October is the time of seeding and of ripening. Brown husks stand up from the steeple bushes around the lakes and in the moist road ditches, and brown seeds hang pendant from the goats beard and the ocean spray. The tall spikes of foxglove, an escapee, have gone to seed, and the fronds of the sword fern are dotted with orange spore cases. Along the shore, the leaves of the bitter cherry drop onto the surface of the water and are carried away by the ebb tide, and the clusters of alder cones hang like ornaments.

Change comes so slowly that one forgets how it was last year, or five years ago, or ten. That which was passable trail has become alder thicket. The logged-over areas that we found unsightly two years ago have healed over with broadleaf evergreens and elder. Little firs are already thrusting their pinnacles above the stumps. Even the power lines that laced the Island like cats' cradles and that seemed an intrusion two or three Septembers ago are scarcely noticeable among the conifer boughs.

Along the shore, lazy smoke arises from Island chimneys, or leans away from the prevailing wind. Piles of cordwood are ricked outside the doors. "You can't warm a kitchen on a damp day with an electric burner, and who knows when a tree is going to topple across a power line?" Of nights, now, Islanders who boast no television sets gather at the homes of those who do. For those who have never seen the time when they could stack the supper dishes and go off to a movie, television has been something of a miracle. But no one is addicted to it. Unaccustomed to night life throughout their youth, Islanders go to bed early.

Periodically, you hear some long-time Islander grieve over the changes that have come about in his lifetime. "There used to be work for young people to do, so they could stay on here," he says, taking it for granted that no one would want to leave this best of all possible worlds. And truly I have met but one Islander who expressed a desire to live elsewhere; and he would have been a malcontent anywhere. I suspect that the real reason for intra-Island marriages has not so much to do with the fact that young Island men remain unexposed to mainland girls, as that they are taking no chances on a wife who might find Island living too circumscribed for her taste.

Islanders speculate uneasily at times concerning the Island's future. Will it be, one day, a haven for summer people and week-enders, with only geographical identity? Or will some miracle keep it alive as the kind of quiet, close-knit, rural community they have made of it? Perhaps the miracle lies in the faith of these people. Disturbing reflections arise to plague the mind whenever a piece of Island property changes hands or the sounds of hammer and saw announce the erection of a new dwelling. But the inhabitants who love the green serenity of their world find it difficult, if not impossible, to believe that it can ever change.

Frequently during the week on the mainland, I find or make occasion to visit the slip from which the *Tahoma* sets sail. Cradled in fog or rain or low-lying cloud, the Island (if it can be seen at all) looks withdrawn and mysterious, a world apart. So it must have looked to Helda Christensen on that day in 1872 when she walked down the hill as a bride and stepped into the rowboat that was to take her across the channel to her new home in the clearing.

On the last day of our summer stay on the Island this year, a Monday, I took my noon sandwich and drove to the turn off the Ekenstam-Johnson road that leads up the rutted hill to the cemetery. Because the narrow road was lined on either side with color, I parked my car at the foot and walked the rest of the way.

The day was mild, with no wind. Sunshine, emerging after morning fog, cast leaf patterns on the roadway. I walked in through the always open gate and made my way methodically up and down the rows of graves. As I read the inscriptions, I counted those I had known in life and was surprised and dismayed that they came to so many.

I thought that day, though, that I had never seen a more serene place. When we first came, a log arch with a hand-lettered, carved sign that read CEMETRY marked the gate. Someone noticed the spelling eventually, and erected a sign down below that read CEMETARY. Now, a neatly painted county placard, correctly spelled, stands inside the cemetery itself. But I liked the earlier, hand-carved sign better.

At the back and sides, the fence lines have been all but obliterated by a growth of salal and huckleberry, seedling fir and madroña and Oregon grape, sword fern and bracken. The wild grass is mowed a few times a year, especially if there is to be a burial, but the charm and the serenity come of a not-too-well-tended look. It looks not so much neglected as let alone.

I have gone in the early summer to find the center section of the grassy driveway carpeted with the rich purple of wild violets. In the open area between the fence and the graves, deer tongue, which the children call Easter lilies, blooms thick in early spring, and all around the edges the bright yellow blossoms of the mahonia mingle with the clustered pale-pink urns of huckleberry among the rust-tinted bright green foliage.

The first Island funeral I attended was that for Ernie Ehricke. The preliminary service had been held in a chapel on the mainland, with only graveside services at the cemetery. I was a newcomer then, with little knowledge of the Island, and the occasion marked my initial visit to the burial ground and the first time I had seen all of the Islanders gathered together.

As the procession of cars that had crossed on the *Tahoma* turned off the Ekenstam-Johnson road, I could see a line of Island vehicles parked along the shoulder all the way down the hill to the schoolhouse, and the cemetery itself seemed to be filled with people.

One fact that was impressed upon me during this first look at the Islanders assembled together was that of their advancing years. The mainland minister, himself an octogenarian, must have noticed this too. For in his few words, he drew a comparison between life and the hillside upon which we stood. "Some of you . . . some of us," he said, "have almost reached the summit." Many of those who stood there that day have joined Ernie at the top. It is easy to see why the Island population is dwindling.

As I moved on down along the row, it occurred to me that here, in these "closed books," the story of the Island is written. Because of the maze of relationships, the Scandinavian majority, the names on the markers run to Johnson and Anderson, Larsen and Christensen and Carlson, names that represent the foundation upon which the community was built. Some of these lives were brief and of little influence. But whether it had been written that one should die at eight and another live to eighty, whatever pain and anxiety and turbulence they had known, each had contributed his part.

I stopped at the grave of young Guy Gardner, who had died at seventeen during a cattle drive across the Cascades. His parents went away and left him here. Where do *they* lie buried? Six-year-old "Cunnie" Lindstrom lies beside the father who cut short his young life. How was it that day for Helda, who lies next, beside her first husband Christian, for whom she made the long journey from Denmark? The news of the murder-suicide must have rocked this little world to its foundations.

I thought of Ellen Ehricke's conviction that it is the good, the worth while, in all of us that has its continuance. There were other tragedies, sudden and violent, that must have jolted the living. But the epitaphs, simple ones, often seen, do not reflect this. "Our loved one." "Blessed are the peacemakers." "Sweet be thy slumber." A child's stone reads: "For of such is the kingdom of Heaven."

Many bear no epitaph, only the words "Father," "Mother," "Sister," "Brother." Near the salal-smothered fence, "Brother Frank" and "Brother Charlie," who lived together in life, lie together for eternity. One marker reads simply and lovingly, "Our Pop." I like that. And so would he, I wager. On this sunlit slope, surrounded by green woods, death seemed a circumstance as natural as the annual going over of the bracken.

As I always do before I leave the burial ground, I made my way to the top of the rise, near the back fence, where the fern and the grape come creeping down the slope, to visit the double grave of William and Elsie Baskett. Standing beside Mr. Baskett's grave, I saw his face clearly for a moment—his piercing dark eyes, his high cheekbones—and heard in memory the echo of the toast he proposed as he raised his glass (how many times?) at our kitchen table or at his own table in the little poultry house feed room he called home during the last years of his life. "Here's kindness!"